WOMEN AND IMMIGRATION LAW

This book examines immigration law from a gender perspective. It shows how immigration law situates gender conflicts outside of the national order, projecting them onto non-western countries, exotic cultures, clandestine labour and criminal organisations. In doing so, immigration law sustains the illusion that gender conflicts have moved beyond the pale of European experience. In fact, however, the classical feminist themes of patriarchy, the gendered division of labour and sexual violence are still being played out at the heart of Europe's societies, involving both citizens and migrants. The essays in this book show how the seemingly marginal perspective of immigration law highlights Europe's unresolved gender conflicts, and how a gender perspective helps us rethink immigration law.

Sarah van Walsum is Senior Researcher in Migration Law.

Thomas Spijkerboer is Professor of Migration Law. Both work at the Vrije Universiteit Amsterdam, the Netherlands.

T0347236

WOMEN AND IMMIGRATION LAW

New variations on classical feminist themes

Edited by
Sarah van Walsum and
Thomas Spijkerboer

Routledge
Taylor & Francis Group

LONDON AND NEW YORK
a Glass House book

First published 2007 by Routledge
2 Park Square, Milton Park, Abingdon, Oxon OX14 4RN

Simultaneously published in the USA and Canada
by Routledge
711 Third Avenue, New York, NY 10017, USA

A Glasshouse book

*Routledge is an imprint of the Taylor & Francis Group,
an informa business*

© 2007 Van Walsum and Spijkerboer

Typeset in Times by
RefineCatch Limited, Bungay, Suffolk

British Library Cataloguing in Publication Data
A catalogue record for this book is available from the British Library

Library of Congress Cataloging in Publication Data
A catalog record for this book has been requested

ISBN10: 1-904385-64-8 (pbk)
ISBN10: 1-904385-65-6 (hbk)

ISBN13: 978-1-904385-64-6 (pbk)
ISBN13: 978-1-904385-65-3 (hbk)

CONTENTS

LIST OF CONTRIBUTORS

Laura María Agustín has been doing research on migration, service work and commercial sex for 13 years. She publishes widely in English and Spanish, is author of the forthcoming *Sex at the Margins: Migration, Labour Markets and the Rescue Industry*, and editor of a special issue of *Sexualities* investigating cultural issues in commercial sex. She has carried out programme evaluations for the ILO and European Commission and belongs to several international networks on migration, sexuality, rights and 'trafficking'. She is currently Lecturer in Sociology at the University of Liverpool and Principal Investigator on an ESRC project researching migrant workers in the UK sex industry.

Rutvica Andrijasevic is currently an ESRC post-doctoral Fellow at the Centre on Migration, Policy and Society (COMPAS), University of Oxford, where she is revising for publication her PhD manuscript entitled 'Trafficking in Women and the Politics of Mobility in Europe'. Rutvica holds a doctorate in Women's Studies from Utrecht University and is specialised in the areas of gender, migration, citizenship and asylum, with trafficking in women being her main area of expertise. Her work has been widely published in various European languages and journals: *DeriveApprodi, Studi Culturali, Multitudes, REMI, Treca, Prokla* and *Feminist Review*. She is part of the NextGENDERation and the Frassanito networks and one of the organisers of the NextGENDERation activities at European Social Fora in 2002, 2003 and 2006.

Jacqueline Bhabha is a Jeremiah Smith Jr Lecturer in Law at Harvard Law School and Executive Director of the Harvard University Committee on Human Rights Studies. She is co-author of the book *Women's Movement: Women under Immigration, Nationality and Refugee Law* (Trentham Books, 1994).

Linda S Bosniak is Professor of Law at Rutgers University. She has published and lectured widely on the subjects of immigration, citizenship, equality and nationalism in law and in political theory. She has served as Acting

Director of Rutgers University's Center for the Critical Analysis of Contemporary Culture at Rutgers University, and as Faculty Fellow and Visiting Professor at the Program on Law and Public Affairs at Princeton University. Her latest book is entitled *The Citizen and the Alien: Dilemmas of Contemporary Membership* (Princeton University Press, 2006).

Isabel Crowhurst is currently a PhD student at the Department of Sociology and a researcher at the Centre for Civil Society, London School of Economics and Political Science. Her research interests include gender and violence, women's international migrations, and gender and civil society.

Betty de Hart holds a doctorate in legal sociology. The title of her PhD thesis is *Foolhardy Women. Mixed Relationships in Nationality and Immigration Law* (Aksant, 2003). She is currently carrying out research on dual nationality and teaching at the Centre of Migration Law, Radboud University, Nijmegen.

Aisha Gill received her PhD at the University of Essex. She currently holds a lectureship in Criminology at the University of Surrey Roehampton. Her main areas of interest and research are health and criminal justice responses to violence against black and ethnic minority women in the UK. She has been involved in frontline services for South Asian women for many years and sits on numerous government working groups on 'honour'-based violence and forced marriages. Her current research interests focus on gender, trafficking, missing women, violence and the social construction of so-called 'honour' killings.

Bettina Haidinger has studied economics, social anthropology and political science. She is presently working on her PhD at the Institute for Advanced Studies, Vienna. The topic of her research is transnational household strategies of migrant domestic workers from Eastern Europe.

Nora Markard has studied law in Berlin, Paris and King's College London. She is currently working for Professor Baer at the Humboldt University of Berlin, where she is also doing research for her PhD. Her fields of interest are comparative, international and refugee law.

Siobhán Mullally is a Senior Lecturer at the Faculty of Law, University College Cork, Ireland, where she teaches Immigration and Refugee Law, International Human Rights Law and International Criminal Law. She has previously lectured at the University of Hull and the University of Peshawar, and has held visiting appointments at Harvard Human Rights Program, Cornell Law School and Sydney University Law School. Her latest book is *Gender, Culture and Human Rights* (Hart Publishing 2006).

Guy Mundlak is Professor of Law at the Faculty of Law and the Department of Labour Studies, Tel Aviv University. He teaches and studies the role of law in the design of social policy, and its effects on labour market institutions. He also serves as the Director of the Minerva Center for Human Rights, and he writes and actively advocates the advancement of social human rights and equal treatment, primarily in the field of work and social work. He is the editor of the annual publication on labour in Israel, *Labour, Society and Law*, and is currently editing volumes on the topics of citizenship and empowerment.

Catherine Raissiguier is teaching and coordinating the Women's and Gender Studies Program at New Jersey City University. The author of *Becoming Women/Becoming Workers: Identity Formation in a French High School* (State University of New York Press, 1994), she is currently working on a book that explores how concepts of citizenship and nationality intersect with gender and immigration in twentieth-century France.

Judith Resnik is the Arthur Liman Professor of Law at Yale Law School, where she teaches about federalism, adjudication, procedure, feminism, and local and global interventions to diminish inequalities and subordination. Prior to Yale, she taught at the University of Southern California and visited at NYU, Harvard, Chicago, and the University of Toronto Law Schools. Her recent books include *Processes of the Law: Understanding Courts and their Alternatives* (2004); *Adjudication and its Alternatives: An Introduction to Procedure* (with Owen Fiss, 2003); and *The Effects of Gender* (1993). She is currently (with Dennis E. Curtis) working on the book, *Representing Justice: From Renaissance Iconography to Twenty-First Century Courts*. Her recent essays include 'Law's Migration: American Exceptionalism, Silent Dialogues, and Federalism's Multiple Ports of Entry' (*Yale Law Journal*, 2006), and 'Trial as Error, Jurisdiction as Injury: Transforming the Meaning of Article III' (*Harvard Law Review*, 2000).

Kaveri Sharma is a lawyer trained in India and has represented women fleeing violent situations in India. She is currently working on a PhD at the London Metropolitan University, where she is researching the interaction of Asian women escaping domestic violence with the legal system in the UK. She also works as a legal adviser at an East London based charity, Newham Asian Women's Project.

Thomas Spijkerboer is Professor of Migration Law at the Vrije Universiteit Amsterdam. He has written extensively about immigration and refugee law. Apart from general issues in this field, he has also focused on gender issues, separated children seeking asylum and asylum procedure. He is author of the book *Gender and Refugee Status* (Ashgate 2000).

Sarah van Walsum is currently working as a senior researcher in Migration Law at the Vrije Universiteit Amsterdam. She has published widely on gender and immigration law and on transnational family relations and immigration law. She is presently doing historical research, comparing changes that have taken place since the Second World War in family norms in Dutch immigration law, nationality law and family law. An English publication of hers is: 'Transnational mothering, Dutch migration policy and the European Court of Human Rights', in Prakash Shah and Werner F. Menski (eds) *Migration, Diasporas and Legal Systems in Europe* (Routledge-Cavendish, 2006).

ACKNOWLEDGEMENTS

First of all we would like to thank all the participants at the Gendered Borders Conference held from September 29 to October 2, 2004, at the Vrije Universiteit Amsterdam. It was their commitment and passion that made the conference such a success, and without the conference, we could never have produced this volume. The conference, in turn, would not have been possible without the hard work and enthusiasm of Joukje van Rooij and Mardin Smayel, the facilities provided by the Vrije Universiteit and De Balie, the generous funding given by the Dutch Ministry of Social Affairs and Employment (Directorate Coordination Emancipation Affairs) and the Netherlands Organization for Scientific Research, and further contributions made by SDU Publishers, the Hague, and Everaert Immigration Lawyers, Amsterdam. In preparing the manuscript for this book, we greatly benefited from the precise and prompt work of Lieneke Slingenberg.

A number of chapters in this volume have appeared earlier elsewhere, or form modified versions of earlier publications. Chapter 6 was first published as: Augustín, Laura (2004) 'A migrant world of services', *Social Politics* 10 (3), pp. 377–96, and is included in this volume by permission of Oxford University Press. Chapter 7 is a modified version of: Mudlak, Guy (2005) 'Re-Commodifying Time: Working Hours of "Live-in" Domestic Workers', first published in: Conaghan, J. and Rittich, K. (eds): *Labour Law, Work and Family*, pp. 125–56, also included in this volume by permission of Oxford University Press. Chapter 5 is a translated version of: Adrijasevic, Rutvica (2005) 'La traite des femmes d'Europe de l'Est en Italie: analyse critique de représentations', *REMI* 21 (1), pp. 155–75, included in this volume by permission of the Revue Européene de migrations internationales (REMI).

Thanks to Alessandro Dal Lago for use of 'Figura 1: Manifesto della Lega nord, agosto 1998: "fermiamoli, arrivano a milioni"' published in *Non-persone,* by permission of Feltrinelli.

A final word of thanks goes to Jean Plantu and the publishers of *Le Monde* for allowing us to include the cartoon, previously published in *Le Monde* of August 14, 1996, in Chapter 11.

INTRODUCTION

Sarah van Walsum and Thomas Spijkerboer

In the fall of 2004, the Vrije Universiteit Amsterdam organised an international conference on women and immigration law in Europe, entitled 'Gendered Borders'. Traditionally, studies on migration and immigration law have focused on male migration. Yet women have always played an important role in international migration, and there is evidence that their share in the total number of migrants has increased in recent years. It is estimated that in the more developed regions of the world – among others Western Europe – women now represent at least 50 per cent of all migrants. The estimated total number of female migrants living in Western Europe was estimated at 9,229,682 in 2000.[1]

The purpose of the 'Gendered Borders' conference was to analyse and evaluate immigration law in Europe from a gender perspective. In the course of the conference, it became clear that the issues that emerged were not only relevant to immigration law, but referred back to some classical issues of second-wave feminism: labour, equality and sexual violence. Moreover, during the discussions held at the conference, we realised that many fundamental questions of feminist debate remain unresolved. What started as a conference over the apparently marginal theme of women and immigration law ended in reflections on the continuing relevance of classical feminist issues and of the undiminished urgency of the theoretical questions raised in the classical feminist debates.

These reflections provided the inspiration for this book. The chapters in this volume are revised versions of a selection of papers presented at the conference. They address a variety of issues relevant to immigration law: asylum, family reunification and labour migration,[2] and do so from perspectives ranging from abstract and theoretical to down-to-earth empirical. What they all share is a specific rendition of feminist themes: one presented from the periphery. As they make clear, many issues that have been declared (at least partly) resolved in dominant discourse have kept their original urgency when presented from a subdominant perspective.

In this introduction, we shall try to make clear how immigration law affects classical feminist themes and, conversely, how feminist theory and

1

activism might help make current-day immigration law in the EU less vulnerable to the neo-conservative political agenda. In this introduction, all cross-references to authors relate to chapters in this book.

New variations on classical feminist themes

Since World War II, feminists in Europe have managed to place a number of issues on the political agenda, including the hierarchical nature of family relations, the skewed nature of the labour market, and reproductive rights and protection against gendered violence. In terms of formal equality, they have made important gains, such as equal rights in family law and equal treatment in labour law and social security law. Moreover, thanks to modern contraceptives, their hard-won access to paid labour, and social benefits provided by the welfare state, women in the European Union (hereafter EU) have won a certain degree of autonomy vis à vis male partners. One of the results of this increased autonomy has been the establishment of shelters from domestic violence, and penal reforms expressing a more responsive attitude towards victims of gendered violence. The dominant perception is, then, that most feminist issues have been (at least partly) resolved.

But viewed from the perspective of most women, many of the classical feminist issues retain their urgency. This is particularly true for those women who are simultaneously confronted with both gendered and other modes of exclusion such as sexual orientation, ethnicity/race, immigration status and/ or class. For, in order to acquire or maintain their autonomy, women in the EU must be able to both maintain control over their reproductive capacities and have access to sources of income and/or material support outside of their family relations, that is: to paid employment and/or social benefits (Gill and Sharma). Particularly those women who must contend with multiple forms of exclusion are hard pressed simultaneously to hold their own in all the spheres of activity that shape the life of a full adult participant of society.

Those women who, in some way, engage with immigration law, must contend with at least two modes of exclusion: gender and nationality. By adopting their perspective, we aim to bring the ongoing gendered tensions in European societies back into view.

Nation and patriarchy

Increasingly, women in the EU have gained access to paid labour. However, a hierarchy in types of labour remains, and women's work still assumes a subdominant position. If anything, the male-dominated sector of regulated, full-time, steady employment has gained in stature as the major prerequisite for citizenship in the social rather than the formal sense of the word, i.e. in the sense of full membership of a society (Bosniak).

2

Social citizenship is associated with a separate sphere of its own, defined in terms of human dignity and individual freedom, which allows for self-fulfilment, social interaction and civil involvement (Mundlak). Immigration law and notions of social citizenship are related, since immigration law regulates legal admission to a national society. This is a selective process, and the criteria used to select immigrants are related to notions of social citizenship. Thus a criminal record, for example, will often preclude admission. Hence, immigration law can give an insight into how the dominant concept of social citizenship is being constructed.

A major project of social and Christian democracy has been to ensure its citizens of the rights and privileges associated with social citizenship (Mundlak). But both the sphere of paid labour and the sphere of freedoms that social citizenship implies can only exist thanks to the reproductive labour that is traditionally performed by women within family relations – labour that is unacknowledged, unseen and unpaid (Bosniak). This reproductive sphere is not pre-determined, but constructed along with, and in apposition to, the male-dominated spheres of paid labour and social citizenship.

Although paid labour and social citizenship are explicitly linked to each other as interdependent spheres, the reproductive sphere is still largely constructed as radically distinct from both. Involvement in the reproductive sphere provides little or no credentials for integration into social citizenship, so that women who are heavily committed to responsibilities in the reproductive sphere receive at best marginal support from the welfare state. On the other hand, the dominant model of full-time paid labour does not accommodate competing commitments in the reproductive sphere.

Performances that take place within the reproductive sphere are not accredited a market value; nor are they perceived of as aspects of human dignity inherent to social citizenship, that should be protected through services and/or measures of social security provided for by the welfare state (Mundlak; Haidinger). As a result, important components of women's identities as adult participants in society are excluded from the dominant model of social citizenship. At the same time, by keeping the predominantly reproductive sphere largely isolated from both market and state involvement, the European welfare state preserves patriarchal notions of men's identity as adult participants in society: that of breadwinner and head of the family.

In a number of ways, immigration law reveals how relevant patriarchal relationships still are, and how intimately they have become tied in with processes that regulate access to membership, in both the formal and the social senses of the word. As Mullally's contribution shows, family norms, reproductive rights and freedom of movement are closely linked. By leaving a country, women can escape the control of a patriarchal moral order, thus challenging and disrupting that order by claiming certain freedoms abroad. On the other hand, by entering another country, migrant women pose a challenge – as potential mothers – to rules that link national belonging to birth and/or family bonds. The immigration and nationality law regimes of receiving countries reveal anxieties concerning the uncontrolled sexuality of female migrants (Mullally).[3]

Immigration law also exposes how the right to establish one's domicile within the nation – surely a prerequisite for social citizenship – continues to be the privilege of those who adhere to the dominant male model of citizenship, defined in terms of a full-time breadwinner. This is evident in the income requirements that apply in rules regulating family reunification (De Hart; Mullally). Immigrant wives, for their part, are kept in a dependent position within their family relations during the first years of their stay in the EU (Raissiguier; Gill and Sharma). In some EU countries they are even excluded from regulated labour relations and the accompanying securities offered by the welfare state (Haidinger).

Class and the gendered division of labour

As argued above, in order to resist patriarchal authority and win autonomy within the reproductive sphere, women must have access to paid employment and/or social benefits. But to do that, women must comply with a dominant model of social citizenship that provides little or no scope for meeting responsibilities in the reproductive sphere. To the extent that they are committed to such responsibilities, they remain dependent on their (male) partner and/or other family members, either to provide the material security that they are unable to acquire for themselves, or to relieve them of at least some of their reproductive responsibilities, or both at the same time.

Some women in the EU, particularly those who form part of dual-earner households, have been able to avoid or at least diminish such dependency by shifting their reproductive responsibilities onto shoulders even less visible than their own – those of outsiders with no access to citizenship at all (Haidinger; Mundlak). As Agustín argues in her chapter, this shift involves not only a transfer of care work, but of sex work as well.

The work of both domestics and sex workers is tainted by its association with the reproductive sphere. At the same time, both types of work disrupt the construction of the reproductive sphere as distinct from the male-dominated spheres of paid labour and social citizenship. In the case of domestic workers, this happens by bringing paid work into the intimate sphere of the home; in the case of sex workers, by bringing those acts of intimacy most strongly associated with the reproductive sphere outside of the home and into the sphere of paid labour. The resulting tension is resolved in the case of domestic workers by denying that their work is to be placed on a par with paid labour (Haidinger; Mundlak); in the case of sex workers, by treating their work as an aberration and thus refuting its worth as a qualifier for social citizenship (Agustín; Crowhurst).

Denied legitimacy, these women cannot benefit from even the limited

4

protection provided by family relations, nor from the protection provided by labour law and the accompanying security net provided by the welfare state (Mundlak; Haidinger). Such an arrangement can only exist as long as the women involved are prepared to accept it. Lack of legal status is clearly one of the factors that explains their willingness to do so. In combination with their exotic identity, the illegitimate nature of their work also helps obscure the tensions within EU societies that they have been enlisted to resolve. As long as the reproductive work that they do is perceived as taking place somehow outside of the nation, the legitimacy of full-time labour as the primary mode of access to social citizenship can continue to go unchallenged (Mundlak).

Although women have been granted formal equality, the possibility of even approaching substantive equality as full participants in society threatens to become the privilege of a specific class of women: those with legal status and sufficient means to hire the services of those lacking both status and access to alternative sources of income. For those EU women who cannot afford to delegate their reproductive responsibilities, full integration into social citizenship is becoming increasingly problematic. Hence denial of the work being done by migrant domestic workers not only leads to a sharpening of the class distinctions between those workers and their citizen employers, but to a sharpening of the class distinctions between their citizen employers and the less affluent citizen women as well.

Ethnicity and gendered violence

As argued above, a current project of European welfare states is to enable a specific mode of social citizenship, based on the male model of the full-time breadwinner. To the extent that state and semi-state institutions must confirm whether or not applicants qualify for help or support, they are not only agents of welfare, but also of control. Immigration law ties into this project in two ways: first, by conferring legitimacy on women who enter as citizens' wives, but then only to the extent that they are prepared to relinquish their autonomy; and second, by denying legitimacy to those women whose labour threatens to expose the inherent contradictions in the dominant mode of social citizenship.

One of the themes that is reflected most consistently throughout this book is how migrant women who lose legitimacy by leaving their citizen husbands and women who are denied legitimacy because of the work that they do, are alternatively demonised or represented as victims of manipulation, deceit, and/or violence at the hands of non-European men (Crowhurst; Mullally). Concern with the violence that many immigrant women have to contend with has rekindled an ongoing feminist debate concerning gendered violence, but now from a specific, culturalist perspective (Bhabha).

The core of this debate concerns the nature of gendered violence. Should it be seen as the expression of men's inherent aggression and women's vulnerability? Or should it be seen as the expression of an ongoing struggle for control: over women's labour, their sexuality and reproductive capacities, their access to resources, their children? Those who adhere to the first view advocate further state repression of male aggression and more protection for (potential) female victims. Those who adhere to the latter view call for measures to support women in their struggle to gain control over the various facets of their lives.

In immigration law, the terms of this debate have shifted in the sense that where formerly men and women have been essentialised in biological or psychological terms, now they are being essentialised in ethnic terms. Through a gendered representation of the alien Other, immigration law – and in its wake, feminist debate – have become closely entwined with a growing preoccupation, within the EU, with matters of ethnic identity. To an increasing extent, distinctions between EU citizens and third-country nationals are being constructed through contrasting representations of gender relations. European societies are being drawn in terms of gender equality and women's autonomy, while male 'third-country nationals' are being represented as archaic, patriarchal and/or violently misogynist, and female 'third-country nationals' as passive, vulnerable, and oppressed. Ironically, those wishing to gain residency rights within the EU for themselves or their families have to play the roles that portray their ethnic difference: that of a full-time breadwinner with a dependent spouse, or that of the passive victim of male aggression (De Hart; Raissiguier; Crowhurst). As a result, ethnic tensions are reinforced, rather than being resolved.

Gender conflict: not resolved but denied

Immigration law forms one of the techniques used to delineate a national society. One of its effects is to stamp all who engage in this branch of law with the mark of the outsider, expressed in both legal and ethnic terms. As a result, issues that mesh with immigration law tend not to be acknowledged as pertinent to the national society involved, but are viewed as specific to those branded as outsiders. The same applies to those gendered tensions, within EU societies, in which immigrant men and women play their part.

Lines of nationality and ethnicity have come to interfere with the distinctions of gender and class, linking legal access to the nation to patriarchal relations, and defining social citizenship in terms that exclude many women. In the process, the relevance of the resulting gender conflicts for the national societies involved are being denied. However, once we accept that gender conflicts involving immigrants are being played out in the heart of European societies, it becomes clear that gender conflicts have not been resolved there, but have simply been projected onto people who have been symbolically placed on the outside.

6

In addressing these unresolved tensions, we run up against a number of questions. Already familiar to feminist theorists, they re-emerge in the context of immigration law. Should sex be defined as work? Should care be defined as a civic virtue? And should women strive to have the reproductive sphere integrated into the sphere of paid labour and/or into that of social citizenship, or is the price – in terms of privacy and family life – too high to pay, not only for men, but for women as well?

Women and immigration law in present-day Europe

Towards the end of the 1990s, immigration law in the EU bore the stamp – albeit in varying degrees – of neo-conservative thought. By this we mean a way of thinking that declares European (or western) arrangements to have universal value; that aims to protect European identity against the invasion of the foreign, inherently non-European (hence non-universalist) legacies of particularly male immigrants; and which assumes this is best done by giving the state considerable discretionary powers.

Gradually, this way of thinking came to incorporate the issue of women and immigration law into its political agenda. As argued above, the western feminist project has come to be seen as finished, by both media and dominant political fora. The purportedly emancipated position of European women is being contrasted with that of their immigrant (especially Muslim) sisters, who supposedly differ in that they are still suffering under a patriarchal system and are in urgent need of consciousness raising. Part of this process has been a selective sensitivity to the issue of gendered violence in the context of immigration and asylum law.

Women in asylum law

Asylum seekers in Europe come predominantly from countries that have freed themselves from European colonisation within the past 50 years, and from states that have emerged from the former communist countries (former Yugoslavia, Chechnya). These frequently fragile states have been further disrupted by structural adjustment policies imposed upon them over the past few decades by the International Monetary Fund (IMF).

Frequently, the resulting tensions have sparked off coups or civil wars, where particular groups (often defined in terms of religion or ethnicity) have sought to oust the sitting regime or to establish an independent territory of their own (Sri Lanka, Chechnya, former Yugoslavia). Such civil wars have often involved sexual violence against 'enemy' women in order to undermine enemy morale and/or promote ethnic purity. In the subsequent struggle to (re)establish and maintain national coherence, moral precepts regarding women's behaviour have often been stressed as normative markers of shared identity, with far-reaching consequences for both women's freedom to participate in public life and their position within family relations. This has been evident in countries as diverse as Iran and Croatia.

In some regions, most notably the Horn of Africa and Western Africa, national coherence has collapsed completely, resulting in continuous warfare, often fuelled by foreign supplies of arms, in which violence becomes an end in itself. In such situations, women have become particularly vulnerable to (sexual) violence, while dependence on their own militias has made them vulnerable on that front as well. This has resulted in a radical limit to women's freedom of movement within such war zones (Markard). In sum, many women flee situations in which they feel threatened by members of their own families, by militias putatively set up to defend them, or by enemy fighters in a civil war.

Feminist critique of western asylum law has long argued that the concepts used to apply the refugee definition recognise women only as the wives or daughters of male refugees. Women's political activism is ignored, and sexual violence is relegated to the private sphere, beyond the scope of asylum law.

In the end, feminist campaigns have proved quite successful in getting regulations introduced, stipulating that sexual violence – whether instigated by militias, family members or enemy forces – qualifies as an act of persecution as defined by the Refugee Convention. Consistent to this, the need for asylum procedures that enable women to talk about their experiences with sexual violence has become widely acknowledged. However, quite independent from these developments, asylum procedures in Europe have by now deteriorated to such an extent that it has become questionable whether women will be able to benefit from these substantive improvements.

So while current asylum policies are explicitly attentive to those asylum seekers who can provide graphic illustrations of the inadequacy of 'non-western cultures' (e.g. victims of female genital mutilation), they have at the same time incorporated so many barriers to admission, that many asylum seekers never make it to the EU in the first place (third-country policies, pre-boarding checks). Of those who do make it that far, few, including women, stand a fair chance during the sharpened procedures.

Trafficking, family migration

Recently, other areas of immigration law have also come to express concern for gendered violence, but again in highly selective ways. Thus images of sexual slavery and abuse connected to the issue of human trafficking help legitimise further restrictions on immigration, increased border control, and the ongoing criminalisation of unregulated travel. The expressed concern for the women involved, however, only reaches as far as this repressive agenda goes. Women are offered protection if, and only as long as, they can be of use in the prosecution, conviction, and incarceration of those charged with transgressing criminal and immigration laws. Only those women who are willing and able to attest to their status as victim, and thus confirm the legitimacy of these repressive acts, are granted even this degree of protection (Crowhurst). What is consistently denied is that the repressive measures these women are asked to support actually exacerbate the problems they must confront (Andrijasevic; Agustín).

Another example of the hypocrisy of immigration law has been the reaction to increased gender equality within family and nationality law. Ironically, such reforms have not resulted in women citizens enjoying a right to domicile equal to that held previously by men. Anxious to prevent foreign men from gaining easy access to legal residence by marrying citizen women, immigration authorities have placed new restrictions on family reunification. Among other things, protection against the expulsion of foreign family members following a criminal conviction has been reduced. As a result, citizen women married to foreign men still lack security of residence for their families, while citizen men have acquired a new possibility to achieve patri-archal authority within their marital relations, namely by marrying an immigrant wife who will be dependent on them for her right of residence (de Hart).

In most EU countries, immigration law is starting to express some aware-ness of immigrant wives' vulnerability to domestic violence. However, the underlying cause of this vulnerability – these women's dependent status – remains unacknowledged. Instead, the violence they are subjected to is depicted as typical of 'non-western culture'. Again, policies that are puta-tively introduced to protect the women involved focus on prosecuting and incarcerating male perpetrators and further limiting possibilities for family migration. In some instances (for example, in the Netherlands) a woman's right to continued residence depends on her initiating criminal charges against her husband, an act that is not necessarily to her advantage (Gill and Sharma).

In sum, immigration law in Europe is currently responsive to those gender issues that can serve to dramatise the perceived inadequacies of 'non-western cultures' or prove the need for increased immigration control. However, it masks the many ways in which it creates and reinforces migrant women's dependencies and vulnerabilities, and how it weakens women's position vis à vis men.

Taking on the neo-conservative challenge

The rise of coherent forms of neo-conservatism that incorporate issues of gender and migration creates a problem for those feminists who oppose the neo-conservative agenda. First, the focus on migrant women's oppression reinforces an implicit assumption that feminist goals have been achieved within the EU nations. Second, it reinforces essentialist notions of culture, portraying Muslim culture in particular as hostile to feminism, helping to legitimate western economic and military hegemony over other parts of the world. Third, it may be used to support the introduction of restrictive immigration law measures, under which women will, directly or indirectly, become the victims.

However, such dilemmas should not discourage us from pursuing the feminist agenda. As Bhabha argues, we must deal with the dilemmas that immigration law confronts us with. A liberal family migration regime can offer men opportunities to re-establish patriarchal authority. If we think restrictions on family reunification are not the right answer, can we explain why? Is repressive state intervention the only way to protect women's autonomy within family relations, or can we come up with alternative proposals to increase the scope of women's agency? We would like to propose two ways in which feminist aims could be pursued in the field of immigration law.

First, as Resnik argues, law is made and applied at several levels that interact. Since neo-conservatives seem to be most powerful at the national level, it may be strategic to seek political support on other levels. The European Union, for example, offers an alternative framework. On the local level too there may be possibilities for resisting national policies; after all, that is where the harsh results of those policies are most directly felt. It may be also that the national judiciary is prepared to protect human rights endangered by national measures. And specialised (quasi-judicial) instances, such as the European Court of Human Rights or the CEDAW (Convention to Eliminate All Forms of Discrimination Against Women) Committee, may offer options in asylum and family reunification law that are not always available at a national level.

Second, as Bosniak argues, legal concepts are not one of a piece, and the inconsistencies in dominant discourse can be exploited. The fact that women's emancipation is a central motif in the neo-conservative project of legitimising European hegemony bolsters the argument that restrictive measures actually encourage women's oppression. Similarly, the argument that procedural rules rob sexual violence victims of the protection granted them by substantive policy rules can be used to invalidate these procedural rules.

Feminists have been campaigning for three decades on issues relating to immigration law. Recently, the topic of women and immigration law has finally made it onto the dominant political agenda, but mainly to the extent that this theme helps legitimate western hegemony abroad and the prosecution, incarceration, and deportation of foreigners at home. What European law and policy makers have been slow in acknowledging is that there are issues to be dealt with regarding immigration law itself.

Moreover, by locating gender conflict outside of the national order – that is, in a 'non-western' country, in an exotic culture or in the clandestine realms of criminal activity – present-day immigration law deflects attention from the gendered tensions inherent in current EU societies – tensions that involve both citizen and immigrant women.

The challenge then is twofold. First, to make clear how the seemingly marginal perspective of immigration law highlights those classical, unresolved feminist themes that reach to the heart of the EU's present-day societies. Second, to make use of the multiple levels of law making, and the inconsistencies in law, to articulate feminist issues through immigration law, to propose alternatives, and to make some impact on the dominant immigration law agenda. That gender has made it onto that agenda is an accomplishment in itself. The question now is how to influence the way gender affects that agenda. This book hopes to make a first step in meeting all these challenges.

Part I includes three essays that deal with the topic of women and immigration law on a level of abstraction that transcends the European context and takes geopolitical power relations into account. These chapters offer conceptual insights into the dilemmas that feminists face when addressing immigration law, the contradictions of legal discourse, and the multiple levels of law making and application. Part II includes articles about asylum, sex work, domestic work and family life that reflect a European perspective and it suggests strategies that apply to the EU as a whole. Part III provides concrete illustrations of women's interactions with national immigration law regimes.

Notes

1 *UN 2004 World Survey on the Role of Women in Development: Women and International Migration*, New York: United Nations, 2005, p 10.
2 The chapters on labour migration focus on domestic workers and sex workers. Obviously, many migrant women in Europe are employed in other sectors. In terms of immigration law, however, most current debates in Europe presently focus on those sectors of the transnational labour market that are being (partially) excluded from regulation, i.e. domestic work and sex work, although some work is being done on labour migration law and female skilled workers. For references see: Eleonore Kofman (2003) 'Women Migrants and Refugees in the European Union', available at: http://www.oecd.org/dataoecd/15/2/15515792.pdf.
3 In the Netherlands, for example, the child of a foreign mother and a Dutch father only acquires Dutch nationality automatically when its parents are legally married at the moment of its birth. When this is not the case, the child can only acquire Dutch nationality via option, and only after having spent at least three years in the company of its Dutch father (Rijkswet op het Nederlanderschap, Art 6).

Part I

GEOPOLITICAL CONTEXT

1

BORDER RIGHTS AND RITES

Generalisations, stereotypes and gendered migration

Jacqueline Bhabha

The same physical act can have opposite effects. Boiling an egg makes it harder; boiling a potato makes it softer.[1] It all depends on what is being boiled. So it is with migration. The physical act of crossing a border between one country and another can be a life saver or a death sentence; a threshold to fame and wealth or a prelude to isolation, ostracism and destitution. The act of moving is in itself (morally, economically, legally and emotionally) neutral, neither good nor bad. Contrast this with situations that clearly are good or bad, such as having a home on the one hand or forced labour on the other. These situations bring with them clear public duties and obligations, irrespective of the merits of individual circumstances. Take housing. The right to adequate housing is considered a cardinal human right.[2] Legal experts, politicians and activists may debate who owes the duty to provide shelter (the state, the employer, the family?); what constitutes 'adequate' shelter (does it include sanitation, heating, privacy?), and to whom the duty is owed (only citizens, residents, asylum seekers, minors?). But no one would defend the advantages of homelessness over those of having a home, and no sensible political platform could advocate this. The right to shelter is uncontroversial. Many, however, would rather not cross a border than migrate and most would rather not have to cross a border. So the right to move, if it can be said to exist at all, is different from the right to shelter – there are circumstances that make it critical, but there may also be circumstances that make moving potentially lethal. Unlike with housing, the luxury of not moving may be as coveted as the right to move.

Forced labour provides the opposite type of contrast. It is prohibited by international law and states have an obligation to take steps to abolish it.[3] Again, there is debate about the boundaries of the concept: the distinction between forced labour and exploitative but voluntary labour; the scope of the concept as applied to different categories of worker (children, pregnant

15

women, the disabled, prisoners); the boundary between forced labour and some types of hazardous or socially stigmatised work. But there is no disputing the state's obligation to intervene to prevent it, and to take steps to protect those affected by it. Labour organisations and industrial relations experts do not question the legitimacy of state intervention or the importance of enforcing sanctions against coercive employers. Not so with migration. Migrant workers, and advocates concerned with their rights, disagree on the merits of state intervention to block or restrict potentially exploitative labour migration. Some argue that the state has an obligation to intervene to prevent migrants clearly destined for forced labour; others argue that selective exit controls targeted at particular members of the population are inherently discriminatory, paternalistic and motivated by racist or conservative political pressures. There is no consensus.

These contrasts are instructive. They capture the difficulties inherent in framing migration in general in terms of absolute rights or state obligations. And they emphasise the importance of specificity in any meaningful discussion of migration issues. There are many vectors of specificity in migration: the 'where' – analysing the migration route; the 'why' – considering the purpose of migration; the 'when' – the length of migration. At different times and in different contexts each of these vectors is the focus of political and legal attention: 'where' – the construction of fortress Europe as a shield against the South and the East; 'why' – the denigration of refugee protection as a foil for 'economic migration'; 'when' – the insistence on classifying long-term labour migrants as 'guest workers'. But the cardinal political concern that dominates all the others is nearly always the 'who' of migration – the demographic characteristics of migrants. At the centre of all debates about migration, as an element in globalisation, as an aspect of human rights or of xenophobia, as a feature of regional integration, as a correlate of development or trade regulation, as an ingredient in cultural exchange and transformation, is the preoccupation with *who* is migrating. Nationality/race/ethnicity (or the fashionable contemporary proxy for these categories, 'culture') is the prime discriminatory criterion: according to one US study, immigration inspectors prejudge passengers according to the geographic region where the flight started – dividing them into 'clean' or 'dirty' (IOM, 2002: 36, citing Gilboy, 1991: 583). Class, gender and age follow close behind as key elements in profiling stereotypes.[4]

Decision making about eligibility for exit, transit, entry and stay is dominated by regulatory and classification systems, both implicit and explicit, which reflect assumptions about legitimacy, vulnerability and desirability related to these demographic characteristics. As a study of decision making by US immigration inspectors found, inspectors rely on 'known categories', usually nationality but often gender and age, to 'sift' or 'winnow' out suspicious people with a minimum of time and effort (Gilboy, 1991: 578–80). One interviewed inspector said: 'Any male from [country x] you secondary. You don't waste your breath. They're not going to tell you anything. They're going to give you a sing-song language, or they are going to lie to you anyway' (Gilboy, 1991: 586). Demographic characteristics of course impact on decision making at both ends of the migratory chain: they affect the choices and pressures that impact on the migrant him or her self, as well as the regulatory framework applied by individual decision makers, be they visa officers, immigration adjudicators or judges.

So, the options and constraints that impinge on an impoverished rural Moroccan 20-year-old will govern the migration choices made, just as the political and cultural attitudes to this demographic group will dictate the immigration procedures the Moroccan is exposed to when leaving, travelling and crossing the border. The two pictures – the migrant's and the immigration officer's – may be transparent and match closely (as with German corporate transnational transfers or contract labour agreements for workers from the Philippines where the migration package – visa, job, accommodation, salary, family accompaniment, length of stay – are fixed in advance); they may be radically divergent (wealthy urban Egyptian visitor detained as Al Qaeda member; Bangladeshi family member travelling to join settled spouse); or they may overlap but require extensive negotiation, delay, litigation to merge (Sri Lankan Tamil fleeing persecution by the LTTE in Jaffna; Nigerian accountancy student).

How does gender play into this complex set of demographic equations that determine the relationship between the migrant's self-perception and actual situation on the one hand, and the immigration officer's mental picture and actual legal framework and classificatory rules and quotas on the other? Make a thought experiment: at the simplest level, the examples of different migrant situations I just presented were not gendered, but did you gender them as you read the paragraph: the rural Moroccan crossing the border; the German transnational corporate executive; the contract worker from the Philippines; the wealthy Egyptian detained post 9/11; the Sri Lankan Tamil seeking asylum from the Tigers; the Bangladeshi spouse seeking family reunion; the Nigerian accountancy student? If yes, then why? Because stereotypes are so fundamental to our use of language that they structure our thought and comprehension processes automatically?[5] Is this good or bad or morally neutral? In other words, are we 'cognitive misers' (Fiske and Taylor, 1984), using stereotypes to do just enough mental work to get by but cutting corners in terms of accuracy? Or are we 'motivated tacticians' (Fiske and Taylor, 1991), using stereotypes as a sensible simplifying strategy for coping with a large amount of data? What are the consequences? For example, does our assumption that the Egyptian visitor suspected of terrorism is male mean that a woman would be less likely to be stopped at the airport or detained on entry, that she would be favoured, and would be likely to benefit? Is this gender discrimination? Does the stereotype of the Bangladeshi wife trailing rather than leading the family migration mean that a woman sponsor seeking to bring her spouse to join her would encounter greater obstacles than a man? If so, then this is gender discrimination, but is it discrimination against the woman sponsor, the male spouse or both?

I pose these questions not to engage in semantics but to illustrate how easy it is to slip into simplistic but incorrect assumptions about gender discrimination and migration. Many of us, myself included, assumed for years that gender discrimination was synonymous with discrimination against women – that female migrants were disadvantaged at all stages of the migration process by a patriarchal migration paradigm. We had good reason for this assumption. We saw British immigration officers subject South Asian women seeking to enter the UK as fiancées to 'virginity tests', following official government policy, because the stereotype was that a South Asian fiancée had to be a virgin (Bhabha and Shutter, 1994: 111–13). Ergo, if a young woman applying to enter in that category turned out, on inspection, not to be a virgin, then she was deemed by definition not to be a 'real' fiancée. We saw Dutch asylum officers refuse Eritrean women refugee status because their form of participation in the liberation struggles – cooking, washing, hiding male comrades – was considered insignificant and purely personal, by contrast with the qualifying behaviour of the male activists. We saw American immigration judges deny refugee protection to a Salvadorian woman raped by government paramilitaries after they killed her guerrilla relatives because the rape was not considered 'political' but a private issue of personal attraction; or we found gross disparities in the percentages of Mexicans who were subjected to expedited removal (85 per cent of women versus 35 per cent of men between 1997 and 1999) (Thomas J. White Center on Law and Government, 2001: 15).We saw family reunion policies which assumed that the head of household was male, that women should follow their husbands and not vice versa, that single parents (of course overwhelmingly female) who had migrated to seek work and left their children in the care of grandparents but supported them by sending most of their earnings back home could not sponsor their children to come and join them because they could not prove that they had had 'sole responsibility for them' – a contradiction in terms! We saw Italian authorities returning women to Nigeria within 48 hours of arrival, simply on the presumption that they were Nigerian nationals and therefore sex workers (Pearson, 2002: 147) – a compelling example of the interaction between race and gender stereotypes (Crenshaw, 1991).

Even temporary visas were discriminatory – in the UK, male students could bring their spouses with them and get permission to work but female students could not (Bhabha and Shutter, 1994). Bangladesh, India, Indonesia and Pakistan prohibited women from taking jobs abroad as domestic workers to pre-empt the possibility of domestic abuse or trafficking, forcing women to bribe their way out of these restrictions (Charnowitz, 2002). In the US, young women entering to visit friends of the family and claiming that they would do some babysitting were automatically referred for further questions under suspicion of being 'nannies' (Gilboy, 1991: 590–1). We also had to contend with citizenship laws that reflected patriarchal assumptions about family structure – women losing their nationality of origin when marrying non-national men (but not vice versa), discriminatory rules about the transmission of citizenship from parent to child (in some countries, only fathers could transmit their nationality to their foreign-born, illegitimate children, in other countries only mothers could do so) (Kerber, 2003).

And it was not just the black letter of the law that was discriminatory. Immigration procedures exacerbated the unfairness of the law by adopting processes that were on the face of it gender neutral but had profoundly prejudicial effects for women. For example, male interviewers questioning immigration applicants unaccustomed to interacting with unrelated men; aggressive cross-examination of trauma and rape victims in confrontational settings after long transcontinental flights; the machinery of immigration control operated through gendered and racialised mechanisms that targeted certain applicants disproportionately. There is no clearer example of this than the discovery that in the 1990s US Customs officers at major airports searching for transporters of illegal drugs wrongly subjected disproportionately large numbers of African-American women to thoroughly intrusive body cavity searches (Schauer, 2003: 176). The overwhelming majority were completely innocent, targeted simply because of their race and gender.

But as our thinking has progressed, and as we have moved from denunciation to investigation, from certainty to a more nuanced questioning, certain flaws in our original schematic approach have became apparent. Our assumption that gender discrimination always disadvantaged women compared to men was wrong, or at least simplistic. We had been too quick to assume, along with everyone else, that women were perennial 'victims' of the system – defenceless, vulnerable, naïve agents who were taken advantage of by others. Careful research revealed, for example, that among asylum applicants in a range of developed states, a higher proportion of women than men were granted refugee status. Far from being discriminated against, women were more – not less – likely to be accepted as refugees. Whether this was because women had greater hurdles to overcome to become refugees in the first place, and therefore had stronger claims than their male counterparts; or whether the assumption that women were more 'vulnerable', more likely to be victims of persecution, more candid and honest, more in need of protection, less threatening to the job market elicited more sympathetic responses from the decision makers; or whether the fact that smaller numbers of women than men applied for asylum made them less likely targets of exclusionary hostility – the reasons for the relative advantage of women over men in asylum were not clear. But the facts were, and they contradicted the confident assertion that refugee protection was unfair to women because it was dominated by a male paradigm of the refugee. Our research also revealed that far fewer women than men made applications for asylum in developed states – not because smaller numbers of women were in need of refugee protection, quite the contrary (women refugees outnumber men in all states neighbouring source countries), but because most refugee women never got beyond countries immediately neighbouring their home country (Bhabha, 2004).

So we had to acknowledge that more complex processes of gender discrimination and gendering were at play throughout the migration process, and that they were not limited to the post-entry stage. The pre-migration situation imposed different and often increased restrictions on female migrants than on their male counterparts, less access to the resources necessary for travel, greater obligations towards other family members (children, the elderly) and cultural obstacles to independent travel. In other words, these formed a complex combination of societal, household and individual factors which resulted in different 'migratory probabilities' (Boyd and Grieco, 2003) for men and women – an amalgam of more or less rational choices by individuals, families and societies of origin which affected the timing and the distance of migration. It was not so much a question of individual decision making – women being less adventurous or confident or independent – but rather a matrix of gendered factors affecting motivation, incentive, resources and social options. It also became clear, in the post-Schengen era, as border controls were progressively militarised and migration became increasingly considered an arm of state security and law enforcement, that the dangers inherent in transit situations had increased – risks of intimidation, coercion, extortion, physical and sexual assault – many of them disproportionately impacting women. These risks were pervasive and ubiquitous. Gradually the evidence emerged that immigration professionals, including the staff of international organisations, advocates and decision makers, had been ignoring very serious and cumulative gender-specific human rights violations relating to the migratory process itself – affecting Vietnamese women fleeing to Hong Kong, Somali women seeking protection in Kenya, Chinese women smuggled into the US or France, or Kosovar and Albanian women crossing into Western Europe. And finally we started paying attention to the gendered processes that characterised decision making in destination countries: the embedded assumptions about family size, shape and structure; the intersection between gender, class and race/nationality stereotypes dominating many of the mechanics of the legal adjudication process; and the exploitation of those stereotypes by 'agents', handlers, snakeheads, smugglers and other migration intermediaries who used the complications and idiosyncrasies of the migration control system, and the powerful pressures to master it, to amass quick illicit fortunes.

In response, we engaged in a range of successful campaigns, campaigns that brought together grassroots activists from the trades union, anti-racist, feminist and immigrant rights movements. The western women's movement, after years of solipsistic preoccupation with peculiarly Anglo-European, often middle-class aspects of women's liberation, eventually accepted the criticisms of women of colour and embraced a broader array of feminist preoccupations including refugee protection, immigration exclusion, deportation and racist post-entry internal controls. We were remarkably successful in some respects. As Deborah Anker has pointed out, excellent feminist work on refugee protection, focused initially on the rights of Haitians fleeing the Duvalier dictatorship but then more generally on Central and Latin American asylum seekers, had an enormous impact on refugee adjudication (Anker, 2002). In the space of 15 years this work yielded extraordinary gains: an acknowledgement that the refugee definition could encompass within its scope women fleeing domestic violence, rape, sexual assault, female circumcision, homophobia and other forms of gender persecution. Many immigration and feminist scholars, advocates and organisations, such as Southall Black Sisters, FOWAAD, Greater Boston Legal Services, Kalayan, JCWI, ILPA and Gisti to name just a few, have valiantly battled rising trends of xenophobia and sustained nativism to stem the tide. They have campaigned and initiated litigation, including before the European Court of Human Rights, challenged discriminatory family reunion laws – in England the infamous 'primary purpose rule' which required Asian couples[6] to demonstrate (how could they? how could anyone?) that the 'primary purpose' of a marriage between residents of the UK and India, Pakistan or Bangladesh was not immigration;[7] immigration laws that made it harder for a UK resident woman to bring her spouse to join her than for a similarly placed man; work permit regulations which stipulated that certain categories of (female) workers had to be childless. We have had successes, and proved that – flawed though it is – the law is a living instrument which can be used and improved.

But as we have forged ahead, trying to cement our ranks across different priorities and political positions, taking on key battles against restrictionism and exclusionism, so we have been forced to engage in intense debates within our own ranks. Not a bad development, you may think: any movement has to re-evaluate its premises as it grows in size and experience. But some of our discussions have been acrimonious. Let me briefly mention three. First, the ever thorny issue of universalism versus cultural relativism, ubiquitous in the human rights firmament generally, but particularly evident in discussions of gender and culture. The key problem is best captured by the evocative rhetorical question posed by the late Susan Okin, 'Is multiculturalism bad for women?' (1997). In our field of migration, this discussion has presented itself as a tension. On the one hand are those who denounce practices considered unqualifiedly, absolutely and universally harmful to women, who emphasise the inherently oppressive aspects which in their view characterise cultures of origin, and use this to strengthen refugee protection claims. On the other hand are those who criticise what they consider imperialistic and ill-informed judgements, what Isabel Gunning labelled 'arrogant perception' (1992). We could, perhaps somewhat unfairly, characterise the two camps as the demonisers versus the appeasers – those who term customs such as

21

female circumcision or strict Islamic dress codes or religious/legal norms (e.g. post Khomeini Iran) as barbaric, persecutory in and of themselves; and those who, sometimes deferring to the views and pronouncements of unelected community spokespersons, reject such categorical universals and argue that all cultural practices have a range of meanings which can have value and legitimacy. Note how the use of stereotypes plays into this discussion – the barbaric African, the sexist Muslim, primitive cultures. Or, on the other hand, a meta-liberal abstentionism, toleration, withdrawal from judgement, arm's length 'respect for the other'.

But note too how the legal system pushes advocates to use these stereotypes, to simplify, to engage in just the sort of cognitive miserliness that I criticised earlier. How many of us, as advocates, have not pressed 'our' country experts to simplify their affidavits, to present as clear a picture as possible of a culture, a situation or a danger in an effort to persuade a court? How often do we solicit names of scholars who can confirm that forced marriage in Southeast China is endemic within the culture (to which the expert's response will usually be 'well it is widespread in some areas but not in others' or 'it does occur from time to time but it is not that common'), or experts who are willing to testify about 'the prevalence of FGM in Nigeria' or 'the harshness of Islamic law in Iran'? In fact, advocates, governments and courts often operate with crude, inaccurate and simplistic stereotypes about complex and evolving social and political situations. For example, the House of Lords in deciding the Islam and Shah landmark refugee case[8] famously declared women in Pakistan, as a whole, second-class citizens. And some years earlier, British adjudicators had delivered the same verdict on the position of women in Iran (Bhabha, 1996). Yet we know that there are grass-roots organisations and feminist groups active in Pakistan and Iran, that the law is not as unnuanced and draconian as these advocates have argued as these courts have held. Many Iranian and Pakistani women are contributing to changes in their societies, not because they are 'western' or 'westernised' but because they are part of indigenous social movements for change. Islamic feminism has become an important fact of political life in both countries, and both law and public practice have been – to some extent – impacted by these developments. For example, since the Khomeini revolution, there has been significant reform to Iranian family law expanding the grounds on which women can obtain a divorce (to include maltreatment which renders the marriage intolerable) (Hoodfar, 1995: 29). Similarly, over the last 40 years, Pakistani judges have been redefining a woman's right to divorce' (Haider, 2000: 287). The situation is dynamic and evolving. Yet when asylum seekers from these countries present their claims, a distinction is often drawn between the individual women's western, progressive and enlightened ways and the primitive contexts they are trying to escape. A New Zealand asylum case concerning an Iranian woman contains language which illustrates this point:

The social status of women in many countries in Asia, Africa and even South America is very different from that which pertains in countries such as New Zealand, Canada, United States and much of Europe. Few countries have legislation prohibiting discrimination against women. Attitudes which in New Zealand are regarded as 'sexist' are widespread throughout the globe. In many countries . . . *unenlightened attitudes* have some form of religious sanction.[9]

To characterise these countries as primitive, barbaric or unenlightened is parochial at best and suggests a high level of ignorance or prejudice, or both. But returning to the use of stereotypes: Are we right? Are we wrong? Is simplification and the use of stereotype a legitimate pragmatic strategy to win a client's case, or is it an illegitimate use of imperialist falsifications? Does this false essentialising of 'community', the obscuring of political nuances and developments, perpetuate and exacerbate an East (or South) = primitive, West (or North) = feminist, enlightened mindset? Or is it a necessary device, in a complex world, to simplify and synthesise unfamiliar information; to generalise, to fix the particular in the general, so that novel decisions can be made? There is undoubtedly a case to be made for simplification; neither advocates nor adjudicators can be expected to have the knowledge of post-doctoral scholars about all the disparate countries they make decisions about. However, there is a danger in our strategy. By trying to secure watertight affidavits, by setting the bar so high for what counts as a persecutory country of origin, asylum advocates are driven to simplify, distort and even falsify the complex societies from which their clients originate in order to persuade decision makers that their clients qualify for protection. Not only is this unsatisfactory as an exercise in accuracy, it also risks jeopardising the basis of asylum in the future, as the background depictions of asylees' countries of origin become more and more removed from the complex multifaceted reality that exists. This strategy also creates too high a benchmark for access to asylum. After all, the standard of proof required by the Refugee Convention is simply that of a reasonable chance or possibility of persecution; we should not fall into the trap of trying to paint a picture that suggests inevitability or even probability of persecution.

A second discussion has proved equally contentious – the debate over arranged and forced marriages. This has a direct impact on border crossing because only legally valid marriages can provide the basis for family reunification (still the dominant mode of entry into most developed countries – accounting for two-thirds of migration into the US, for example (Kofmann, 2004: 243–4)). There is a broad consensus against forced marriages, and in favour of arranged marriages; the critical issue (as with all marriage) is free or genuine consent. On this, feminists, human rights activists, governments, ethnic and religious minority organisations, and most members of the public agree. But how easy is it to isolate free consent from pressure bordering on coercion? What is genuine consent? And how should one evaluate the quality of consent in relation to the costs of not consenting?[10] Does it deteriorate as the consequences of refusing to comply mount? Is reluctant or resentful consent still consent? Can we justify the equation more coercion = less genuine, voluntary, free consent? If this is so (and I believe it is), then the line between arranged and forced marriage is not as clear-cut as many of us have long argued, though of course marriages at the extremes of the spectrum are totally distinct. If the price of refusing a suggested marriage partner is rejection by the entire extended family, or losing the love of one's parents, or even the shame that comes from disobeying an older relative, what should we consider to be too high a price for the marriage to count as consensual? Another way of getting at this problem is to ask the question: 'What makes the exit option real' (Kukathas, 2003) as opposed to too costly to contemplate? Interestingly, it has been pointed out that British courts have moved from a clear dichotomy to a more nuanced position on the subject. They no longer require gross physical pressure, threat to life or limb, as a necessary correlate of a forced marriage, but assess whether the future spouse's 'mind has been overborne, however that was caused'. As a result, many marriages that were once considered valid arranged marriages would now be considered void or voidable forced marriages.[11] This shift is a result of activist pressures from within the communities affected against forced marriage.

The tough question is to what extent, if any, immigration law should play a part in this decision-making process, given that the fundamental issues are human rights concerns which have nothing directly to do with migration? Is the validity of a marriage, its consensual nature, irrelevant to decisions to grant family reunion visas? Should intervention against forced marriage only take place after family reunification has taken place? Is it conceivable that state immigration controls could operate in a rights-enhancing manner to forestall forced marriages and to assist reluctant, resentful future spouses from additional duress? Does any state have a duty to explore the possibility of this situation, given the well-established and widely publicised patterns of matchmaking? Or is it naïve and dangerous to suggest this, because alleged concerns about the validity of marriages (which the state is unlikely to explore adequately) will result conveniently in justifications for immigration restrictionism, and in encouragement for confusion between legitimate arranged marriages and coercive forced ones? On balance, the latter concerns seem to win the argument for most of us, though we should be mindful of the serious difficulties in accessing legal protection against abusive spouses and coercive marriages post family reunion.

This is not as straightforward and easy a set of alternative choices as some of us once thought. Related to this dilemma is the topic of mail-order brides, and the many variations of commercially mediated matchmaking that generally transport impoverished but desirable young women into marital relationships with older and richer men. Again we are back to the coercion/consent conundrum – how do we distinguish? How do we avoid falling into the Scilla of infantilising women's choices and agency without landing up with the Caribdes of criminal negligence and complicity in forced labour, or sexual slavery? Marriage migration is clearly a free and rational exit choice for many and may represent a net improvement in life chances and quality, an emancipatory strategy. This is true across continents and decades. Already in 1984, it was clear that:

> 'For women [taking part in the emigration from Ireland] it was more than a mere flight from poverty. It was an escape from an increasingly patriarchal society whose asymmetrical development as a colony generated insufficient social space for women even as wife and mother.'
>
> (Morokvasic, 1984: 898)

But are there any duties of care at the border and, if so, to whom? Is a brief restriction of freedom, to clarify future arrangements or provide documentary confirmation of the account, compatible with respect for the right to freedom of movement (as proposed by Human Rights Watch, 2002)? This is an uncomfortable topic but one that goes to the heart of border rites and rights.

This debate leads directly into the third contentious topic that I would like briefly to touch on – the debate about sex work, slavery and trafficking. This topic has just about eclipsed all others in the migration field over the last few years – to the extent that there is now, in the public imagination, a seamless stream of vast numbers of hapless refugee and other third world and East European women and children being forcibly trafficked into developed states by exploitative criminal gangs. Trafficking has become virtually synonymous with forced sex work, despite the evidence of large-scale trafficking for domestic and agricultural purposes.

Separating fact from fiction is not easy. There is no denying that large numbers of domestic and sex workers from overseas enter and work in developed states.[12] We know that there is a huge sex and pornography industry – of unprecedented dimensions – which provides a seemingly insatiable, demand-driven economic magnet for one part of this migration. Considering some of the data helps one to realise why the prospects for success in curbing sex trafficking or seriously addressing and improving the human rights needs of migrant sex workers are very slim. According to an MSNBC poll in February 2002, 84 per cent of American men pursue sex-related activities online. These include dating and escort services, locating sex clubs and adult videos – all activities involving sex workers, with an increasing number of them being migrants. The profits from this industry are mind-boggling: $57 billion globally every year, of which $12 billion in the US. Porn revenue in the US exceeds the joint income from all professional football, baseball and basketball franchises. The industry simply has an overwhelming need for person power. As radical Swedish MEP Marianne Eriksson (an active campaigner for gay rights and not a moralist at all) put it recently: 'There is a lack of knowledge about the link between porn, which has become normalised in every country and gets into every home, and the commercialisation of women and child trafficking ... It is not upper-class rich people that get damaged by porn; it is a poverty issue.'[13] We know that within the industry, very serious human rights violations take place with regularity; that young women and children particularly (but not exclusively) are subjected to forced labour, sexual violence and gross brutality in many metropolitan centres. We also know that large numbers of such migrants are grossly unprotected by domestic law enforcement and welfare institutions. They are allowed to work in unsafe surroundings, pressured into potentially compromising situations as prosecution witnesses in the hope of securing legal immigration status, and are vulnerable to removal and deportation once they come into contact with law enforcement authorities. At the same time, protestations against the evils of trafficking in persons are ubiquitous. Yet the phenomenon, if this is what it is, continues unabated: the solutions as unclear and elusive as ever. We seem to be in a stalemate. Why is this?

First, it is clear that public pronouncements and concerns have been in some ways disingenuous. Whatever the well-intentioned motivations of individual political players, the collective drive behind curbing trafficking and convicting traffickers has been fuelled by immigration control rather than human rights concerns. This is evident from the emphasis of the international conventions agreed and the political contexts in which the issue has been addressed: organised crime and state security rather than labour rights and enhancement of migrant legal protections. With a few exceptions, the latter have attracted no extra funding or resources. Labour inspectors, housing inspectors, shelters, clinics, legal status for trafficked persons are scarce and face constant funding constraints. Governments have been interested in demonstrating their concern to curb undocumented migration not to protect the rights of abused migrant workers but to attract support from xenophobic lobbies, fuelled by domestic employment insecurities. This has dictated the choice of interventionist policies, directed at exclusion and delegitimisation rather than inclusion or protection. The failure materially to increase assistance for trafficked persons has been such that some women's rights and sex worker advocates are now arguing that the 'trafficking' terminology is more harmful than beneficial and should be disposed of.

Second, the demand for migrant sex labour has not been addressed or curbed. The sex and pornographic industry is massive and growing; it is unchecked and undeterred. There is in practice no political will to curb or restrict it. Significant numbers of beneficiaries of the industry, as profiteers or consumers, are doubtless present within the ranks of the regulatory state bodies. As a recent human rights report on trafficking at the Burma–Thai border documents:

For some of the sex workers at one particular brothel the 'greatest fear' was 'working for free', that is providing sexual services for Thai police and soldiers ... The owner of a restaurant where sex was regularly sold was 'a colonel in Thai immigration'.

(Physicians for Human Rights, 2004: 38)

Unlike drugs, which threaten the lives of the sons and daughters of parliamentarians and immigration officials, sex work is confined to the poorer social strata. It does not really threaten the family life of most policy makers in a comparable way. Given the incentives and the overpowering demand, attempts at curbing the supply are likely to be unsuccessful unless the vested interests in maintaining supply are addressed. But we have no idea of the real numbers, despite the industry that has developed to churn them out. And we do not know how many migrant sex workers are prisoners, sex slaves in effect, and how many are working in mutually advantageous if exploitative relationships, exercising a desired and rational exit strategy from economically, politically or socially oppressive situations.

Third, I am not sure that we can maintain a clear-cut distinction between persons who have been smuggled and persons who have been trafficked, though here again there is a seemingly easy dichotomy that revolves around consent: smuggled migrants are complicit in their illegal travel, they have chosen it and consented; trafficked persons are coerced, involuntary prisoners of cruel racketeers.[14] So much for the theory and international law.

In practice, though, the dividing line is much less clear. How should we categorise the very sizeable numbers of migrants who agree to be smuggled for enormous fees (the current rate from Fujian China to New York City is $40,000; from the Wenzhou region of Zhejiang to Paris, it is FF 500,000 (Yun, 2004: 7)) and then work for years to repay the fee with exorbitant rates of interest and vicious threats for late payments? Are they consensual smugglees, who are making a tough choice in tough circumstances, or are they trafficked persons? Again this discussion is not purely academic, not a doctrinal dispute over definitional niceties. International (and some domestic) law now distinguishes sharply between the two categories – trafficked persons, usually referred to as trafficking victims, are objects of compassion and in some cases assistance; they are considered eligible for a range of human rights protections and benefits, for state-funded protective services, even – in some cases – for permanent immigration status (though the annual quota of 5,000 US T visas is grossly underutilised). Smuggled persons, by contrast, are unproblematically considered illegal migrants who have willingly sought professional assistance to evade immigration control ('sneaking across the border' in popular parlance) and who therefore do not have strong claims to human rights protection let alone immigration status. They only become objects of compassion once dead or at death's door. Moreover, since they are not coerced, they are considered fully responsible for their situation.

However, and herein lies the difficulty, consent at one point should not be taken as consent forever. How then do we categorise the indentured Chinese worker? Does her initial interest in agreeing to the smuggling contract preclude her from challenging the terms of her forced labour? Can an exploitative, mutually advantageous agreement (such as the one between the 'snakehead' who arranges for the smuggling and the smugglee who is transported from China to the west) also count as slavery or forced labour? One way of addressing this difficult question is to recognise that consent and coercion are always contextual, they are not freestanding. Different existential starting points can affect our assessment of individual responsibility or consent.[15] A person who is threatened with 'your money or your life' cannot be said to have consented when handing over the money. A person who says 'yes' to a marriage proposal to avoid being beaten or burnt cannot be said to have consented. As the philosopher Alan Wertheimer points out, citing Aristotle, 'one acts involuntarily when one must choose between alternatives that are contrary to the range of alternatives one's moral will would permit ... On the other hand, one cannot be said to have acted involuntarily simply because one does not *like* the available alternatives' (Wertheimer, 1987: 302).

Let us translate this discussion into a migration situation. Consider a large family in Albania in which a young woman agrees/chooses to become a sex worker in Italy. If the family is poor, the possibility of sex work in Italy might appear attractive, an offer the woman cannot refuse – her baseline of expectations is exceedingly low. For a better-off woman, with a comfortable life and adequate resources, the same possibility is unlikely to appear remotely attractive, rather something she would only do if seriously threatened – her baseline of expectations is much higher. So whether something constitutes an offer or a threat depends in large measure on the baseline of the person to whom the suggestion is made, not simply on the nature of the suggestion itself.[16] Sometimes the alternatives may be less stark: the baseline may be less desperate, the comfortable life less appealing. What constitutes an improvement in one's situation may be far from obvious. Indeed, 'making a hard choice may constitute an important aspect of autonomy' (Wertheimer, 1987: 233). But could one ever justify interference with such a choice? This is the challenging dilemma at the heart of the debate. To quote Wertheimer again: 'Under extreme conditions, the presumption that noncoercive agreements should be enforced might be overridden by considerations of exploitation' (1987: 238). So if the Albanian woman became an indentured labourer, interference might be justified. But what if she consented to work 16 hours a day for €5 a month? Would we want to argue that the woman is responsible for her decision, should not be infantilised by protective policy and should be free to act on her choice, however reluctant or reticently made? Or would we want to argue that this is really no choice at all but coercion under a different name – because the alternative is no alternative? Hiding behind the veil of 'consent' does nothing to address concretely the substantial risk of serious harm.

Glorifying choice, independence and autonomy may be naïve or even callous if it means disregarding the morally unacceptable dilemmas that lead to the choices. On the other hand, one risks consenting to state interference that is likely to restrict the mobility of some sections of the population unfairly and in a discriminating way, which is in reality restrictive immigration control under the guise of human rights protection. In Burma, for example, all women between the ages of 16 and 25 are required to travel with a legal guardian. The government justifies this as an anti-trafficking measure, but women interviewed by an opposition NGO (Democratic Voice of Burma) said that the regulations did not prevent travel but made it more difficult for them in terms of additional bribes and harassment at the border. Changes to the regulations have made it approximately four times more expensive for women to get a passport than for men (Wertheimer, 1987: 198–9). So border controls do not solve the problem of gendered migrant abuse, they just exacerbate it. They also risk displacing what should be a struggle for political and social change within and between communities to a discussion of the merits of different forms of border control, when the fact of crossing a border is not the significant rights issue. The difficulty with either position is that neither fully represents the interests of the affected parties. As Human Rights Watch commented in a recent report on Thai women trafficked into debt bondage in Japan:

> In determining the appropriate treatment of suspected victims of trafficking, it is important to emphasise that such persons have not been charged with any criminal activity and that their treatment must be consistent with the intent of protection ... *While briefly restricting a woman's freedom of movement for the purpose of factual clarification and document verification may be appropriate*, any further deprivation of liberty must be consistent with the right to be free from arbitrary detention.
>
> (Human Rights Watch, 2002: 236; emphasis added)

The only thing worse than an exploitative agreement is no agreement at all (Human Rights Watch, 2002: 237). Exploited workers do not welcome greater state interference because, far from enhancing their rights, it simply leads to immigration restriction, unemployment and a risk of retaliatory violence from the employer. That is why many undocumented workers fear the migration and health and safety inspectors above all else. Migrant sex workers in particular have found the protection of host states, in situations where they are linguistically, socially and politically isolated, to be elusive and patchy. They occupy very weak negotiating positions in foreign countries. Immigrant networks, often presented in an idealised form as instances of immigrant initiative and will to succeed (like families in an earlier time), in practice frequently silence women migrants' voices, by participating in and concealing domestic abuse, by adopting the pre-existing gendered hierarchies, even by exploiting newly arrived, undocumented relatives. Moreover, undocumented workers have an additional vulnerability: the insecurity that comes from not having documents – the depressing refrain 'no tengo papeles' (Mendelson, 2004: 139). The panacea of participation in the public sphere, celebrated as the key to empowerment by activists against domestic violence, is no panacea at all but a potentially dangerous exposure.

In this situation of double threat – within the home and on the street – mainstream legal remedies and institutional supports are simply not available (Mendelson, 2004: 138). Turning to the police, the courts or to the home environment are potentially equally dangerous. The only alternative is to improve the background situation – but how? By restricting entry in the first place (e.g. through carefully profiled, brief screenings at the border)? By granting unconditional amnesty and residence permits to those who come forward (something we might well call for but that states have been very wary of)? By improving the background situation? But in a context where, as *The Economist* recently revealed, any migrant moving from the South to the North is likely to add at least $300,000 to his or her lifetime earnings (Cairncross, 2002: 4), finding a human rights justification for blocking choices that can lead to life improvements is hard. So the argument against intervention or interference with choice is a powerful one.

Enforcing rights protection irrespective of migration status is of course the optimal solution for undocumented workers, male and female. But this flies in the face of the current dominant contradiction at the heart of the immigration question: the tension between the racist political imperative to exclude unskilled migrant workers and the economic imperative to include them; in other words, the tension between political aversion and economic need. It is this unresolved tension that produces the distinctive pattern of gendered migration that we have been considering: large-scale migration, both documented and undocumented, of disenfranchised and highly exploitable workers to service a range of economic, social and personal needs – from textile sweatshops, to fast-food takeaways, to hospitals, childcare facilities and the sex industry. Of course, there are also the many highly skilled migrants, both male and female – doctors, computer programmers, scientists, technicians, lawyers, actors, industrialists – a full range of professionals and business people who glide through relatively effortlessly. But they are the globalised elite, not the restricted majority with whom we need to be concerned.

Changing demographic and gendered employment patterns in both the developing and the developed states drive this complex migration picture, producing fractured families and new migration routes, and a growing demand for migrants – baby girl adoptees from China and Russia (at a rate of 30,000 per year); male labourers for building and agriculture; women for an ageing population with double income earners and no space for the care of the young, or the elderly, or perhaps for non-commercial sexual pleasure. Maybe we need to return to our political roots: many of the battles of the early women's movement that some of us took part in decades ago – regarding collectivisation of housework, reorganisation of the working day and week, shared childcare, carer leave – remain to be addressed. And while we ignore them, some of the old divisions between the beneficiaries and the losers of the fight for women's rights – divisions that reflect race and class barriers – reappear to remind us that our collective activism is as critical as it ever was.

Acknowledgements

I am very grateful to Molly Curren and Kate Desormeau for superb research assistance and comments. I am also grateful to participants at the Gendered Borders conference in Amsterdam for helpful and provocative questions and discussion. I would like to dedicate this article to three friends who worked long and hard on gendered migration and whose contribution we sorely miss today – Arthur Helton, Joan Fitzpatrick and Mary Diaz.

Notes

1 I borrow this wonderful metaphor from the late German Jewish refugee poet Eva Ehrenberg, who used it to illustrate how people react differently to adversity, some by hardening and others by softening.

2 See especially the Universal Declaration of Human Rights (Art 25(1)) and the International Covenant on Economic, Social, and Cultural Rights (Art 11(1)).

3 See especially the 1926 UN Slavery Convention and the 1956 Supplementary Convention on the Abolition of Slavery, the Slave Trade and Institutions and Practices Similar to Slavery; ILO Convention C 29 on Forced or Compulsory Labour; the Universal Declaration of Human Rights (Art 4); the European Convention on Human Rights (Art 4(1)) ILO Convention C 105 on the Abolition of Forced Labour; and the Rome Statute (Art 7).

4 Typically a range of other more particular factors are included to construct the stereotypes that are used for selective immigration 'profiling'; but race, gender, class and age are often key to the 'algorithm of complex factors' that guide the exercise of official discretion (see Schauer, 2003: 187).

5 Certainly stereotypes seem to function in this way; they are not fixed, immutable constructs but rather implicate both the viewer and the viewed, structuring the experience of both (see Homi Bhabha, 1983).

6 There is no case where the rule has been applied to two white spouses (Menski, 1999: 83).

7 It is worth noting, in passing, that some within the immigrants' rights lobby were ambivalent about the merits of repealing the primary purpose rule, because they saw it as a protection against forced marriage to cousins and other relatives abroad for British-Asian girls.

8 *Islam (AP) v Secretary of State for the Home Department, Regina v Immigration Appeal Tribunal and Another ex p Shah*, [1999] 2 All ER 545.

9 Re SY [1994] NZAR 915/92, in Mimi Liu and Laura Black (eds), *Gender Asylum*

Law in Different Countries: Decisions and Guidelines (1999), London: Women Refugees Program of RLC, p 491.

10 Many of the reflections in this paragraph are drawn from an anonymous journal manuscript, submitted to the author for review, entitled 'UK initiatives on forced marriage: regulation, dialogue, exit'. On file with the author.

11 See unpublished manuscript, cited in note 10.

12 Estimates of numbers of trafficked sex workers vary enormously: this is a function of definitional differences as well as the inherent difficulty of obtaining reliable data on a criminal activity; numbers range from 700,000 to 4 million trafficked persons per year globally, including an unknown but substantial number of trafficked sex workers (UNESCO, 2003).

13 'Porn to Die', *Sunday Herald*, 11 April 2004.

14 See the difference in the definitions in the two Palermo protocols, on trafficking and smuggling respectively, to the UN Convention on Transnational Organized Crime.

15 These examples are drawn from Wertheimer (1987: 5–6).

16 I am very grateful to Michael Blake for illuminating conversations clarifying this point.

References

Anker, Deborah (2002) 'Boundaries in the field of human rights: Refugee law, gender, and the human rights paradigm', *Harvard Human Rights Journal* 15, pp 133–54.

Bhabha, Homi (1983) 'The other question', in Barker, Francis (ed), *The Politics of Theory. Proceedings of the Essex Conferences on the Sociology of Literature, July 1982*, Colchester: University of Essex

Bhabha, Jacqueline (1996) 'Embodied rights: Gender persecution, state sovereignty, and refugees', *Public Culture* 9, pp 3–32

Bhabha, Jacqueline (2004) 'Demography and rights: Women, children and access to asylum', *International Journal on Refugee Law* 16(2), pp 227–43

Bhabha, Jacqueline and Shutter, Sue (1994) *Worlds Apart: Women under Immigration, Nationality and Refugee Law*, Stoke on Trent: Trentham Books

Boyd, Monica and Grieco, Elizabeth (2003) *Women and Migration: Incorporating Gender into International Migration Theory*, Migration Policy Institute, accessed at: http://migrationinformation.org/Feature/print.cfm?ID=106

Cairncross, Frances (2002) 'The longest journey: A survey of migration', *The Economist*, 2 November, p 4

Charnowitz, Steve (2002) 'WTO norms on international migration'. Paper prepared for IOM workshop on existing international migration law norms, accessed at: http://www.wilmer.com/files/tbl_s29Publications%5CFileUpload5665%5C3835%5Ccharnovitz.pdf

Crenshaw, Kimberly (1991) 'Mapping the margins: Intersectionality, identity politics, and violence against women of color', *Stanford Law Review* 43, pp 1241–99

Democratic Voice of Burma (n.d.) *Migration and Trafficking of Women and Girls*, accessed at: http://emg.osj.dvb.no/e_docs/122gs.pdf

Fiske, Susan T and Taylor, Shelley E (1984) *Social Cognition*, Reading, MA: Addison-Wesley

Fiske, Susan T and Taylor, Shelley E (1991) *Social Cognition*, New York: McGraw-Hill

Gilboy, Janet (1991) 'Deciding who gets in: Decisionmaking by immigration inspectors', *Law and Society Review*, 25(3), pp 571–99

Gunning, Isabel (1992) 'Arrogant perception, world-travelling and multicultural feminism: The case of female genital surgeries', *Columbia Human Rights Law Review*, 23(189), pp 189–248

Haider, Nadya (2000) 'Islamic legal reform: The case of Pakistan and family law', *Yale Journal of Law & Feminism*, 12, pp 287–341, cited in Marouf, Fatma (2000), 'The challenge of constructing "the position of women" in Iran and Pakistan in gender-based asylum claims', unpublished class paper on file with the author

Hoodfar, Homa (1995) 'Reforming from within: Islamist women activists in Iran', in Gah, Shirkat (ed) *Women Living under Muslim Laws. Reconstructing Fundamentalism and Feminism: The Dynamics of Change in Iran* 12, Special Bulletin, p 29, cited in Marouf, Fatma (2000), 'The challenge of constructing "the position of women" in Iran and Pakistan in gender-based asylum claims', unpublished class paper on file with the author

Human Rights Watch (2002) *Owed Justice: Thai Women Trafficked into Debt Bondage in Japan*, section X, accessed at: http://www.hrw.org/reports/2000/japan/10-response-thailand.htm

IOM (2002) *International Comparative Study of Migration Legislation and Practice* (commissioned by the Department of Justice, Equality and Law Reform, Republic of Ireland), Dublin: International Organization for Migration

Kerber, Linda (2003) 'The asymmetries of citizenship', unpublished manuscript on file with the author

Kukathas, Chandran (2003) *The Liberal Archipelago: A Theory of Diversity and Freedom*, Oxford: Oxford University Press

Mendelson, Margot (2004) 'The legal production of identities: A narrative analysis of conversations with battered undocumented women', *Berkeley Women's Law Journal* 19, pp 138–216

Menski, Werner (1999) 'South Asian women in Britain, family integrity and the primary purpose rule' in Barot, Rohit, Bradley, Harriet and Fenton, Steve (eds), *Ethnicity, Gender and Social Change*, Basingstoke: MacMillan and St Martin's Press, cited in unpublished manuscript, 'UK initiatives on forced marriage: regulation, dialogue and exit', on file with the author

Morokvasic, Mirjana (1984) 'Birds of passage are also women', *International Migration Review* 18(4), pp 886–907

Okin, Susan (1997) 'Is multiculturalism bad for women?', *Boston Review* 22(5), pp 25–40

Pearson, Elaine (2002) *Human Traffic, Human Rights: Redefining Victim Protection*, London: Anti-Slavery International

Physicians for Human Rights (2004) *No Status: Migration, Trafficking and Exploitation of Women in Thailand: Health and HIV/AIDS Risks for Burmese and Hill Tribe Women and Girls*, Boston: Physicians for Human Rights

Schauer, Frederick (2003) *Profiles, Probabilities and Stereotypes*, Cambridge, MA: Belknap Press of Harvard University Press

Thomas J. White Center on Law and Government (2001) 'The expedited removal study: Report on the first three years of expedited removal', *Notre Dame Journal of Law, Ethics and Public Policy* 15 pp 50–1

UNESCO (2003) *Fact sheet No. 1: Worldwide trafficking estimates by organization*, accessed at: http://www.unescobkk.org/culture/trafficking/GraphWorldwide.pdf

Wertheimer, Alan (1987) *Coercion*, Princeton: Princeton University Press

Yun, Gao (2004) 'Chinese migrants and forced labour in Europe', Geneva, unpublished manuscript on file with the author

2

CITIZENSHIP, NONCITIZENSHIP AND THE STATUS OF THE FOREIGN DOMESTIC

Linda Bosniak

In any discussion of gendered borders, one of the things we inevitably talk about is citizenship, even if we don't address it as such. In my contribution to this volume, I reflect upon the idea of citizenship as it bears on borders and gender. My specific focus is the condition of immigrant domestic workers in Europe and other developed countries – a great many of whom are *noncitizens* as a matter of status. I shall argue that the practices and institutions and experiences associated with immigrant domestic labour implicate citizenship – and noncitizenship – in a variety of ways which include, but extend beyond, legal status and its absence. Immigrant domestic workers experience compound forms of noncitizenship, the characterisation of which contributes to conceptualising the relationship between gender and borders.

The duality of citizenship

Citizenship is an idea that looks both inward and outward.[1] The term 'citizenship' is commonly used to refer to aspects of a community's relations with the world beyond the borders of the political community (we say, 'I am a citizen of X country', or, 'she is trying to take out citizenship in Y country'; here, citizenship is more or less interchangeable with nationality). But we also use the term 'citizenship' to talk about the relationships prevailing among people already assumed to be community members. For instance, we talk about campaigns for 'social citizenship' or a commitment to achieving 'democratic citizenship'; here, we're talking about relations among already presumed members. Citizenship is therefore Janus-faced; it looks to the inside and the outside simultaneously. We might say that as an idea, citizenship sits at the boundary between the foreign and the domestic, and implicates them both.

The fact of citizenship's dual orientation – toward the inside and the outside, toward the domestic and toward the foreign – can be confusing analytically. It's not always clear which sort of citizenship is at stake in any given conversation. In addition, citizenship's dual orientation presents certain challenges at the level of normative political theory. Who, exactly, is and is not included in this category 'citizen'? How far does the category of citizenship extend? Who are citizenship's subjects?

The answer we give tends to vary depending on the analytical orientation we start with. When we are talking about citizenship in the *domestic* sense, we understand citizenship, at least ideally, to stand for universalist values – for the inclusion and recognition of 'everyone'. We know in practice that this is an unachieved universality, but universalism is still the normative standard we understand to be relevant here. In contrast, when we are talking about citizenship in the *foreign* sense, we understand it to entail some degree of exclusivity and boundedness. Citizenship of a nation presumes the existence of national outsiders by definition (see generally Bosniak, 2004).

The concept of citizenship is thus comprised of contrasting analytical and normative understandings – the domestic–universal, on the one hand, and the foreign–exclusive, on the other. Much of the richness and difficulty of the term results from the interplay between these understandings.

To examine this interplay in relation to gendered borders, it is useful to further explore the idea of the 'domestic'. So far, I have been using the term 'domestic' in a geopolitical sense – to refer to the world inside the national political community, as distinct from its outside – as distinct from the foreign. But we also need to engage with the domestic in the social reproductive sense – where 'domestic' refers to the world traditionally denominated the 'private realm', the household, the *oikos*. This, of course, is a domain long associated with women and it is a principal locus of women's subordination – as well as women's agency. Thinking about the confluence of both forms of domesticity brings questions of women's citizenship into especially sharp relief.

The revival of citizenship discourse

To set the stage, however, I must first say a few more words about citizenship itself. The idea of citizenship has come to play a central role in social, political and legal thought over the past two decades in both the Anglo-American world and in Europe (Bosniak, 2004). At least from an outsider's perspective, there is a great preoccupation among scholars and activists in Europe with citizenship. Whether the focus is on 'democratic citizenship', 'social citizenship', 'equal citizenship', 'dual citizenship', 'multicultural citizenship' or 'postnational citizenship', citizenship is now vital to the intellectual and political projects of many – particularly on the left, though not exclusively. As to what citizenship means, exactly, things aren't entirely clear. Sometimes the word is used to describe the enjoyment of individual rights; sometimes, participation and active engagement in the process of self-government; sometimes it is meant to refer to group identity and solidarity; and sometimes to a formal legal status. Given the range of uses to which the term is put, it is clear that citizenship is an exceptionally versatile idea – probably excessively so.

At the same time, though, citizenship has a remarkably consistent evaluative meaning: citizenship is almost always portrayed as an object of the greatest aspiration – as the highest fulfilment of democratic and egalitarian desire. The trouble is that this habit of citizenship romanticism (as I have called it) tends to obscure the normative duality that lies at the heart of the citizenship idea. 'Citizenship' evokes a state of democratic belonging and inclusion, it is true. But this belonging or inclusion is usually premised upon a conception of a community which is itself bounded and exclusive. These boundaries are established and policed pursuant to a set of social practices and institutions that we also call 'citizenship'.

Unfortunately, in a lot of the citizenship-talk in the academy and in political discourse, the existence of these boundaries is simply not acknowledged. The national society – or sometimes, as in the case of Europe, the supranational society – is treated as the total universe of analytical focus and normative concern; and citizenship then has to do with the nature of the relationships prevailing among already assumed community members. Campaigns for social citizenship, for democratic citizenship, generally look inward, and are relevant to the already-established 'we'. Citizenship's boundary questions, on the other hand, are usually the grist of a specialised group of scholars and activists, namely the immigration scholars or immigration activists. We are the folks who make borders the specific object of our attention. In contrast, almost everyone else talking about citizenship tends to presume away the boundaries, or more often, they presume away any world outside the political community altogether.

I have argued elsewhere that citizenship romanticists need to acknowledge and contend with the often repressed reality of bounded, exclusionary citizenship in their political projects (Bosniak, 1998). But this isn't a one-way street; I also believe that those of us who focus our attention on citizenship in the bounded, exclusionary sense need to engage with the aspirational, universalist visions of citizenship that animate so much political thought. What we need to do, in short, is to deepen the conversation – in both directions – between the universalist and exclusionary understandings of citizenship in order to see each of them more clearly and understand what they have to say to each other. The subject of international domestic labor provides a useful context for doing this.

Citizenship and domestic work

Any discussion of immigrant domestic workers needs to be situated in the broader debates in feminist thought over women and work, so that's where I will begin.[2] First, it bears noting that in the vast literature from the Anglo-American world and Europe about the status of women – about women's oppression and women's empowerment and equality – the idea of citizenship has figured very prominently. Here, the term citizenship is meant to represent liberty, democracy and justice. Speaking of women's citizenship is usually understood as a way of speaking about women's emancipation from subordination. Achievement of citizenship means achievement of justice. This, of course, is the universalist, inward-looking rendering of the idea of citizenship.

Now, the citizenship-for-women literature is itself diverse and contains a range of theoretical and disciplinary concerns. But one of its persistent themes is a concern with women's economic well-being, which is often expressed as a concern with women's 'economic citizenship' or women's 'social citizenship'. Sometimes the focus is on meeting women's basic needs, or providing a 'basic income' for women. But more often, the concern is to ensure the opportunity for women to find and sustain 'decent work'. As the feminist political theorist Carole Pateman wrote several years ago, 'Paid employment has become the key to citizenship, and the recognition of an individual as a citizen of equal worth to other citizens is lacking when a worker is unemployed' (Pateman, 1989: 10). Likewise, the feminist historian Alice Kessler-Harris has recently stated that 'access to economic equality' through work is 'a necessary condition of citizenship' for women (Kessler-Harris, 2001: 283).

This is the classical feminist, integrationist paradigm, one that is widely accepted and clearly important. But in some of its aspects, the integrationist vision has generated controversy among feminist theorists. Some scholars have posed a powerful and inescapable question to its proponents: how, structurally, is women's participation in the workforce made possible? Work in the traditionally conceived public domain is enabled by essential, often invisible care-work in the domestic sphere – work that includes childrearing, household management, food preparation, social capital development and other physical and organisational and emotional maintenance tasks. Women have traditionally performed the overwhelming share of this work, whether or not they work in the paid labour force. In fact, some feminists have argued that women can achieve equal citizenship only when this care-work is itself recognised and socially valued (though there are still others who regard this as a recapitulation of the old cult of domesticity and a bad idea) (Harrington, 2000).

But the crux of the critique is that, to the extent that we view women's economic citizenship as best achieved through decent market employment, we need to keep the domestically based preconditions for this employment in mind. And when we do this, what we see (to make a long story short) is that as women have increased their participation in the paid labour market in many of the developed societies in the past couple of decades, a lot of the domestic work they would otherwise have done (or that the men they live with would have had to do) has *itself* become the object of commodification – by which I mean that it is delegated to others to do in exchange for a wage. And the others involved are almost always women.

Of course, delegation of domestic work from some women to others is not a new phenomenon in Europe or elsewhere. However, as more women have entered the labour market in recent years, domestic work has become increasingly commodified. Certainly, there are relevant country differences here. In some countries in Europe, a great deal of childcare is provided or funded by the state. However, in most developed countries childcare is largely privatised. And childcare aside, a great deal of what we think of as care-work or domestic work is never state provided or subsidised. So with certain qualifications, it is clear that the work of social reproduction has become increasingly commodified over time.

The story of this commodification can be told in a variety of ways. It is a story about class stratification and about racial domination, as well as about gender inequality – and all of these have to be addressed. But there is another part of the story that particularly interests me: that is the fact that the market in domestic labour in many countries has become increasingly transnational. A great number of the domestic employees (in Europe and in other developed economies) are transnational migrants: they are people who have crossed national borders, often specifically for the purpose of work.[3] Which means that the increasing participation of women in the market economies of many developed countries, including many European countries, has drawn upon – and is now significantly reliant upon – a globalised market in domestic labour.

Of course, once we pay attention to the transnationalisation of domestic labour, we necessarily introduce a different strand of citizenship discourse into the conversation. We are now talking about citizenship not only as an aspirational ideal of egalitarian relations in a pre-given political society, but also, from a boundary-conscious perspective, as a status premised on societal closure and exclusivity. It is, after all, the exclusivity of citizenship which prevents many prospective immigrants – including immigrant domestic workers – from entering the country, or requires them to wait for years to enter, or compels them to enter surreptitiously, or imposes time and occupational constraints on their presence. Their exclusion derives precisely from their lack of citizenship in the country (or in the European case, in any EU country). So the transnationalisation of domestic labour is deeply tied up with the operation of an exclusive citizenship, which operates in gatekeeping fashion at the territorial borders of the nation or supranation.

But what immigrant rights advocates and immigration scholars know is that the gatekeeping associated with exclusionary citizenship doesn't merely operate at the territorial borders. Noncitizens who are present within the territory, who are on the territorial *inside*, still remain subject to the operation of the border laws there. As status noncitizens – as 'aliens', in legal terms – they are always potentially subject to deportation; and they are more vulnerable to the abuse of power in various domains (including the domestic workplace) because they fear enforcement of the immigration law against them. The fact of their alienage also means that they are denied important rights, including access to the vote and important social benefits, which limits their social power in various ways. All of this describes the experience of a great many immigrant women who work in the domestic-care arena in Europe and elsewhere, whether they are present temporarily or permanently, lawfully or unlawfully.

Compound noncitizenship

This scenario I have described of transnational domestic labour thus implicates two very different conceptions of citizenship. The question I want to pose is: how should we think about the relationship between them? We have seen that, as a structural matter, the pursuance by women in the developed world of 'economic citizenship' or 'equal citizenship' by way of paid work in the public sphere is often, and increasingly, facilitated by the domestic employment of other women, many of whom are from third world countries and many of whom are themselves in a condition of noncitizenship as a matter of status. What exactly does this mean? Does it mean, as some observers have suggested, that first world women acquire their citizenship *at the expense of* the citizenship of their domestic workers? Does it mean that there is some kind of citizenship expropriation going on?

I don't believe this is a useful way to think about the issue. There is no doubt that the transnational organisation of reproductive labour reflects systemic inequality and privilege between classes of women internationally. And arguably, there are expropriations from South to North involved. These are expropriations of labour, of care – and maybe even of love (as Arlie Hochschild suggests, 2001) – all in the context of a market exchange. Ordinarily, these are expropriations that often work to the greater benefit of the employer than the employee.

But it is labour and care, not citizenship itself, which are transferred from one group of women to another. In fact, I think we have to conclude that the citizenships – and noncitizenships – at stake are not transferable in this way at all because they are simply not the same species of thing. We use the word 'citizenship' here to talk about two distinct sets of social relationships and commitments. When scholars like Pateman and Kessler-Harris talk about women's lack of citizenship, they are critiquing a general situation of social and economic powerlessness experienced by many women within contemporary societies. Yet of course, immigrant domestic workers experience this same kind of social and economic powerlessness, often, far more acutely than their employers. Likewise, when feminists talk about women's pursuit of economic citizenship through wage-work outside their homes, it goes without saying that paid domestic workers are pursuing the same objective.

But many immigrant workers are noncitizens in an additional and distinct way. The fact of their noncitizenship status – their alienage – means that they are always subject, or potentially subject, to the immigration regulatory authority of the state. And this, in turn, serves to render them even more socially and economically powerless than they would otherwise be. For these immigrant women, their lack of status-citizenship often functions as an additional axis of inequality and exploitation.

Recognising the compound nature of these women's noncitizenship is important, I think, for at least two reasons. First, in order effectively to support social justice efforts on their behalf, we need to understand the structure of their subordination. But in addition, the case of immigrant domestic labour is theoretically instructive because it is a site that brings together various citizenship discourses and allows us to consider the relationships among them.

Citizenship and the domestic

A good way to begin to think about this relationship among citizenship discourses is to focus on the idea of 'the domestic' itself. As I said earlier, we conventionally talk about 'the domestic' in a couple of different senses. On the one hand, when counterposed to the foreign, 'the domestic' refers to a country's internal affairs. On the other hand, when counterposed to the public domain or the market, 'the domestic' refers to the internal life of the household or family. In both cases (whether we're talking about citizenship in the geopolitical sense or in the broadly reproductive sense), the domestic sphere is defined by contrast to something outside of it: it represents the internal side of a larger, divided whole.[4] And in both cases, the term connotes 'home'.

Feminists, of course, have famously dismantled the purported divide between the domestic and public spheres. They have shown that the fiction of separate spheres does not hold up either descriptively or normatively. The practices and experiences associated with each are in fact intertwined and mutually constitutive in all kinds of ways. And they have shown that efforts to enforce such a divide have been a central feature of regimes of gender subordination.

I think many scholars of globalisation (including some immigration scholars) have undertaken an analogous intellectual project with respect to the domestic/foreign divide. Here, too, they have said, the ideology of separate spheres just doesn't hold up empirically. Borders are porous and mutable. There is no truly insular national space; the foreign and the domestic are interwoven in innumerable ways. And they have pointed out that very often, enforcement of the line between the foreign and the domestic produces injustice on a transnational scale.

Thus, in deconstructing the prevailing ideologies of separate spheres, both the feminist and globalist projects fundamentally reconceive the scope and meaning of the domestic itself. What is so important about the case of immigrant household workers is that it shows how intimately these projects are linked. The reproductive domestic and the geopolitical domestic are themselves tightly interconnected by way of what we might call a transnational political economy of household work; and of course, it is a gender-structured system in which both the transnational domestic workers and their employers participate.

This kind of social reality requires advocates for social justice, including feminists, to develop political responses. In doing so, we need to figure out where the borders of our social solidarity begin and end. Citizenship for whom, exactly? Answering these questions, I think, implicates the gender of borders in the fullest sense of the term.

Notes

1 For a more elaborated discussion of citizenship's divided character, see Bosniak, 2006.
2 Much of the ensuing discussion is drawn from Bosniak, 2006: Ch 5 ('Borders, domestic work, and the ambiguities of citizenship').
3 There is a large literature concerning domestic work and immigration. For a sampling, see Chang, 2000; Ehrenreich and Hochschild, 2002; Anderson, 2000; Hondagneu-Sotelo, 2001; Harrington Meyer, 2000; Milkman *et al.*, 1998.
4 See Kaplan, 2002: 25 ('*Domestic* has a double meaning that links the space of the familial household to that of the nation, by imagining both in opposition to everything outside the geographic and conceptual border of the home'.)

References

Anderson, Bridget (2000) *Doing the Dirty Work: The Global Politics of Domestic Labour*, London: Zed Books

Bosniak, Linda (1998) 'The citizenship of aliens', *Social Text* 56, pp 29–38

Bosniak, Linda (2004) 'Citizenship', in Cane, Peter and Tushnet, Mark (eds), *Oxford Handbook of Legal Studies*, Oxford: Oxford University Press, pp 183–201

Bosniak, Linda (2006) *The Citizen and the Alien: Dilemmas of Contemporary Membership*, Princeton: Princeton University Press

Chang, Grace (2000) *Disposable Domestics: Immigrant Women Workers in the Global Economy*, Boston: South End Press

Ehrenreich, Barbara and Hochschild, Arlie R (eds) (2002) *Global Woman: Nannies, Maids and Sex Workers in the New Economy*, New York: Metropolitan Books

Harrington Meyer, Madonna (ed) (2000) *Care Work: Gender, Labor, and the Welfare State*, New York: Routledge

Hochschild, Arlie (2001) 'The nanny chain', *American Prospect* 11(4), p 32

Hondagneu-Sotelo, Pierrette (2001) *Domestica: Immigrant Workers Cleaning and Caring in the Shadow of Affluence*, Berkeley: University of California Press

Kaplan, Amy (2002) *The Anarchy of Empire in the Making of U.S. Culture*, Cambridge: Harvard University Press

Kessler-Harris, Alice (2001) *In Pursuit of Equity: Women, Men and the Quest for Economic Citizenship in 20th-Century America*, Oxford: Oxford University Press

Milkman, Ruth, Reese, Ellen and Roth, Benita (1998) 'The macrosociology of paid domestic labor', *Work and Occupations* 25(4), pp 483–510

Pateman, Carole (1989) *The Disorder of Women: Democracy, Feminism and Political Theory*, Cambridge: Polity Press

3

GENDERED BORDERS AND UNITED STATES' SOVEREIGNTY[1]

Judith Resnik

Fearing the foreign

In Europe, the talk is about the harmonisation of laws and co-operation among nation-states. Around the world, transnational lawmaking, convention-drafting, and norm-sharing have a long and complex history that spans colonialism, the Commonwealth, the formation of the United Nations and, now, the new and still contested European Union. Adjudication has become a central aspect of the enterprise of border-crossing legal norms. Courts (both national and transnational) are vested with jurisdiction to enforce the obligations of public and private actors. Transnational legalism is often celebrated as a positive artefact of globalisation and of the development of human rights, even as decisions about how and when to use precepts crafted elsewhere entail difficult judgments.[2]

But in some sectors of the United States, the prospect of transnational lawmaking affecting domestic norms through the importation of rules by judges or by other government actors is unwelcome. Illustrative of this attitude is a proposed statute, called the American Justice for American Citizens Act, introduced in the winter of 2004 in the United States Congress and then again in 2005. The 2004 draft bill proclaims: 'The American people are rightfully entitled to be governed by the Constitution, not as amended by judges through the process of "transjudicialism" '.[3] A companion bill, the Constitution Restoration Act of 2004, would instruct judges that, when

> interpreting and applying the Constitution of the United States, a court of the United States may not rely upon any constitution, law, administrative rule, Executive order, directive, policy, judicial decision, or any other action of any foreign state or international organization or agency, other than English constitutional and common law.[4]

As of this writing, none of these bills have been enacted. But they provide evidence that advocating these positions pleases some lawmakers' constituents.

In this chapter I examine the anxiety, occasioned repeatedly in American history, about transnational human rights regimes and their potential to influence American conceptions of rights. Despite such regular efforts to shore up the political and legal boundaries of the United States, the American polity is inevitably affected by developments from abroad. Whether expressly acknowledged or not, constitutional democracies are import and export nations – of people, of law, and of conceptions of equality.

Such a prospect is appealing for Americans seeking expansive understandings of the causes of and remedies for women's subordination. Some transnational innovations, such as the Convention on the Elimination of All Forms of Discrimination Against Women (CEDAW), have a broader reach than do current understandings of the US Constitution. As a consequence, legislators supporting bills such as the American Justice for American Citizens Act are right to worry that worldwide efforts to generate new remedies could well alter the status quo in the United States.

As the proposed bills hostile to those efforts also illustrate, opponents often couch their objections in jurisdictional terms. Whether in the language of 'states' rights' or in the terms of nationalism, a common trope is the assertion of a 'sovereign' power to make laws free from 'outside' influence.[5] These debates about jurisdiction entail two arguments, one about what the *substantive norms* of a democracy should be, and another about what the *legitimate sources* for such norms are. Extricating those concerns from the shorthand prohibitions and directives is required to address the underlying concerns about political legitimacy and identity.

What ought to be done about the reticence of lawmakers in the United States to participate in international conventions such as CEDAW? Many human rights advocates in the United States urge ratification and participation at the national level. As I explain below, those interested in engaging the United States in a generative project of rights-expansion should look beyond the national government. Localities – both cities and states – have been an important and under-appreciated site of both the import and export of persons, laws, and culture. To interrupt status inequalities in an arena as large as the United States requires interaction with local as well as with national actors. This approach should be familiar to Europeans, as the commitment to what is in European law called 'subsidiarity', to policy and lawmaking at the level closest to individuals, expresses a parallel insight.

Further, non-Americans may well be wary of US engagement with transnational conventions. As illustrated in this chapter through discussion of the American involvement in contemporary anti-trafficking efforts, engagement by the United States has resulted in efforts to promote a prosecutorial and punitive approach rather than a focus on the economic, social, and political conditions that human rights advocates argue would undercut the abilities of traffickers to procure women and girls. The paradigm is criminal law, not development and human rights. Were the United States to become more active in other UN conventions, the United States might similarly try to impose its approach and could use its resources to limit or narrow interpretations of the reach of equality norms.

I have chosen to use the phrase 'gendered borders' in this chapter's title for three reasons. First, it denotes the differential impact on women and men of rules by which nations and federations admit or reject people. Second, the phrase adverts to practices within a single state or a federation that allocate authority to subdivisions, thereby deciding which aspects of its populace's lives are to be governed by norms that transcend all of its subparts and when, in contrast, variations in norms are permitted. In the United States, a claimed constitutional 'right' of states to govern certain aspects of social ordering has been used to argue for rejection of international human rights norms. Moreover, national prerogatives to decide when to participate in 'foreign affairs' are claimed to preclude local efforts by states and cities to incorporate international human rights in their governing documents. Third, 'gendered borders' also refers to the boundaries created by the sex-gender system, which relies on delineated roles for women and men to vary opportunities of both. For those sharing an interest in eroding or reconfiguring any of these boundaries, the diverse borders within and between nation-states have to be analysed with a specificity sensitive to the various histories, practices, and theories of each to identify when such delineations mark barriers *to* change and when they create opportunities *for* change.

Centuries of anxiety

Hostility to foreign influences is not a new phenomenon in the United States. Time and again, as ideas about human rights develop around the world, the battle inside the United States is cast in terms of borders. Repeatedly over the last 300 years, protests against great human rights movements have been couched in the language of jurisdiction, of the 'rights' of the states or of the national government to decide their fate independent of 'foreign influences'.

In the nineteenth century, opponents of emancipation for slaves resented the international liberation movement. They argued that foreign critics of slavery ought to stay out of affairs which they did not understand (Keck and Sikkink, 1998). Even after the Civil War, as women pursued the vote, parallel objections were made – that the international suffragist movement ought not influence US policy and, in turn, that the national government ought not decide the issues for states (Sneider, 2002). In the 1870s, such jurisdictional claims prevailed in the Supreme Court, which held that despite the ratification of amendments to the US Constitution to prohibit states from infringing on the 'privileges and immunities' of citizenship or depriving persons of equal protection of the laws, Virginia could refuse to let women vote.[6]

Some 75 years later, in the early 1950s, after the promulgation of the Universal Declaration of Human Rights, a Republican Senator from Ohio,

John Bricker, proposed to amend the US Constitution to make it unlawful for the United States to enter into treaties that could affect the 'rights of citizens of the United States'.[7] Senator Bricker's supporters wanted to ensure 'that international agreements would not lead to United Nations interference or more liberal social and economic policies and legislation in the United States'.[8] Although the Bricker Amendment did not become law, the influence of its approach can be seen today, as the United States imposes reservations on its participation in certain international conventions (Henkin, 1995). Repeatedly, international and transnational human rights movements have been met in the United States with a xenophobia founded on anti-immigrant, anti-socialist, anti-Semitic and anti-feminist attitudes (Bickel and Schmidt, 1984: 229).

Permeable borders

But the vehemence of the protests cannot stop law's seepage. Inevitably, judges – and all of us – are influenced and affected by judgments from abroad. Take, for example, the use of the term 'dignity', a key word in the 1948 Universal Declaration of Human Rights, which begins with the recognition of the 'inherit dignity' of all people.[9] Dignity is central to many other transnational agreements, including the International Covenant on Economic, Social and Cultural Rights,[10] the International Covenant on Civil and Political Rights (ICCPR),[11] the Convention on the Elimination of All Forms of Racial Discrimination (ICERD),[12] and the Convention on the Elimination of All Forms of Discrimination Against Women (CEDAW).[13] Similarly, many countries have constitutions and basic laws that also make express a commitment to human dignity. Examples include Germany[14] and Israel.[15]

In contrast, the term dignity is not used in the US Constitution, which was written during the eighteenth century. While ideas now understood as intrinsic to the concept of dignity can be found in the Constitution's commitment to liberty, equality, and to other personal rights (Neuman, 2000), protection of individuals came through other phrases in the Bill of Rights. For example, the Eighth Amendment prohibits 'cruel and unusual punishment'. The Fourteenth Amendment, our major equality provision, guarantees the 'privileges and immunities of citizens' and gives rights of due process and equal protection to all 'persons'.[16]

Yet the word 'dignity' can be found in the jurisprudence of the US Supreme Court (Resnik and Suk, 2003). Indeed, the term appears some 900 times in Supreme Court decisions issued since 1789. But during the eighteenth and nineteenth centuries, the Supreme Court mentioned the word dignity only when discussing entities, rather than individuals. That usage continues. According to the Supreme Court, nations, states, legal institutions, courts, judges, the flag, and even God have dignity interests.

Only in the 1940s, as people around the world asserted human dignity against the horrors of fascism, did the Supreme Court use the word 'dignity' to capture individuals' rights protected by the American Bill of Rights. The first uses in 1942 and in 1943 were in the context of criminal defendants' rights to counsel[17] and to see a neutral third person when subject to detention.[18] Since then, the term has become commonplace in US constitutional law. One can find references to 'dignity' in decisions interpreting the Fourth Amendment's right to be free from search and seizure and in the Eighth Amendment's ban on cruel and unusual punishment as well as in its protection against horrific conditions in prisons and its constraints on the imposition of the death penalty.

The language of personal dignity has also played an important role in discussions of equal protection and due process under the Fourteenth Amendment, of personal privacy, of reproduction and of sexual orientation. Indeed, in the 2003 Supreme Court decision holding that states cannot criminalise private consensual sex between two adults of the same sex, the majority opinion written by Justice Anthony Kennedy explained: 'adults may choose to enter upon this relationship in the confines of their homes and their own private lives and still retain their dignity as free persons'.[19]

The development of the discourse of dignity in the application and interpretation of personal constitutional rights is an example of influences from abroad on American law.[20] While foreign sources are not much cited in the cases, the turn to dignity is borne from world experiences. This example is not idiosyncratic; several scholars have documented how the civil liberties tradition of the earlier part of the twentieth century in the United States was affected by developments abroad (e.g., Witt, 2004). Moreover, interpretations of the US Constitution are examples of both import and export. The country has incorporated dignity into its rights regime and influenced the jurisprudence of constitutional courts around the world[21] as a contributor and a recipient in an interactive constitutional jurisprudence (L'Heureux-Dubé, 1998).

Innovations from abroad

Given the permeability of America – from its physical borders to its legal ones – the questions are not *if* or *whether* the United States will be affected by international and transnational human rights movements but rather *how* the United States will be affected, and *when*. That effects will be felt is heartening for some inside the United States, because a great deal of important innovation – especially related to women's rights – comes from outside the United States. And, for those who fear the foreign, they have a basis for that fear; some strands of thought developed transnationally have richer understandings of the role governments should take to engender equality than those currently embraced by many American lawmakers.

The changing status of women provides a ready example. Over recent decades, women have not only gained recognition as rights holders but have also changed the meaning of rights and the content of obligations. The International Criminal Court (ICC), from which the United States has now withdrawn, is illustrative of the 'mainstreaming' of women's rights. The Rome Statute that chartered the ICC is an important human rights document for women,[22] for it is 'the first international treaty to recognize a range of acts of sexual and gender violence as among the most serious crimes under international law'.[23] Within its definition of 'crimes against humanity' (which involve knowingly launching a 'widespread or systematic attack directed against any civilian population'), the ICC's enabling statute specifies harms to women, including 'rape, sexual slavery, enforced prostitution, forced pregnancy, enforced sterilisation, and any other form of sexual violence of comparable gravity'.[24] Further, the crime of enslavement is explained with specific reference to trafficking in 'persons, in particular women and children',[25] and the social groups protected against persecution are defined in terms of gender as well as other categories. Moreover, the ICC Statute not only identifies women as victims but also as witnesses in need of protection and as decision makers holding the power of judgment. Party states must, when selecting judges, 'take into account the need . . . for . . . [a] fair representation of female and male judges'.[26]

A second transnational document, more often identified as feminist, is the UN Convention on the Elimination of All Forms of Discrimination Against Women (CEDAW), entered into force in 1981. CEDAW requires signatory states to take 'in the political, social, economic, and cultural fields, all appropriate measures, including legislation, to ensure the full development and advancement of women, for the purposes of guaranteeing them the exercise and enjoyment of human rights and fundamental freedoms on a basis of equality with men'.[27] Further, the Convention calls for 'temporary special measures aimed at accelerating de facto equality between men and women'.[28] CEDAW's focus is on purpose and effect rather than intentionality.[29] Private actors as well as public actors are called upon to change, as CEDAW aspires to alter women's experiences from early education to old age as they work in households and in wage markets.

CEDAW itself has not been static. In 1992, in General Recommendation 19, the expert committee charged with overseeing CEDAW's implementation specified that violence directed at women was a form of discrimination to be redressed by signatory states.[30] Beginning in 2000, states could also join an 'Optional Protocol' that permits individuals or groups, after exhausting national remedies, to file complaints directly against countries and authorises the oversight committee of CEDAW to initiate investigations.[31] As of 2006, 183 countries had ratified the basic provisions of CEDAW, albeit sometimes with reservations limiting obligations on particular aspects. Seventy-nine nations had also agreed to participate in the Optional Protocol.

But not the United States. Although President Jimmy Carter signed CEDAW for the United States in 1980, subsequent administrations have either not succeeded in convincing Congress to ratify CEDAW or have opposed its ratification.[32] Opponents rely, in part, on the language of jurisdiction: that because the United States is a federation, committed to respecting roles for states, CEDAW is particularly pernicious. Even when the Clinton Administration proposed that the Senate ratify CEDAW in the 1990s, the Executive also submitted 'reservations, understandings, and declarations' ('RUDs', or caveats used in international treaty making to enable selective adherence to treaty provisions) to state that ratification would not result in 'changing US law in any respect'. Further, in what is termed a 'federalism understanding', the proposed RUDs specified that joining CEDAW would not alter the allocation of authority between state and national governments.[33]

States' rights are one set of prerogatives delineated; adherence to bounded gender roles is another on which opponents of CEDAW rely. According to a 2001 monograph entitled *How UN Conventions on Women's and Children's Rights Undermine Family, Religion, and Sovereignty* and published by an organisation called the Heritage Foundation, the expert committee implementing CEDAW undervalues the nuclear family by encouraging mothers to 'leave their children in the care of strangers' to enter 'the workforce'.[34] Arguing that the 'United Nations has become the tool of a powerful feminist-socialist alliance that has worked deliberately to promote a radical restructuring of society', this monograph called on Congress to protect against the dangers the United Nations poses to the sovereignty of the United States.[35]

From the vantage point of US lawmakers opposed to innovative developments of human rights, the Heritage Foundation has identified (albeit by deploying a hyperbolic attack) one of CEDAW's conceptual innovations, which is to challenge the premise that women are obliged first and foremost to their roles within households. CEDAW does expect both women and men to take responsibility for the 'upbringing and development of their children'[36] and, further, that signatories should enable women to have access to a host of activities beyond family life. Were the United States to become a member of the Convention, it would – like nations around the world – have to make periodic reports to and take questions from a committee of 23 experts, examining the ways in which the Convention's mandates were (or were not) being met.

Furthermore, CEDAW's openness to affirmative interventions, its definition of discrimination based on the effects of actions rather than proof of the intent of the actor, and its application to all spheres of activity make that document's approach to equality broader than current interpretations of the equality mandates in the US Constitution. CEDAW defines discrimination to include any 'distinction, exclusion, or restriction made on the basis of sex' that generates an inequality in any field – 'political, economic, social, cultural, [and] civil'.[37] Pursuant to these mandates, the inquiries made of countries are far-reaching, seeking accounts of how gender affects the delivery of healthcare and family planning, safety, education, employment, recreation and sports, government benefits and political power. CEDAW proposes an understanding of women's lives that encourages legal interventions in a manner not yet common in the United States.

Multiple borders and border crossings

The anti-foreign attitudes held by many national lawmakers in the United States is increasingly anomalous when contrasted with the involvement of many other countries in international lawmaking. The foundational documents of several countries commit themselves to looking at comparative sources as they interpret domestic laws. South Africa's constitutional provision is an oft-cited example, requiring its courts – when interpreting its own Bill of Rights – to consider international law as well as 'foreign law'.[38] Other countries have constitutions stating commitments to what the Constitution of the Netherlands terms 'development of the international rule of law'.[39]

But the very barriers created by the federated form of American government also contain possibilities for various methods by which to develop transnational norms. Although the United States has not ratified CEDAW, the City of San Francisco has adopted aspects of CEDAW and made them a part of its own domestic laws. Local law of that city now requires reports on the role women play in its various departments, including Public Works, Adult Probation, Arts, the Rent Board, Environment and Juvenile Probation.[40] In a 2003 'action plan' from the Department on the Status of Women, the City and County of San Francisco stated its ambitions to review 'federal, state, and local laws and public policies to identify systematic and structural discrimination against women and girls'; to 'integrate gender into every city department to achieve full equality for men and women through the city-wide budgeting process'; to 'increase opportunities for non-traditional and higher-paid employment for women'; to develop 'and expand work/life policies that impact women at all levels'; to increase 'women's access to financial resources', and to increase protection for women's 'bodily integrity', safety, and 'well-being'.[41]

Dozens of other cities have called for the national government of the United States to ratify CEDAW. As of March 2004, some 44 cities, 18 counties and 16 states had local legislation relating to CEDAW (Milani et al., 2004: 74). These efforts are illustrative of an important phenomenon: that state and local governments have often been instrumental in affecting US policies, both domestic and international. During recent decades, many localities have promulgated resolutions on issues such as apartheid in South Africa, the use of land mines and the mistreatment of labourers.

As in the example of CEDAW, local action on human rights can take different forms. One is expressive, calling on the United States to take a particular action, such as ratification of a treaty. Another approach is to enact local laws that incorporate concepts from abroad into domestic law, for example, by mandating that a state will not purchase goods made by countries condoning forced labour (Resnik, 2006).

In the United States, not only has the national government's involvement in international law been contested; actions of localities have also been challenged on jurisdictional grounds. Opponents of local incorporation of transnational rights have argued, with some success in the US Supreme Court, that the national office of the Presidency in conjunction with Congress has exclusive control over 'foreign affairs', thereby pre-empting local action. Recent decisions have stopped Massachusetts's efforts to ban its own purchase of products made by labourers forced to work in Burma[42] and have prevented California from requiring insurance companies doing business in that state to disclose information from the Holocaust era.[43] Thus, the claimed importance of state primacy over certain arenas of law is used as a reason to reject national acceptance of certain international norms, and a claimed national authority over international relations is used to justify limiting local involvement in transnational human rights movements.

What these diverse legal actions help to underscore is that looking only to Washington misses important facets of American political life. The struggles over equality and transnationalism are not confined to the US Congress. Advocates need to focus on the many borders of the United States, their varying permeabilities, and the relative desirability of using different government actors (judges, executive officials, legislators at national and local levels) as norm entrepreneurs.

Fears of the foreign, reciprocated

From the vantage point of an equality advocate in the United States, I can aspire to more openness to interactive exchanges across borders – at both national and state levels – than currently exists. But as a participant in transnational efforts to engender new understandings of the meaning of equality, bringing the United States into a prominent role in the development of international norms may have less appeal.

Current efforts to persuade the United States to ratify CEDAW rely heavily on the argument that, because the country's constitutional and statutory laws of equal protection are more or less comparable, the United States is already CEDAW-compliant.[44] While conceptually and strategically appealing (aimed at making 'foreign' law appear less foreign), I find the claim overstated. My hope for joining CEDAW is grounded in the aspiration that such affiliation will influence and in some respects bring about change in the United States.

But there is a possibility that rather than CEDAW changing the United States, the United States might change CEDAW. We know from the experience of the drafting of the ICC Statute, and from other actions of the United States at the United Nations, that American involvement often entails efforts to dominate agendas. Were the United States to ratify CEDAW, the country could attempt to constrain its import, perhaps through influencing appointments of experts to the panel of 23. The United States might attempt to place on the panel individuals committed to the current narrow constructions of American constitutional equality law and opposed to affirmative action or other kinds of targeted interventions.

A basis for concern comes from analyses of recent actions by the United States on trafficking. From early in the twentieth century, the United States has been deeply involved in efforts to end what was, in 1904, called the 'white slave trade'.[45] In addition to joining the International Agreement for the Suppression of White Slave Traffic, the United States changed its domestic criminal law in 1910; Congress enacted legislation known as the 'Mann Act' (its sponsor's name) to make illegal the transportation across state lines of 'any woman or girl for the purpose of prostitution or debauchery, or for any other immoral purpose'.[46]

More recently, the United States became a party to the UN's Convention Against Transnational Organized Crime, supplemented by two protocols, one to 'Prevent, Suppress, and Punish Trafficking in Persons, Especially Women and Children' and the other addressed to 'The Smuggling of Migrants'.[47] In 2000, Congress enacted the Trafficking Victims Protection Act (TVPA), which created an interagency Task Force chaired by the Secretary of State to monitor and combat trafficking by facilitating 'cooperation among countries of origin, transit, and destination' to prevent and prosecute traffickers.[48] Congress obliged the President to undertake 'international initiatives to enhance economic opportunity for potential victims' by funding programmes 'in foreign countries to assist' victims of trafficking to reintegrate or resettle.[49]

In addition, Congress has imposed 'minimum standards' on other countries and announced that the United States would not 'provide nonhumanitarian, nontrade-related foreign assistance' to governments that had neither met the standards nor made 'significant efforts' to do so.[50] The Secretary of State reports on such compliance efforts, and the President has discretion to withhold various forms of aid.[51] Further, Congress has made 'victims of severe forms of trafficking' eligible in limited circumstances for certain benefits, such as legal assistance, otherwise unavailable under US law.[52] The 2003 reauthorisation imposed new criminal penalties on traffickers and created a new civil remedy enabling individual victims of trafficking to bring lawsuits for damages against perpetrators.[53]

The involvement of the United States in international anti-trafficking work should not be seen as a counter-example to its refusal to ratify CEDAW. Rather, unlike the expansive vision of CEDAW that would entail the reorganisation of power to redress the structural subordination of women, anti-trafficking activities place women in conventional roles – in need of protection from sexualised aggression perpetrated by 'outsiders'. These laws also presume that the United States itself needs protection against the importation of 'foreign immoral' practices. The approach is prosecutorial[54] rather than focused on the human rights of victims, who are in need of economic and political assistance to alter their conditions at home and in need of opportunities to migrate in search of better lives.[55]

Entering into agreements with foreign nations to oppose trafficking is a method of working with outsiders to maintain the borders of nation-states by policing entry. Further, the United States is using its anti-trafficking efforts to combat prostitution, a policy different from some countries that have promoted regulation of sex workers. The United States' legislation on trafficking (TVPA) requires recipients of anti-trafficking grants to affirm that their programmes do not 'promote, support, or advocate the legalization or practices of prostitution'.[56] Thus, contemporary anti-trafficking laws in the United States continue to incorporate anxieties about foreign influences, mobile women, disruption of families, and the impositions placed by sex on women.

To describe anti-trafficking efforts as founded on such traditional assumptions is not to minimise the harms they address nor to denigrate the contributions made by efforts to prevent forced labour and slavery achieved by transporting people far from their homes. But the ability to enact such provisions stems in part from the congruence between anti-trafficking laws and anti-immigration policies in the United States, as well as from presumptions that individuals, and particularly women, do not wish to leave their countries of origin or to use their bodies in sexualised ways to gain income.[57]

High stakes, variegated borders and democratic ordering

This brief overview of US involvement in transnational human rights law has, I hope, made plain both the permeability of legal traditions and the intensity of conflicts about the legitimacy of import and export. In contemporary democracies, genuine differences exist about the relationships among government, courts and individuals. The meaning of equality and the techniques for its realisation are contested, within nation-states and within transnational organisations, both public and private.

What I hope has also become clear is the importance of avoiding a romantic view about any level of lawmaking – local, national, federated or transnational. In this chapter, I have stressed innovation outside the United States, but I should not be read as glorifying those locations. International bodies and domestic governments have repeatedly failed to address a host of injuries, from the injustice of wartime exploitation of 'comfort women' (Chinkin, 2001: 335) to the sadly ordinary violence,[58] poverty, and illiteracy that lace women's lives throughout the world. In the words of a UNICEF report, violence against women remains 'one of the most pervasive of human rights violations, denying women and girls equality, security, dignity, self-worth, and their right to enjoy fundamental freedoms.'[59] And the many words about equality, committed on paper in transnational documents such as CEDAW, do not necessarily translate into conditions of equality in the lives of women and men. Indeed, several of the countries that have ratified CEDAW are identified with highly oppressive conditions for women.[60]

The borders of the nation-state order much of our lives, just as the borders of the sex-gender system continue to shape people's experiences around the world. International and transnational lawmaking has both utility and limits; their implementation and enforcement require local action. For change, all levels of power – the international, the transnational, the national and the local – need to be enlisted in the project of giving meaning to the promise of equality.

This multiplicity is itself an opportunity, as gaps in governance and alternative governments are spaces in which all power-seekers, be they entrenched or newly fabricated, try to gain a foothold. Globalisation and increased reliance on federated forms of government have enhanced the capacity for networks to crisscross multiple levels and wide geographic areas. In sum, the concept of jurisdiction is not singular but multivalent. Jurisdiction can simultaneously function as an obstacle to reform and as a vehicle for reform. Those seeking to redefine rights need to dislodge long-entrenched definitions of the bounded roles assigned to women, men, and to various levels and kinds of government.

Notes

1 All rights reserved, © Judith Resnik, July, 2006. My thoughts here have been informed by exchanges with Dennis Curtis, Vicki Jackson, Karen Knop, Reva Siegel, Kathryn Sklar, and Seyla Benhabib. Appreciation is also due to Elizabeth Brundige, Josh Civin, Paige Herwig, Anita Khandalwal, Alison MacKenzie, Marin Levy, Bertrall Ross, Julie Suk, Katherine Desormeau, Hannah Hubler, and Laura Heiman for able research assistance, to Gene Coakley for innovative library assistance, to Marilyn Cassella who facilitated the communications among us all, and to Sarah Van Walsum for her invitation to participate and her helpful comments on an earlier draft.

This chapter grows out of related work, specifically my articles 'Categorical Federalism: Gender, Jurisdiction, and the Globe' (2001) 111 Yale Law Journal 619; 'Law's Migration: American Exceptionalism, Silent Dialogues, and Federalism's Multiple Ports of Entry' (2006) 115 Yale Law Journal 1564; and the chapter 'Sisterhood, Slavery, and Sovereignty' in Sklar, K and Stewart JB (eds), *Women's Rights and Transatlantic Antislavery in the Era of Emancipation* New Haven: Yale University Press (forthcoming 2006).

2 See Resnik (2006, 1612–1625).

3 See American Justice for American Citizens Act, HR 4118 (2)(7), introduced in the 108th Cong, 2d Sess in April 2004. Section 3 of this bill provides that:

Neither the Supreme Court of the United States nor any lower Federal court shall, in the purported exercise of judicial power to interpret and apply the Constitution of the United States, employ the constitution, laws, administrative rules, executive orders, directives, policies, or judicial decisions of any international organization or foreign state, except for the English constitutional and common law or other sources of law relied upon by the Framers of the Constitution of the United States.

The bill was introduced by Republican Members of the House of Representatives – Ron Paul of Texas and Marilyn Musgrave of Colorado. See also Constitutional Restoration Act (2005) S 520, introduced in the 109th Cong, 1st Sess in March 2005).

4 See Constitutional Restoration Act (2004) S 2082, introduced in the 108th Cong, 2d Sess, in February 2004. The specific provision, Title II is entitled 'Interpretation of the Constitution'. Enforcement provisions (Title III) threaten judges with impeachment if they engage in 'any activity that exceeds the jurisdiction of the court'. Section 302 is entitled 'Impeachment, Conviction, and Removal of Judges for Certain Extrajurisdictional Activities'. The bill was sponsored by Republican Senators Richard Shelby of Alabama, Sam Brownback of Kansas, Lindsey Graham of South Carolina, Jim Inhofe of Oklahoma, Wayne Allard of Colorado and Democrat Zell Miller of Georgia.

5 As a sponsor of the American Justice for American Citizens Act explained, 'harmonizing American law with foreign law could undermine individual rights and limited, decentralized government'. Statement of the Hon Ron Paul, in the House of Representatives, 1 April 2004, 150 Cong Rec. E 512 (2 April 2004).

6 See *Minor v Happersett*, 88 US 162, 171 (1875). The Court concluded that, while women were 'citizens,' the Constitution was silent on the issue of whether that status required states to permit women to vote. Given no action by Congress, the Court did not address whether 'such interference' into state practices would have been constitutional.

7 SJ Res 130, introduced in the 82nd Cong, on 7 February 1952 and reproduced in Tananbaum, 1988: 222, Appendix C.

8 Proponents included leaders of the American Bar Association, a coalition of 'Republican and conservative, mostly southern, Democrats, businessmen who created an entity called The Foundation for Study of Treaty Law, a group of doctors fearing 'socialized medicine', and the Vigilant Women for the Bricker Amendment, a group opposed to International Labour Organisation's effects on the United States. See Tananbaum: 1988, 43, 116–20. The proposed amendment failed in the Senate by one vote and analysts believe that President Eisenhower's opposition stemmed from an interest in preserving presidential powers and flexibility.

9 That text provides: '[w]hereas recognition of the inherent dignity and of the equal and inalienable rights of all members of the human family is the foundation of freedom, justice and peace in the world.' Universal Declaration of Human Rights, Preamble, GA Res 217(A) at 71 (1948), UN GAOR, 3d Sess, 1st Plen mtg, UN Doc A/810 (12 December 1948). Its first Article declares: 'All human beings are born free and equal in dignity and rights.' Ibid., 72.

10 GA Res 2200A (XXI), 21 UN GAOR Supp (No 16) 49; UN Doc A/6316 (1966), 993 UNTS 3 (entered into force 3 January 1976).

11 GA Res 2000A (XXI), 21 UN GAOR Supp (No 16) 52; UN Doc A/6316 (1966), 999 UNTS 171 (entered into force 23 March 1976).

12 660 UNTS 195 (entered into force 4 January 1969).

13 1249 UNTS 20378 (entered into force 3 September 1981).

14 The first article of the Basic Law of Germany, adopted in 1949, states: 'The dignity of man is inviolable. To respect and protect it is the duty of all state authority'. Grundgestez [GG] [Constitution] Art 1 (FRG).

15 Basic Law, s 1(a) (Israel). Section 2 declares, 'There shall be no violation of the life, body or dignity of any person as such', and Section 4 entitles all persons to the protection of 'their life, body, and dignity'.

16 US Constitution, Fourteenth Amendment, s 1.

17 See *Glasser v United States*, 315 US 60, 89 (1942). In dissent, Justice Felix Frankfurter objected to the Court's holding that federal felony defendants had a Sixth Amendment right to counsel; he argued against a blanket rule, stating: 'The guarantees of the Bill of Rights are not abstractions. Whether their safeguards of liberty and dignity have been infringed in a particular case depends upon the particular circumstances'.

18 In *McNabb v United States*, 318 US 332, 343 (1943), Justice Frankfurter, there writing for the majority, explained that the right to appear promptly before a committing authority was required: 'A democratic society, in which respect for the dignity of all men is central, naturally guards against the misuse of the law enforcement process'.

19 *Lawrence v Texas*, 539 US 558, 567 (2003).

20 I am not suggesting that, had the word 'dignity' been used in the constitutional text, the weight accorded to it would be the same as in current US case law. As Aharon Barak, President of Israel's Supreme Court, has explained, when 'human dignity is expressly mentioned in a constitution' it can be given independent force (Barak, 2002: 45).

21 See, e.g., Henkin (1998) (arguing the influence of the US Constitution on the Universal Declaration of Human Rights). See generally Glendon (2001).

22 See United Nations Diplomatic Conference of Plenipotentiaries on the Establishment of an International Criminal Court, Rome Statute of the International Criminal Court, UN Doc A/CONF 183/9 (adopted 17 July 1998 and as corrected through July 1999) [hereinafter ICC Statute] (Koenig and Askin, 1999, vol. 2, 3–29).

23 Steains (1999, 357). See also Chesterman (2000: 10) (describing the inclusion of 'rape and sexual violence' as 'the most controversial offenses' that were to be covered by international law).

24 ICC Statute, supra note 22, Art 7 (1).

25 Ibid., Art 7(2)(c). Persecution is defined as 'against any identifiable group or collectivity on political, racial, national, ethnic, cultural, religious, gender . . . or other grounds'. Ibid., Art 7(1)(h).

26 Ibid., Art 36 (8)(a)(iii). Judicial selection criteria also include equitable geographic distribute and forms of legal expertise. Ibid, 36 (8)(a)(i) and (ii).

27 CEDAW, see above n 13, Art 3.

28 Ibid., Art 4; see also Art 2(e) and (f). When equality is achieved, these measures are to be discontinued.

29 A comparative analysis is provided by Ginsburg and Merritt (1999).

30 See Report of the Committee on the Elimination of All Forms of Discrimination Against Women (1992), General Recommendation 19, 11th Sess UN Doc A/47/38. That CEDAW as first drafted did not address violence reflects that, in the 1970s, women's transnational networks were then not focused on that topic, which would later move to the forefront. See Keck and Sikkink (1998: 166). In 1993, the UN Commission on Human Rights created the Office of Special Rapporteur on Violence Against Women.

31 Adopted by the General Assembly in October 1999 and entered into force (after obtaining the requisite ten first signatories) in December 2000. See Optional Protocol to the Convention on the Elimination of All Forms of Discrimination Against Women, 6 October 1999, 2181 UNTS 83. See also United Nations, The Convention on the Elimination of All Forms of Discrimation Against Women: The Optional Protocol, Text and Materials at 1–2, 6–7, 110–18 (UN Publications, 2001) (detailing the process and stating in Art 17 that any member state signing the protocol could not impose reservations).

32 The Clinton Administration supported ratification, with reservations. See Halberstam (1997). The Bush Administration has not sought congressional ratification; when involved in the war in Afghanistan, the Administration stated its support of CEDAW and subsequently indicated that it was reviewing the impact CEDAW might have on US law. See LaFranchi (2002).

33 Convention on the Elimination of All Forms of Discrimination Against Women: Hearing Before the Senate Committee on Foreign Relations, 103d Cong 13 (1994) (Statement of Jamison S Borek, Deputy Legal Advisor, Department of State); Senate Executive Report No. 103–38 (1994). Additional proposed reservations include rejecting regulation of what is termed 'private conduct' beyond that already recognised under US law, imposing no further duties for equality in employment and providing no guarantees on treatment of family planning. See Mayer (1996: 727).

34 Fagin (2001: Executive Summary).

35 Ibid., 21.

36 CEDAW, above n 13, Art 5.

37 Ibid., Art 1, and Art 3.

38 Constitution of South Africa, ch 2, s 39 (1996) ('When interpreting the Bill of Rights, a court, tribunal or forum (a) must promote the values that underlie an open and democratic society based on human dignity, equality, and freedom; (b) must consider international law; and (c) may consider foreign law.'

39 Grondwet [GW] [Constitution] Art 90 (Netherlands).

40 See, e.g., Government of San Francisco (1998) *Local Implementation of the United Nations Convention on the Elimination of All Forms of Discrimination Against Women (CEDAW)*, Ch 12K, Ordinances of the City and County of San Francisco (California, US) (approved 13 April 1998, modified 27 December 2000), accessed at http://www.sfgov.org/site/dosw_page.asp?id=19794.

41 See San Francisco Commission on the Status of Women, CEDAW Action Plan, (approved 1 February 2003), accessed at: http://www.ci.sf.ca.us/site/cosw_page asp?id=17146.

42 *Crosby v National Foreign Trade Council*, 530 US 363 (2000). The Massachusetts' statute addressed companies doing business in Burma and provided some exceptions. The provision was challenged by the National Foreign Trade Council, which represented companies involved with foreign commerce, of which 34 were on the restricted purchase list of Massachusetts (ibid.: 369–70).

43 *American Insurance Association v Garamendi*, 539 US 396 (2003).

44 See *Ratification of the Convention on the Elimination on All Forms of Discrimination Against Women: Hearing Before the Senate Committee on Foreign Relations*, 107th Cong at 32–9 (13 June 2002) (Statement of Harold Hongju Koh). Further, some argue that the US Constitution could be interpreted differently. See West (1994). In contrast, opponents argued that CEDAW was the Equal Rights Amendment 'on steroids'. See Catholic Family and Human Rights Institute (2002); McElroy (2002) accessed at http://www.foxnews.com/story/0,2933,60218.00.html.

45 According to Alain Corbin (1990), the first international conference on 'white

slave trade' occurred in 1899, when representatives of 12 countries came together and determined to set up an international mechanism to combat the problem. There occurred divisions between those seeking to abolish prostitution and those seeking to regulate it. Corbin argued that trafficking emerged in response to demand that had, prior to that time, been met through brothels. An international agreement followed, entered into in Paris in 1904. This provided that, 'within the limits of law', contracting governments were to create means to centralise information about '*traite des blanches*' and to attempt to apprehend individuals at ports of entry, return the women and girls to their countries of origin, and provide some facility for them in the interim. See International Agreement for the Suppression of the White Slave Traffic, UN Sales No 1950.IV.1 (1904). The 1910 Convention implementing that agreement limited its reach to transportation of women for prostitution. While 'retention, against her will, of a woman or girl in a house of prostitution' was a grave problem, the 1910 agreement did not address that issue because such problems were 'exclusively a question of internal legislation'. International Convention for the Suppression of the White Slave Traffic, Final Protocol, UN Sales No 1950.IV.2 (1910).

46 See *White Slave Traffic*, House Report No 47, Appendix A, 15–18 (1909); Mann Act of 1910, ch 395, 36 Stat 825 (codified as amended at 18 USC sections 2421–24 (2000). The Mann Act remains in use, amended in 1986 to make its terms gender neutral, and supplemented by anti-pornography legislation. See Child Sexual Abuse and Pornography Act of 1986, Pub L No 99–628, 100 Stat 3510, codified at 18 USC section 2251 *et seq.* (2000) and also limiting Mann Act prosecution to cases involving interstate transportation for prostitution or 'any sexual activity for which any person can be charged with a criminal offense' – thereby linking a federal violation with those of state laws governing sexual behaviour. See 18 USC section 2421.

47 Both protocols build on efforts from mid-century. See Convention for the Suppression of the Traffic of Persons and the Exploitation of the Prostitution of Others, 2 December 1949, opened for signature 21 March 1950, 96 UNTS 272, 282 (entered into force 25 July 1951). As of 2006, the more recent protocols had been signed by more than 110 countries.

48 See Pub L No 106–386, 114 Stat 1464, codified at 22 USC sections 7101–10 (2000), as amended by the Trafficking Victims Protection Reauthorization Act of 2003, Pub L No 108–93, 117 Stat. 2875 (2003), codified at 22 USC section 7101 note, at 18 USC section 1595 (creating a civil remedy, discussed below), and elsewhere [hereinafter TVPA].

49 TVPA, 22 USC sections 7104–5.

50 Ibid.

51 22 USC sections 7106, 7107. The 2003 amendments require reports on the numbers of individuals obtaining benefits and visas under the TVPA, as well as on the numbers of convictions obtained. The amendments also call for research by the Executive Branch on the effectiveness of programmes against trafficking and new efforts through international media to broadcast the many harms caused by trafficking and sex tourism.

52 'Severe forms of trafficking' is defined as 'sex trafficking in which a commercial sex act is induced by force, fraud, or coercion, or in which the person induced to perform such an act' is under 18; or 'the recruitment, harboring, transportation, provision, or obtaining of a person for labor or services, through the use of force, fraud, or coercion for the purpose of subjection to involuntary servitude, peonage, debt bondage, or slavery' 22 USC section 7102 (8). To obtain federal services, a person has to meet those requirements and either be 18 or be certified by

the US government that the person is 'willing to assist in every reasonable way in the investigation and prosecution of severe forms of trafficking' and have either a bona fide application for a visa or the Attorney General's agreement that the person is needed to remain in the United States to 'effectuate prosecution of traffickers' 22 USC section 7105(b)(I)(c) and (e).

53 Amended 18 USC section 2423 provides that persons traveling in interstate or in foreign commerce or into the United States to engage in sex with persons under the age of 18 or to obtain financial gains by aiding others to do so could be imprisoned for not more than 30 years.

54 See US Department of State (2004). On its list of 'best practices' are: discouraging the industry in sex tourism; attempting to identify and to intercept potential victims; facilitating co-operation among countries; combating prostitution; battling trafficking through education programmes; confiscating funds from trafficking proceeds to use for financing anti-trafficking programmes; sharing information and protecting victims. The 2004 Trafficking Report also explains (pp 26–28) the criteria used for the United States to rank countries; included are a country's law enforcement efforts demonstrated through the numers of prosecutions and convictions of traffickers and the kinds of sentences imposed on traffickers.

55 See, e.g., Guinn and Steglich (2003) (discussing poverty, unemployment, and civil society as well as prosecution and constraint of traffickers).

56 22 USC section 7110(g)(1–2). See also US Department of State (2004:15) (discussing how 'prostitution fuels trafficking').

57 These multiple rationales for anti-trafficking have caused disagreement among feminists regarding the shape such provisions should take. See, e.g., Balos (2004), Sullivan (2003), Wijers (2000), and Kapur (2002). Within the United States, proponents of the federal legislation include some feminist groups joined by those concerned about the vulnerability of women. See Carnes (2000).

58 See UNICEF, Domestic Violence Against Women and Girls (2000: 2, Overview), As the report explains, most countries have laws prohibiting such violence but violations are common. Moreover, home-based abuse may be condoned by the passivity of state law enforcement. And, although the 'family is often equated with sanctuary . . . [for many] it is also a place that imperils lives, and breeds some of the most drastic forms of violence perpetrated against women and girls'. Ibid.: 3.

59 For every one man who is illiterate around the world, two women are. Seventy per cent of the world's poor are women, and women are 'less nourished than men, less healthy, more vulnerable to physical violence and sexual abuse.' Nussbaum (2000:1). On education and literacy, see Ginsburg and Merrit (1999); UN Human Development Report (1999), and Sen (1999).

60 See White and Blakesley (1999); Schabas (1997). See also Charlesworth et al. (1991). More generally, assessments of enforcement of human rights treaties do not reveal high levels of implementation. See Hathaway (2002).

References

Balos, Beverly (2004) 'The wrong way to equality: Privileging consent in the trafficking of women for sexual exploitation', *Harvard Women's Law Journal* 27, pp 137–75 (now called the Harvard Journal of Law and Gender)

Barak, Aharon (2002) 'Foreword. A judge on judging. The role of a supreme court in a democracy', *Harvard Law Review* 116, pp 16–162

Bickel, Alexander M and Schmidt, Benno C, Jr. (1984), *The Judiciary and Responsible Government, 1910–1921 (Part I)*, New York: Macmillan Publishing Co

Catholic Family and Human Rights Institute, US Pro-Life/Pro-Family NGOs Flood White House Switchboard Against CEDAW, 5 FAX 24, 7 June 2002, at http://www.c-fam.org/FAX/Volume_5/faxv5n24.html

Carnes, Tony (2000) ' "Odd Couple" Politics: Evangelists, Feminists Make Common Cause Against Sex Trafficking', *Christianity Today*, 44 (3)

Charlesworth, Hilary, Chinkin, Christine and Wright, Shelley (1991) 'Feminist approaches to international law', *American Journal of International Law* 85, pp 613–45

Chesterman, Simon (2000) 'An altogether different order: Defining the elements of crimes against humanity', *Duke Journal of Comparative & International Law* 10, pp 307–43

Chinkin, Christine M (2001) 'Women's international tribunal on Japanese military sexual slavery', *American Journal of International Law* 95, pp 335–41

Corbin, Alain (1990) *Women for Hire: Prostitution and Sexuality in France after 1850*, trans. Sheridan, A, Cambridge, MA: Harvard University Press

Fagan, Patrick F (2001) *How UN Conventions on Women's and Children's Rights Undermine Family, Religion, and Sovereignty*, Heritage Foundation, Backgrounder, No 1407, accessed at: http://www.heritage.org/Research/InternationalOrganizations/loader.cfm?url=/commonspot/security/getfile.cfm&PageID=95496

Ginsburg, Ruth B and Merritt, Deborah J (1999) 'Affirmative action, an international human rights dialogue', *Cardozo Law Review* 21, pp 253–82

Glendon, Mary A (2001) *A World Made New: Eleanor Roosevelt and the Universal Declaration of Human Rights*, New York: Random House

Guinn, David E and Steglich, Elissa (2003) *In Modern Bondage: Sex Trafficking in the Americas: National and Regional Overview of Central America and the Caribbean: Belize, Costa Rica, Dominican Republic, El Salvador, Guatemala, Honduras, Nicaragua & Panama*, Ardsley, New York: Transnational Publishers

Halberstam, Malvina (1997) 'United States ratification of the Convention on the Elimination of All Forms of Discrimination Against Women', *George Washington Journal of International Law & Economics* 31, pp 49–96

Hathaway, Oona A (2002) 'Do human rights treaties make a difference?', *Yale Law Journal* 111, pp 1935–2042

Henkin, Louis (1995) 'US ratification of human rights conventions: The ghost of senator Bricker', *American Journal of International Law* 89, pp 341–50

Henkin, Louis (1998) 'The Universal Declaration and the U.S. Constitution', *PS: Political Science & Politics* 31, pp 512–15

L'Heureux-Dubé, Claire (1998) 'The importance of dialogue: Globalization and the international impact of the Rehnquist Court', *Tulsa Law Journal* 34, pp 15–40

Kapur, Ratna (2002) 'The tragedy of victimisation rhetoric: Resurrecting the "native" subject in international/post-colonial feminist legal politics', *Harvard Human Rights Journal* 15, pp 1–37

Keck, Margaret E and Sikkink, Kathryn (1998) *Activists Beyond Borders: Networks in International Politics*, Ithaca, NY: Cornell University Press

Koenig, Dorean M and Askin, Kelly D (1999) 'International criminal law and the International Criminal Court statute: Crimes against women', in Koenig, Dorean M and Askun, Kelly D (eds) *Women and International Human Rights Law* 2, Ardsley, NY: Transnational Publishers, pp 3–29

LaFranchi, Howard (2002), Women's Treaty Revives Old Debates, *Christian Science Monitor* 1

Mayer, Ann E (1996) 'Reflections on the proposed United States reservations to CEDAW: Should the Constitution be an obstacle to human rights?', *Hastings Constitutional. Law Quarterly* 23, pp 727–823

McElroy, Wendy, (2002) Senate Must Not Ratify CEDAW, *Fox News*

Milani, Leila Rassekh, Albert, Sarah C and Purushotma, Karina (eds) (2004) *CEDAW: The Treaty for the Rights of Women*, accessed at: http://www.womenstreaty.org/CEDAW%20Book-%20WHOLE%20BOOK.pdf

Neuman, Gerald L (2000) 'Human dignity in United States constitutional law', in Simon, Dieter and Weiss, Manfred (eds), *Zur Autonomie des Individuums: liber amicorum Spiros Simitis*, Baden-Baden: Nomos Verlagsgesellschaft, pp 249–71

Nussbaum, Martha C (2000) *Women and Human Development: The Capabilities Approach*, New York: Cambridge University Press

Resnik, Judith (2001) 'Categorical federalism: jurisdiction, gender, and the globe', *Yale Law Journal* 111, pp 619–80

Resnik, Judith (2006) 'Law's migration: American exceptionalism, silent dialogues and federalism's multiple ports of entry', *Yale Law Journal* 115, pp 1564–1670

Resnik, Judith and Suk, Julie C (2003) 'Adding insult to injury: Questioning the role of dignity in conceptions of sovereignty', *Stanford Law Review* 55, pp 1921–62

Schabas, William A (1997) 'Reservations to the Convention on the Elimination of All Forms of Discrimination Against Women and the Convention on the Rights of the Child', *William & Mary Journal of Women and the Law* 3, pp 79–112

Sen, Amartya (1999) *Development as Freedom*, New York: Knopf

Sneider, Allison L (2002) 'Women suffrage in Congress: American expansion and the politics of federalism, 1870–1890', in Baker, Jean (ed) *Votes for Women*, Oxford and New York: Oxford University Press, pp 77–89

Steains, Cate (1999) 'Gender Issues', in Lee, Roy S (ed) *The International Criminal Court: The Making of the Rome Statute: Issues, Negotiations, Results*, The Hague and Boston: Kluwer Law International, pp 357–64

Sullivan, Barbara (2003) 'Trafficking in women: Feminism and new international law', *International Feminist Journal of Politics* 5, pp 67–91

Tananbaum, Duane (1988) *The Bricker Amendment Controversy: A Test of Eisenhower's Political Leadership*, Ithaca, NY: Cornell University Press

United Nations Development Program, *Human Development Report* 1999 at 138–141 (Gender-Related Development Index)

UNICEF, *Domestic Violence Against Women and Girls*, Innocenti Digest, No. 6 (May 2000)

United States Department of State, Trafficking in Persons Report (June 2004), at http://www.state.gov/documents/organization/34158.pdf

West, Robin (1994) *Progressive Constitutionalism: Reconstructing the Fourteenth Amendment*, Durham, NC: Duke University Press

White, John Valery and Blakesley, Christopher L (1999) 'Women or rights: How should women's rights be conceived and implemented?', in Koenig, Dorean M and Askun, Kelly D (eds) *Women and International Human Rights Law* 2, Ardsley, NY: Transnational Publishers, pp 51–75

Wijers, Marjan (2000) 'European Union policies on trafficking in women', in Rossilli, Mariagrazia (ed) *Gender Policies in the European Union*, New York: P Lang, pp 209–29

Witt, John F (2004) 'Crystal Eastman and the internationalist beginnings of American civil liberties', *Duke Law Journal*, 54, pp 705–63

Part II

EUROPEAN PERSPECTIVES

4

GENDERED VIOLENCE IN 'NEW WARS'*

Challenges to the Refugee Convention

Nora Markard

The 1951 Refugee Convention[1] is a product of the Cold War. Drafted to deal with those displaced by the Nazi ravages, it was at the same time an ideological instrument of the West against the Warsaw bloc. Eurocentric in conception, it was therefore premised on 'peacetime persecution' by oppressive regimes as they were then known (Sztucki, 1999: 57). The Convention definition of a refugee is based on the idea that an organised state persecutes in a discriminatory manner a group of the population that seeks subsidiary protection abroad.

Today, however, the situation has changed as many flee abuse from civil wars (UNHCR, 1997a: ch. 7). Many of these wars are characterised by a multitude of warring factions and large-scale abuse of civilians, including killings, mutilations, abductions, rape and forced displacement. The state, where it can still be said to exist, often takes part, directly or indirectly, in the abuse. Such wars pose significant problems to the definition of a refugee as envisaged in 1951. The relevance of non-state persecution has not been undisputed. Also, although human rights abuses in these wars often hit men and women in particular ways, gendered persecution[2] meets particular problems with respect to the applicable 'Convention reason' and the nexus to it. A new European directive[3] has incited important steps, while posing further problems.

This chapter argues that a proper analysis of the new forms of civil wars and a gender-sensitive reinterpretation of the Refugee Convention in the light of human rights developments and humanitarian law could fill remaining protection gaps.

Gender-based violence in civil wars and the Refugee Convention

Gender-based violence and armed conflicts are two aspects that count as problematic with respect to the Refugee Convention. The legal issues arising

---

* This chapter is based on a research project which is on-going.

in the application of the Convention concern the persecutory measures, the agents of persecution, the applicable Convention reason, and the nexus clause.

The harm feared as persecution

The atrocities of today's civil wars include many forms of gendered abuse against both sexes. For reasons of space, however, the focus of this chapter will be limited to the specific problems of rape.

The term 'persecution' is not defined in the Refugee Convention. While various definitions have been proposed, the common tenor is that persecution is an infliction of harm or suffering by interference with the human body or a limitation of a person's activities that is graver than discrimination. Perhaps the most persuading definition has been given by Hathaway, who phrases it as a 'sustained or systemic violation of basic human rights' (Hathaway, 1991: 101). In his framework, violations of first-generation human rights, aiming at the physical integrity and freedom of the person, always constitute persecution (Hathaway, 101–10).

It is clear that rape as a serious human rights violation aimed at the human body constitutes persecution (UNHCR, 2002, para 9; ExCom, 1993, para d; Excom, 1995, para f). Sexual violence is also explicitly mentioned in the 2004 European Directive on Minimum Standards for the Qualification of Third Country Nationals as Refugees (the Qualification Directive)[4] that had to be transposed into the national law of the member states by October 2006 (Art 38). Article 9 (2) provides that '[a]cts of persecution ... can, *inter alia*, take the form of: (a) acts of physical or mental violence, including acts of sexual violence; ... (f) acts of a gender-specific or child-specific nature'.

The agents of persecution

Persecution by state agents is clearly covered by the initial conception of the Refugee Convention. However, there is a strong tendency to 'privatise' sexual violence carried out by officials (see Ankenbrand, 2002: 51; Mees-Asadollah, 1998: 144–5; Crawley, 2001: 35). If rebel groups have replaced the state in parts of or the whole territory and have established a more or less stabilised rule, persecution by such de facto authorities can be deemed to be equal to state persecution.

Beyond this, UNHCR and most states have recognised that the Convention is not confined to state persecution (UNCHR, 2001: para 19). If a third party acts with the backing of the state, such as paramilitaries, this is usually accepted as indirect persecution by the state. If the state is unable to protect against third-party persecution within the area of its own rule, or if the state has dissolved altogether ('failed state'), the issue is more difficult.

Arguably, the purpose of the Convention is to grant substitute protection abroad where the home state either is the persecutor or does not provide protection against third-party persecution, being either unwilling or unable to do so. However, until recently, this issue was contested (Wilsher, 2003; Vermeulen et al., 1998). In particular, France and Germany traditionally favoured an accountability approach, until the Qualification Directive required changes in the law.

In the 1983 leading case *Dankha*, the French Council of State (*Conseil d'État*) required that acts of persecution by private persons be 'encouraged or tolerated by the public authorities so that the applicant is in fact not able to obtain the protection of the state'.[5] This approach concerned many Algerian asylum-seekers who fled the terror of Islamic groups. Where the state claims to take measures against such persecution by rebel factions – such as the Sudanese government against the Janjaweed – such a requirement makes it hard to obtain recognition as a third-party refugee. However, the French Refugees Appeals Board (*Commission des recours des réfugiés*) recognised as refugees applicants of Croatian or Muslim origin who were no longer able to claim protection from the Bosnian authorities against the militias of the Bosnian-Serb de facto authorities.[6]

Until 2005, the German Federal Administrative Court (*Bundesverwaltungsgericht*) accepted only persecution by a state or by an organisation with state-like powers. If the persecution was carried out by a private person, it had to be attributable to the state as a form of indirect action (*mittelbare Rechtsgutsverletzung*).[7] With reference to Article 31 of the Vienna Convention on the Law of Treaties, the Court considered the purpose of the Refugee Convention at the time of the ratification, when the Convention became German federal law. At that time, according to the Court, what made an alien a refugee was the disruption of the connection between the person and her home state. If the state was just unable to provide protection in situations of instability or disintegration, its lack of accountability excluded persecution. Later developments of state practice dropping the requirement of state 'complicity' would not change the content of German federal law, since the German legislator had declined to give suit to this development. This German position even found its way into the 1996 Joint Position of the European Council.[8] In cases of civil war, the German jurisprudence considered state authority to be generally ineffective.[9] This excluded persecution even by state agents, for this would require an effective state authority. Such effective authority is only present if the rule of a faction has durably stabilised in a particular area, constituting a 'de facto state' or 'quasi-state'.[10] Today's civil wars, however, often lack clear frontlines and stable rule: 'rebel-held' or 'government-held' areas or garrisons are constantly contested; various factions move among each other. The state may even have been completely replaced by private actors such as the clans in Somalia.

The outlined approaches thus left large gaps of protection in civil war cases (see Moore, 2003). As a result, in 1998, Ms Adan, a member of a

Somalian minority clan, and Mr Aitseguer, claiming persecution by the Algerian Groupe Islamique Armé, came to the UK from Germany and France respectively where they had been denied recognition. Upon appeal, the House of Lords decided that, upon return under the 1990 Dublin Convention, Adan and Aitseguer would be threatened by expulsion in violation of the *non-refoulement* clause and that, because of their construction of the Convention, France and Germany were not 'safe third countries'.[11]

The Qualification Directive has done much to close this gap. In its Article 6 it lists not only the state and de facto authorities as possible persecutors, but also 'non-state actors, if it can be demonstrated that [the state or the authorities replacing it] are unable or unwilling to provide protection against persecution'. However, the problem of persecution in 'failed states' might persist, since arguably the clause presupposes that there are authorities of some sort – state or quasi-state – from whom protection could be expected. States could argue that such cases could only receive subsidiary protection.

The subsidiary protection provisions address persons who, without qualifying as refugees, fear serious harm in their country of origin. Such serious harm can consist of execution, torture, inhuman or degrading treatment or a 'serious and individual threat to a civilian's life or person by reason of indiscriminate violence in situations of international or internal armed conflict' (Art 15 (c)). The subsidiary protection status is more precarious, and its benefits are reduced. The residence permit is granted for one, not three years (renewable) (Art 24). Access to employment is subject to conditions, social welfare and medical treatment can be reduced to core benefits, and access to integration programmes will only be granted if the state considers this useful (Art 26–33).

France changed its law in 2003 to include non-state persecutors, but accepts non-state protection only from 'international and regional organisations' instead of mentioning the directive's 'parties or organisations . . . controlling the state'.[12]

Germany integrated the most important elements of the directive in the comprehensive new Residence Law on aliens that entered into force in January 2005.[13] This law expressly provides that persecution can emanate from non-state actors whether or not state authorities are existent in the country (60(1)(c) AufenthG). Leave to remain is granted where there is an individualised danger to life, bodily integrity or freedom (60 (7)) in situations of generalised danger, only an (optional) administrative suspension of expulsions can give leave to remain for a renewable six months (60(a)(1)). In reaction to the express mention of the Convention in 60(1), the Federal Administrative Court surprisingly agreed that 'according to settled case law', German law had to be interpreted in consistence with the Refugee Convention.[14] So far, the application of the new law by the lower courts is not quite satisfactory (Bank and Schneider, 2006). First-instance courts decided that family members threatening honour killings could not be non-state actors under the law,[15] and quickly subsumed the violent situation in Somalia under 60(7).[16] This demonstrates how such a provision can lead the courts to a merely summary examination of the refugee clause, quickly jumping to the subsidiary protection clause.

The grounds of persecution and the nexus clause

The Convention explicitly limits its protection to certain groups of people identified by race, religion, nationality, membership of a particular social group (PSG), or political opinion. Gender is not among the mentioned grounds. It has been claimed that the list of 'Convention reasons' reflects a predominantly male paradigm insofar as it focuses on a male-dominated public sphere, ignoring female experiences of oppression in a private sphere (Indra, 1987; Kelly, 1993: 674; Crawley, 2001: 5). The question of how to classify women's cases, where the means of or the reasons for persecution are gender-specific, has therefore been subject to intense discussion.

These cases are mostly examined under the PSG category (UNHCR, 1997b: 105) – probably the most controversial among the five. In the case of countries where there is an institutionalised policy of discrimination against women that involves or denies protection against persecutory acts, it has been held that women in that country constitute a PSG.[17] This approach is supported by the cases of *Ward*[18] and *Acosta*[19] which have been widely followed by common law courts. According to *Ward*, a particular social group can be defined either by an unchangeable characteristic (including a person's past) or one that is not unchangeable but so fundamental to the person's human dignity that she should not be required to change it. *Acosta* explicitly mentions sex as an example of an innate characteristic. Gender as a social role might be a good example for the second PSG category.

The Qualification Directive also uses the *Ward* formula (Art 10(1) (d)), adding that '[g]ender related aspects might be considered, without by themselves alone creating a presumption for the applicability of this Article'. This reference could, on the one hand, suggest that gender aspects would be considered under the PSG category or, on the other hand, that gender alone would not suffice to constitute a PSG, while other categories are not excluded from scrutiny. Interestingly, the new German provision (cited above) expressly includes PSG claims solely based on gender (60(1) AufenthG).

The PSG label bears particular difficulties. Adjudicators are reticent to recognise half of the population as a particular social group, especially since not all women in one country are usually persecuted. In reaction, more narrow definitions are attempted. In the case of female genital mutilation, such a group can be as small as 'young women who are members of the Tchamba-Kunsuntu Tribe of northern Togo who have not been subjected to female genital mutilation, as practiced by that tribe, and who oppose the practice'.[20] Such a narrowed definition seems difficult in civil war cases.

Moreover, the nexus clause constitutes a major obstacle in rape cases generally. Rape is often looked at in isolation. In a situation of chaos and widespread terror against civilians, it is depicted as a spontaneous outbreak of 'private' violence, the perpetrator benefiting from a situation of lawlessness to carry out sexual abuse for personal satisfaction instead of following a persecutory intent. Additionally, claimants from war zones often have to prove that they fear harm that exceeds the 'ordinary risks' that civilians incur in wars. In situations where violence against civilians is widespread, this may be difficult. In facing these problems, it may prove helpful to take a closer look at how these wars work.

Today's civil wars: 'new wars'

Old wars and 'new wars'

Drawing on Voltaire's adage that the Holy Roman Empire was neither holy, nor Roman, nor an empire, one could say that today, many civil wars are neither civil, nor wars as we used to know them. Nor do most of the conflicts that continue to be reported as civil wars have much in common with the features that we associate with this notion. The end of the Cold War and the effects of globalisation have profoundly changed the face of many conflict zones. Instead of two well-organised armies fighting as proxies for two states, or, in the case of classical civil wars, an army and well-organised guerrilla troops, 'new wars' (Kaldor, 2001) feature a multitude of factions who largely involve civilians as targets and who may perceive war not as a means to an end but as an end in itself.[21]

Although ethnicity is today a popular concept to explain violence, it does little to account for long periods of peaceful co-existence (Turton, 1997) and it tends to naturalise an 'imagined community' (Anderson, 1991). Ethnicity can be mobilised in conflicts, but it is not a given, and it can fail to explain the patterns of violence that we find today.

The following section is not supposed to explain all current conflicts, but to highlight important elements of 'new wars' that are present to different degrees in different conflicts. The Kurdish-Turkish conflict, for example, has not been influenced by these changes in the same way as the Liberian civil war. However, where appropriate, adjudicators have to take account of changed mechanisms when assessing a refugee claim with a civil war background.

A weakened state, strengethened insurgents

The states that are the theatres of 'new wars' are typically former colonies that rely on the export of raw materials and agriculture. Falling export prices have led these states to rely on loans, and most of them have fallen into debt. IMF and World Bank adjustment policies, demanding downsizing of the administration, privatisation and tax reductions for foreign investors, have often had adverse effects, reducing sources of revenue without providing the improvement of infrastructure and the knowledge transfer expected. Declining wages for state agents foster corruption that may in extremis lead to a 'shadow state' (Reno, 2000). The restructuring of former state companies has raised the level of unemployment and has widened the income gap. Intense production by foreign investors has wrought drastic effects on the environment, driving an increasing number of people to urban centres in search for better opportunities. Diseases, spreading rapidly in inadequate living conditions in densely populated urban areas, place further strains on social structures and the state.

The effects of globalisation give these tendencies an extra spin. Revolutions in transport technology and finance have made production very flexible and enable investors, in the event of a crisis, to withdraw their funds within seconds. A technical revolution in communication systems have made real-time information widely available. As globalisation brings images and symbols of the western lifestyle to every hut in any country, young people question the traditional society with its system of elders and authority. They want status, not a life of rural struggle. In continually expanding cities, they join a growing underclass of mostly young men who, lacking education, employment and opportunity, develop a spirit of resentment and rebellion (Keen, 1998: 46f; Richards, 1996). As an alleged answer to the overwhelming effects of globalisation, identity politics foment, often encouraged from above as a survival strategy by leaders losing legitimacy, or seeking to spread insecurity by sowing intercommunal conflict for their own financial ends (Kaldor, 2001: 78; Keen, 1998: 24).

Many of the countries affected by 'civil wars' today were once war zones during the Cold War, supplied with weapons and money by the superpowers. The end of the Cold War stripped many of them of their strategic interest. The withdrawing superpowers left stockpiles of weapons behind and made more available 'on sale' due to massive downsizing of the Warsaw Pact armed forces. Other states are affected by spillovers from neighbouring countries, be it by illegal trade circuits, refugees, or identity politics (Kaldor, 2001: 110).

As a result of these developments, the state is greatly weakened. The effect of this on the armed forces is especially critical. Underpaid or unpaid troops will use their arms to procure income through extortion and pillage. Some of them will join armed bands as so-called *sobels*: soldiers during the day, 'rebels' at night. Without effective armed forces, the government often holds only nominal power and its control is reduced to the capital, with large areas falling under the rule of rebels, militias, armed gangs or clans. A gradual erosion of security accompanies a growing privatisation of violence

(Kaldor, 2001: 92) to which government is unable to launch an effective response.

The effect of these developments on insurgents is the exact opposite of its effect on the state. Where insurgents are already active, the end of super-power patronage forces them to seek other ways to sustain themselves. Trade is greatly facilitated by the new means of communication and transport. From the remotest areas of the country, they can direct legal and illegal trade via the internet and mobile telephones. Container transport facilitates illegal trade, and former Warsaw Pact armies sell not only cheap weapons but also small airplanes and jeeps (Mackinlay, 2002: 17–22).

This can dramatically transform 'old-school' popular insurgency movements. Their ideology loses importance, and the economic gain becomes a value in itself instead of a means to fight for change: greed substitutes for grievance. This does not mean that the insurgents do not present themselves in terms of 'liberation movements' or fighters for democracy. But their claims are often belied by their actions. Instead of moving among supportive civilians like 'the fish in the sea' (Mao), their economic activities increasingly entail policies that alienate them from the civil population. But this strategy is also attractive for private 'initiatives'. A withdrawing state leaves increasing sources of income to a new class of entrepreneurs in a sort of zero-sum game in authority and revenue. 'Businessman rebels' step into the vacuum left by the state to build up war economies. (Mackinlay, 2002: 66 ff; Keen, 2000: 24–5, 34–5; Collier, 2000: 91, 100)

Modern war economies: three stereotypes

'Businessman rebels' or warlords

The main actors in modern war economies can be grouped in three stereo-types: 'businessman rebels' or warlords, 'Lumpen rebels' and governments.

Typically, revenues come from the exploitation of resource-rich areas which an armed group or clan conquers. Trade relies heavily on transborder networks with established western companies: Warlords 'act locally, but . . . think globally' (Duffield, 2000: 84; Keen, 1998: 30). To secure this trade, the insurgents have to establish an alternative monopoly of power in the area. They do not necessarily defend a territory against concurring rebel groups or the government (Collier, 2000: 103). Sometimes, rebel groups divide up terri-tory and resources and co-ordinate troop movements, or even sell weapons to the 'enemy' (Keen, 1998: 17–18).

Tactics to secure the area can involve attacks against civilians. Rape plays an important role in such attacks (Nowrojee, 2005; Cockburn, 2004: 36). This appears especially counterproductive where the insurgents claim to fight for a common cause. But given the economic benefits, such tactics make sense. This form of war economy relies on a 'suspension of legality due to insecurity' (Duffield, 2000: 81). Strategies of immiseration of civilians, direct attacks, the spread of a climate of insecurity and forced movements can help depopulate a resource-rich area, attract aid that can be exploited, or simply serve to extort money from the civil population, for example in form of 'war taxes' or 'protection money,' while keeping social structures weak. A textbook example for this kind of war economy is Angola's UNITA. Charles Taylor established similar structures in Liberia.

Lumpen forces

This war business benefits from and employs 'Lumpen rebels' (Mackinlay, 2002: 44), recruited from an urban subclass that has 'nothing to lose, but the world to gain' (Oppenheimer, cited in Mackinlay, 2002: 44). Moving around on pick-ups with a mounted machine-gun, they benefit from a security vacuum and the availability of light weapons to prey on civilians, living off the war hand-to-mouth. Their lives being extremely hard and unstable, these forces are basically recruited and held together by force and fear. A frequent technique to prevent the 'recruits' – often children – from fleeing is to force them to commit atrocities against their family or community. This type of rebel is exemplified by the RUF in Sierra Leone.

Government forces and shadow states

Government forces themselves, though claiming to be fighting the rebels, can also profit from the 'new wars', to a point that government forces equally abuse civilians, seek to incite ethnic strife, and encourage rebel violence, notably by trading with them and selling them weapons (Adebajo and Keen, 2000: 8). War keeps military spending high and protects positions. It masks or explains human rights abuse and the exploitation of particular groups (Keen, 1998: 37; Shearer, 1998: 23). The ensuing looting and pillaging finances 'Operation Pay Yourself' for government troops (Reno, 2000: 50) and provides rewards for supporters who would otherwise join other factions (Keen, 1998: 29). War allows for monopolisation of trade and information and leads to price movements that can be very profitable (Collier, 2000: 130; Keen, 2000: 30). Corruption provides large sources of income. This can lead to the establishment of a 'shadow state' (Reno, 2000: 45 ff) that seeks to monopolise public goods, like security, in order to extract payments from civilians and companies for personal enrichment. Consequently, it will seek to 'make life less secure and more materially impoverished for subjects' (Reno, 2000: 47).

Flawed concepts – flawed responses

A 'new war' thus differs in many respects from what one would expect from a civil war. The situation is characterised by a 'privatisation of violence' (Kaldor, 2001: 94). Both government and rebels have an agenda that is at least as much economic as it is political. War has become a continuation not of politics, but of economics by other means (Keen, 1998: 11). For these reasons, the fighting factions are not always interested in an end to war, but rather in its prolongation. Large-scale civilian casualties do not represent collateral damage but instead a strategy. Civilians constitute a source of income, their displacement replaces their support (Kaldor, 2001: 98), accompanied by abuses, killings, inducement of famines etc. In addition to its economic functions, violence has become a lifestyle. Fighters who cannot return to their community because of their atrocious record identify with this rebel lifestyle; nor is a 'return' to rural life (if they have actually ever lived such life) attractive to them. An Angolan fighter says: 'Go home? I've been fighting since I was 16, now I'm 47. What home would you be talking about?'[22]

These phenomena challenge two traditional notions: that war is about winning, and that it is a collapse of a system rather than the creation of an alternative one (Keen, 2000: 19). Moreover, the notion of 'intra-state' or 'civil war' fails to grasp the growing importance of cross-border effects of the globalisation of trade (Duffield, 2000: 74).

While outdated notions make an adequate response difficult when a humanitarian crisis eventually triggers intervention. Few ceasefires or peace accords are worth the paper they are signed on, serving merely to regain forces or to buy time (King, 1997: 24). Humanitarian goods are routinely extorted or pillaged and peacekeepers attacked (Shearer, 2000). The readiness with which such wars are depicted as unsolvable, either as an outbreak of ancient ethnic hatred (Bosnia) or of pre-modern barbarism (West Africa), may also be grounded in a limited willingness to endanger European trade interests in the area and soldiers' lives.

This sketch shows that the image of civil wars underlying international responses and media reports, but also refugee law application can be inadequate. Unfortunately, it has found its way also into the civil war provisions of the Qualification Directive, which mentions 'indiscriminate violence in situations of international or internal armed conflict'. Rectifying this image therefore has important consequences for the application of the Refugee Convention to war refugees.

The impact of human rights and humanitarian law

Advanced human rights and humanitarian law standards also work to make the Convention more inclusive. According to its preamble, the protection against discriminatory human rights violation is the main purpose of the

Convention. Consequently, as the human rights standards evolve, the Convention itself has to follow, affording 'continuing protection for refugees in the changing circumstances of the present and future world'.[23] As a 'living instrument',[24] adopted 'for a humanitarian end which is constant in motive but mutable in form', it must keep track with contemporary developments, or it will become an anachronism.[25]

These developments include the recognition of rape as a means of terror. Thus, state-backed rape as a method of warfare constitutes torture[26] under the Convention Against Torture (CAT).[27] The right to freedom from torture, in return, belongs to customary international law and therefore binds all states that have not persistently objected. Under international criminal law, rape has been recognised as a war crime and a crime against humanity and even as genocide.[28] This is also explicitly mentioned in the Rome Statute of the International Criminal Court[29] as a result of the Bosnian experience. The contextualisation of rape as a method of terror against civilians will help to de-privatise rape in wartime.

The 1949 Geneva Conventions, in their common Article 3, list minimum safeguards for non-international armed conflicts. These include the prohibition of 'violence to life and person, in particular murder, cruel treatment and torture . . . [and] outrages upon human dignity' inflicted upon civilians.[30] Humanitarian law provides an important standard in international as well as internal wars: there can be no justification for the violation of its provisions (Fitzpatrick, 2001: 6). They are supplemented by lists of non-derogable human rights that cannot be breached even in times of public emergency.[31]

These developments make clear that it is indefensible to conceive of violations of core principles of human rights and humanitarian law that constitute war crimes and crimes against humanity as 'ordinary risks' inherent in civil wars. In the words of the UK Immigration Appeals Tribunal:

> the reference to the word 'ordinary' presupposes a distinction between the ordinary and the extraordinary, and the 'risk to life and liberty inherent in civil war' cannot refer to risks that are extraordinary or abnormal by minimum international standards governing civil war and armed conflict.[32]

Gender-based claims under the Convention

Since gender is not among the listed Convention reasons, the question of the appropriate label for women's cases has been subject to intense debate.

Gender as a separate category

Many national constitutions list, in their anti-discrimination or equality clauses, sex or gender as a category. Why not include sex/gender as a category in its own right in the Refugee Convention (Cipriani, 1993)? In its reform of the asylum provisions in 1997, Sweden introduced a clause that specifically dealt with sex/gender, however, such a move is not without problems. Folkelius and Noll (1998: 625 and *passim*) rightly point out that such a clause risks reducing the female experience of persecution to the sex/gender aspect. This is particularly problematic if, as in the Swedish case, the standard of protection is inferior to the one provided for other categories of refugees. But it also tends to de-politicise female activity (Greatbach, 1989) and reaffirms the division between 'normal' persecution following the male paradigm of a 'real refugee', and 'different', gender-specific persecution of women whose status is merely likened to the one of a 'real' refugee (Spijkerboer, 2000: 128–30; Haines, 2003: 326–7). The 'normal' Convention reasons continue to be 'owned' by mostly men. It therefore appears to be preferable to deal with sex/gender cases within the existing framework.

Sex/gender as a particular social group

There is strong support for treating sex, or gender, or more narrow categories of either, as basis for a 'particular social group' (for Germany, see Ankenbrand, 2002: 54). Some object that this would mean that more than half of the population of a country would count as persecuted – and would be entitled to stay. This argument is invalid for two reasons. One is that it alludes to the floodgate image: it insinuates that for reasons of the sheer number of possible applicants, this cannot be a proper construction of the Convention definition.[33] The other is that there is no mention of numbers in the Convention (Spijkerboer, 2002: 20–9). The categories of race and nationality comprise numbers that are possibly even larger.[34]

Another objection is the fact that not *all* women suffer persecution. Other attempts therefore limit the PSG to certain groups of women.[35] However, as Lord Hoffmann aptly points out in *Shah* and *Islam*, the fact that some members of a PSG escape persecution does not mean that there is no persecution for reasons of membership in that group.[36]

Moreover, how could a more narrow definition of a PSG comprising women risking sexual violence in armed conflicts be framed? And is this the right approach? Is the proper Convention category really PSG defined by sex? This would mean that the sexualised violence against women would not be seen in the context of violence against the rest of the population; rather it would be seen as different, differently motivated and needing a different category. However, sexual violence could also just be a particular means of persecution that is linked to sex because it is directed only at women; but not in that the persecution as such is motivated by the sex of the victim.

The nexus clause requirement

This takes us to the nexus clause requirement. In establishing whether the persecution occurred 'for reasons of' membership in the PSG, causal-link tests such as the Canadian 'but for' test are rather problematic (Hathaway and Foster, 2002b: 471–2). Most probably, the person would not have been raped were she not a woman. The question is, though, whether she would have escaped persecution *altogether*. In the case of civil wars, it seems that rape is just a particular means of persecution directed against women, as a part of a more general pattern of abuse of the civil population as a whole or against certain ethnic or religious groups. Women are often not targeted because they are women, but because they are part of a targeted group (Crawley, 2001: 72–4).

It seems, therefore, that a focus on the PSG category does not do justice to the patterns of violence in civil wars. A more adequate approach is attempted below.

Reinterpretation of the Refugee Convention: a sketch

While the causes of refugee movements have changed in important respects, this does not mean that the Refugee Convention is past its 'use-by date'. Its categories are flexible enough to accommodate many new developments. In the following sections, elements of a more adequate interpretation are given.

The agents of persecution

If governments of embattled states frequently take part in the systematic abuse of civilians, officials committing rape in such context cannot be considered to be acting as private citizens. A state that officially claims to be willing to prevent third-party persecution and to provide protection can in reality be condoning such violence or even collaborating with the perpetrators. Therefore seemingly uncontrolled militia violence may very well be 'encouraged or tolerated' by the state.

Contrary to the German jurisprudence and in line with the new law, it is obvious that the non-existence of a state or of stable de-facto authorities in no way indicates that there is no organised persecution. The violence occurring in civil wars is well targeted, and the fact that neither of the factions establishes quasi-state structures does not diminish this fact.

Persecution 'for' a convention reason

The images of animalism and natural sex drive that underlie the depiction of sexual violence in armed conflict imply gendered and racial stereotypes (Spijkerboer, 2000: 104) which overshadow possible planned effects of rape on the victim and its community.

In the framework of 'new wars', the abuse of civilians, including rape, has become a method of warfare. 'Private' reasons such as sexual gratification or economic motivations are but a part in the bundle of motives. The question is whether a Convention reason is present among these. It seems futile to try and weigh which reason was the 'effective cause' (Hathaway and Foster, 2002b: 474); for example, when in an ethnically charged conflict a particular tribe is driven out of a resource-rich area that a warring faction wants to exploit. Recent developments in human rights and humanitarian law also make clear that such abuses cannot be depicted as an 'ordinary risk' that civilians encounter in armed conflicts. It is therefore important that, when examining a refugee claim relating to a situation of armed conflict, the question of individualised persecution is carefully assessed before subsidiary protection clauses are applied.

With respect to the applicable Convention reason, it appears that it will be more helpful to a comprehensive understanding of the situation to consider women's claims as 'normal cases' (Spijkerboer, 2000: 111, 124, 128–30), in the same way as the cases of male victims of non-sexual violence. As indicated above, the reduction of 'women's cases' to the sex/gender aspect leads to a de-politicisation of these cases and eventually to a dead-end. If, as part of a strategy of terror, women are raped, their sex is the reason for the choice of that particular form of abuse rather than for the abuse itself.

Numbers suggest that gender stereotyping can be detrimental as well as beneficial for women's as well as men's claims (Spijkerboer, 2000: 194). However, structural exclusion would be an indirect violation of the equality clause as enshrined in various human rights instruments. Moreover, the European Community's commitment to gender mainstreaming (Articles 2 and 3 EC)[37] has to guide the interpretation of the Directive. This includes not (only) a sensitivity for women's concerns, but an elimination of all sorts of gender stereotyping.

The question of the proper Convention reason is the same for all group members. They might constitute a PSG, but they might also belong to a certain ethnicity or religious group that is being targeted, or they might be considered to have helped other factions, thus being persecuted for reasons of (ascribed) political opinion. The applicable Convention reasons will vary depending on the context.

Of course, there will be situations where none of the Convention reasons is applicable, simply because the persecution is, in fact, indiscriminate. However, neither the situation of war nor the particular act of persecution prevents a detailed analysis.

The Bosnian exception

Important steps in the right direction have been taken in the case of large-scale systematic rape of Muslim women in Bosnia in 1994. For the first time, rape has been recognised as a strategy of war, and as persecution for a Convention reason, such as nationality or religion (Hullmann, 1997: 49, 81). In Germany, Bosnian victims came not under the 'small asylum' clause that quotes the Geneva Convention definition, but under the constitutional, 'great asylum' for reasons of 'political persecution' (Marx, 1995: 34–8).

However, this has remained an exception. A comparison of Tamil, Sudanese and Bosnian rape cases (Spijkerboer, 2000: 131) reveals differences in legal treatment depending on the ethnicity of the victim. On the whole, the European approach to civil wars has not been satisfactory and will probably persist under the Qualification Directive.

Conclusion

The 1951 Refugee Convention is certainly out of date with respect to the conception of the typical refugee it had in mind. Times have changed since the year of its drafting, and so have standards influencing its interpretation. But to keep up with the times and to prevent an increasing loss of significance, every kind of law or treaty has to be considered as a 'living instrument' that stays true to its purpose in changing times.

The European Qualification Directive has brought some improvements in the field of third-party persecution and gendered persecution. However, its subsidiary protection clause risks attracting all civil war cases and depriving them of a careful assessment of possible individualised persecution. Such second-class protection can be considered positive insofar as it usually covers all those 'defined out of' the Convention (Spijkerboer, 2002: 29–36). On the other hand, the existence of such a status makes it easier to deny refugee claims, knowing that the rejected claimants will be allowed to stay on humanitarian grounds. The Directive's gender-based persecution clause might do the same for the grounds of persecution and make it harder for women to get their claims examined outside of the PSG ground.

The proposed reassessment of civil wars and a gender-sensitive approach that does not reduce women's claims to the gender aspect will help reframe women's claims in rape cases as 'normal cases' deserving 'first-class' protection.

Still, it is in the nature of legal categories that they are not all-inclusive. The inclusion of a list of Convention reasons as well as an exclusion clause means that not every form of persecution renders a person a refugee in all circumstances. This is certainly deplorable, but nothing is currently less probable than an extension of the scope of protection of the Convention. We therefore have to work with what we have. And in a number of cases, a reinterpretation is not only possible, but also an obligation.

Notes

1 United Nations Convention Relating to the Status of Refugees, 189 UNTS 150.
2 The much-used term 'gender-based persecution' is not quite precise, since it confounds not only the terms 'sex' and 'gender' but also the reasons for and the forms of persecution which can primarily concern one sex, such as rape. However, since it is so widely used, the present paper will follow this terminology. Where more precision is required, this will be made explicit.
3 Council Directive 2004/83/EC of 29 April 2004, OJ L 304, 30.9.2004, pp 12–23.
4 See above, n 3.
5 CE, sec, *Dankha*, 27 May 1983; *Recueil Lebon*, p 220; AJDA 1983, p 483 (my translation).
6 CRR, 5 April 1993, 227.353 (*Kurtic*), and 12 February 1993, 232.258 (*Dzebric*), *Chronique, Documentation-Réfugiés* Supp No 223 17/30 August 1993, pp 7, 9.
7 BVerwG, 18 January 1994, BVerwGE 95, pp 42, 45.
8 EC Council, OJ L 63/2, 13.03.96.
9 Federal Constitutional Court (*Bundesverfassungsgericht*), 10 July 1989; BVerfGE 80, p 315; BVerwG, 21 January 1992; BVerwGE 89, p 296.
10 BVerwG, 18 January 1994; BVerwGE 95, p 42.
11 UK House of Lords, *SSHD v Adan and SSHD v Aitseguer*, 19 December 2000; [2001] Imm AR, p 253.
12 Art 2 (3) Loi 52–893 of 25 July 1952; Loi relative au droit d'asile (Law on the Right to Asylum), modified by Loi 2003–1176 of 10 December 2003; *Journal Officiel*, 11 December 2003.
13 Gesetz über den Aufenthalt, die Erwerbstätigkeit und die Integration von Ausländern (AufenthG) of 30 July 2004, BGBl. I 2004, 1950.
14 BVerwG, 8 February 2005, Doc No 1 C 29.03, accessed at www.bverwg.de/media/archive/2956.pdf (26 June 2005), para 15.
15 VG Regensburg, 24 January 2005, Doc No 8 K 04.30779; accessed at http://www.jurisweb.de.
16 VG Aachen, 13 January 2005, Doc No 7 K 4011/04.A; accessed at http://www.jurisweb.de.
17 Most importantly in House of Lords, *Shahana Islam v SSHD; R v Immigration Appeal Tribunal and SSHD ex p Syeda Shah*, 1999, IJRL 11, pp 469–527.
18 Supreme Court of Canada, *Canada (Attorney General) v Ward* [1993] 2 SCR 689, *per* LaForest J.
19 US Board of Immigration Appeals (BIA), *Re Acosta* 1995, 19 I and N 211.
20 US BIA, *re Kasinga*, 21 I and N 357.
21 The adjective 'new' is relative; Münkler (2004: 75–88) points out interesting parallels with the Thirty Years' War. See also Schlichte, 2006.
22 *Guardian*, 21 February 2003.
23 UK Court of Appeal, *Aitseguer, per* Laws LJ, quoted in Symes, 2001: 11.
24 Ibid.
25 Australian High Court, *Shah, per* Sedley, quoted in Symes, 2001: 11.
26 European Court of Human Rights, *Aydin v Turkey* (1998), 25 EHRR 251.
27 United Nations Convention Against Torture, 1465 UNTS 85 (entered into force 1987).
28 International Criminal Tribunal for Rwanda, (ICTR), *Prosecutor v Jean-Paul Akayesu*, 2 September 1998, ICTR-96-4-T; International Criminal Tribunal for the former Yugoslavia (ICTY) *Prosecutor v Kunarac, Kovac and Vukovic*, 22 February 2001, IT-96-23-T& IT-96-23/1-T.
29 Art 7 (1)(g), Art 8 (2) (b) (xxii).
30 See also Art 27(2) Geneva Convention IV Relative to the Protection of Civilian

Persons in Time of War (75 UNTS 287), Art 75(2) and Art 76(1) Additional Protocol I (1125 UNTS 3), and Art 4(1) Additional Protocol II (1125 UNTS 609).
31 E.g. Art 15 of the 1950 European Convention on Human Rights, 213 UNTS 221; Art 4 of the 1966 International Covenant on Civil and Political Rights, 999 UNTS 171.
32 *Rudralingam* (00/TH/02264; 24 November 2000), quoted in Symes and Jorro, 2003: 112–13, against UK House of Lords, *R v SSHD ex p Adan* [1998] Imm AR 338.
33 But see Justice Madgwick's rebuttal of this argument, Federal Court of Australia in *Jama*:

> [E]specially when considering the question of 'social group' the inadmissible questions: 'Where will it all end? How can we accept all such people?', often leap to mind. . . . [But under the law] nobody – Minister, Tribunal or Court – is authorized to deny a person a protection visa as a 'refugee' on the ground that, if one particular person obtains such a visa then, to be consistent, many other similarly-placed people ought to be granted one too.
>
> (Symes, 2001 9–10)

34 Hathaway and Foster, 2002a: 479; McHugh in *Applicant A v Minister for Immigration and Ethnic Affairs* (1997) 142 ALR 331.
35 Cf the discussion in the UK House of Lords, *Islam* and *Shah*, n 15 above.
36 Ibid.
37 Treaty Establishing the European Community (EC; Treaty of Rome), OJ C-325, 24 December 2002 (consolidated version).

References

Adebajo, Adekaye and Keen, David (2002) 'Banquet for warlords,' *The World Today*, July, pp 8–10

Anderson, Benedict (1991) *Imagined Communities: Reflections on the Origin and Spread of Nationalism*, London: Verso

Ankenbrand, Birthe (2002) 'Refugee women under German asylum law', *International Journal of Refugee Law* 14, pp 45–56

Cipriani, Linda (1993) 'Gender and persecution: Protecting women under international refugee law', *Georgetown Immigration Law Journal* 7, pp 511–49

Collier, Paul (2000) 'Doing well out of war: An economic perspective', in Berdal, Mats and Malone, David (eds) *Greed and Grievance: Economic Agendas in Civil Wars*, Boulder/London: Lynne Rienner, pp 91–111

Crawley, Heaven (2001) *Refugees and Gender: Law and Process*, Bristol: Jordan

Duffield, Mark (2000) 'Globalization, transborder trade, and war economies', in Berdal, Mats and Malone, David (eds), *Greed and Grievance: Economic Agendas in Civil Wars*, Boulder/London: Lynne Rienner, pp 69–89

ExCom (Executive Committee of UNHCR) (1993) *Conclusion No 73 (XLIV) 1993, Refugee Protection and Sexual Violence*, Geneva: UNHCR. Accessed at: http://www.unhcr.ch

ExCom (Executive Committee of UNHCR) (1995) *Conclusion No 77 (XLVI) 1995, General*, Geneva: UNHCR. Accessed at: http://www.unhcr.org

Fitzpatrick, Joan (2001) 'Human rights and forced displacement: Converging standards', in Bayefski, Anne F and Fitzpatrick, Joan (eds), *Human Rights and Forced Displacement*, Cambridge, MA: M Nijhoff Publishers, pp 3–25

Folkelius, Kristina and Noll, Gregor (1998) 'Affirmative exclusion? Sex, gender, persecution and the reformed Swedish Aliens Act', *International Journal of Refugee Law* 10, pp 607–36

Greatbach, Jacqueline (1989) 'The gender difference: Feminist critiques of refugee discourse', *International Journal of Refugee Law* 1, pp 518–26

Haines, Rodger (2003) 'Gender-related persecution', in Feller, Erika, Türk, Volker and Nicholson, Frances (eds), *Refugee Protection in International Law: UNHCR's Global Consultations on International Protection*, Cambridge: Cambridge University Press, pp 319–50

Hathaway, James C (1991) *The Law of Refugee Status*, Toronto: Butterworths

Hathaway, James C and Foster, Michelle (2002a) 'Membership of a particular social group: Discussion paper', *International Journal of Refugee Law* 15, pp 476–91

Hathaway, James C and Foster, Michelle (2002b) 'The causal connection ("nexus") to a Convention ground: Discussion paper', *International Journal of Refugee Law* 15, pp 461–76

Hullmann, Klaus (1997) 'Austria', 'Switzerland', in Carlier, Jean-Yves *et al.* (eds), *Who Is a Refugee? A Comparative Case Law Study*, The Hague: Kluwer Law International, pp 11–55, 111–63

Indra, Doreen (1987) 'Gender: A key dimension of the refugee experience', *Refuge* 6(3), pp 3–4

Kaldor, Mary (2001) *New and Old Wars: Organized Violence in a Global Era*, Cambridge: Polity Press

Keen, David (1998) 'The economic function of violence in civil wars', *Adelphi Paper* 320

Keen, David (2000) 'Incentives and disincentives for violence' in Berdal, M and Malone, D (eds), *Greed and Grievance: Economic Agendas in Civil Wars*, Boulder/London: Lynne Rienner, pp 19–41

Kelly, Nancy (1993) 'Gender-related persecution: Assessing the asylum claims of women', *Cornell International Law Journal* 26(3), pp 625–74

King, Charles (1997) 'Ending civil wars', *Adelphi Paper* 308

Mackinlay, John (2002) 'Globalisation and insurgency', *Adelphi Paper* 352

Mackinlay, John and Kent, Randolph (1997) 'A new approach to complex emergencies', *International Peacekeeping* 4, pp 31–49

Marx, Reinhard (1995) *Handbuch zur Asyl- und Flüchtlingsanerkennung*, Neuwied: Luchterhand

Mees-Asadollah, Ursula (1998) 'Frauenspezifische Verfolgung – wird die deutsche Asylpraxis ihr gerecht?', *Streit*, pp 139–55

Moore, Jennifer (2003) 'Whither the accountability theory: second-class status for third-party refugees as a threat to international refugee protection', in van Selm, Joanne *et al.* (eds) *The Refugee Convention at Fifty. A View From Forced Migration Studies*, Lanham, MD: Lexington Books, pp 113–28

Münkler, Herfried (2004) *Die neuen Kriege*, Hamburg: Rowohlt

Reno, William (2000) 'Shadow states and the political economy of civil wars', in Berdal, Mats and Malone, David (eds), *Greed and Grievance: Economic Agendas in Civil Wars*, Boulder/London: Lynne Rienner, pp 43–68

Schlichte, Klaus (2006) 'Neue Kriege oder alte Thesen? Wirklichkeit und Repräsentation kriegerischer Gewalt in der Politikwissenschaft', in Geis, Anna (ed) *Den Krieg überdenken: Kriegsbegriffe und Kriegstheorien in der Kontroverse*, Baden-Baden: Nomos, pp 111–31

Shearer, David (1998) 'Private armies and military intervention', *Adelphi Paper* 316

Shearer, David (2000) 'Aiding or abetting? Humanitarian aid and its economic role in civil war', in Berdal, Mats and Malone, David (eds), *Greed and Grievance: Economic Agendas in Civil Wars*, Boulder/London: Lynne Rienner, pp 189–203

Shearer, David (2001) 'Privatizing protection', *The World Today*, August/September, pp 29–31

Spijkerboer, Thomas (2000) *Gender and Refugee Status*, Aldershot: Ashgate

Spijkerboer, Thomas (2002) 'Subsidiary protection in asylum law: The personal scope of international protection', in Bouteillet-Paquet, Daphné (ed) *Subsidiary Protection of Refugees in the European Union: Complementing the Geneva Convention?*, Brussels: Bruylant, pp 19–42

Symes, Mark and Jorro, Peter (2003) *Asylum Law and Practice*, London: LexisNexis

Symes, Mark (2001) *Caselaw on the Refugee Convention*, London: Refugee Legal Centre

Sztucki, Jerzy (1999) 'Who is a refugee? The Convention definition: universal or obsolete?', in Nicholson, Frances and Twomey, Patrick (eds) *Refugee Rights and Responsibilities*, Cambridge: Cambridge University Press, pp 55–81

Tiberghien, Frédéric (2001) 'La jurisprudence du Conseil d'État sur la Convention du 28 juillet 1951 relative au statut des réfugiés', in Chetail, Vincent and Flauss, Jean-François, *La Convention de Genève du 28 juillet 1951 relative au statut des réfugiés 50 ans après : bilan et perspectives*, Brussels: Bruylant, pp 289–323

Turton, David (1997) 'War and ethnicity', in Turton, David (ed), *War and Ethnicity: Global Connections and Local Violence*, Rochester: University of Rochester Press.

UNHCR (1997a) *The State of the World's Refugees: A Humanitarian Agenda*, Geneva: UNHCR. Accessed at: http://www.unhcr.org

UNHCR (1997b) 'Gender-related persecution: An analysis of recent trends', *International Journal of Refugee Law*, Special Issue, pp 79–113

UNHCR (2001) *Auslegung von Artikel 1 des Abkommens von 1951 über die Rechtsstellung der Flüchtlinge*, Geneva: UNHCR. Accessed at: http://www.unhcr.de

UNHCR (2002) *Guidelines on International Protection: Gender-Based Persecution within the Context of Article 1A(2) of the 1951 Convention and/or its 1967 Protocol Relating to the Status of Refugees*, HCR/GIP/02/01, 7 May 2002 Geneva: UNHCR, Accessed at: http//www.unhcr.org

Vermeulen, Ben, Spijkerboer, Thomas, Zwaan, Karin and Fernhout, Roel (1998) *Persecution by Third Parties*, University of Nijmegen: Centre for Migration Law

Wilsher, Daniel (2003) 'Non-state actors and the definition of a refugee in the United Kingdom: protection, accountability or culpability?', *International Journal of Refugee Law*, 15, pp 68–112

5

PROBLEMATISING TRAFFICKING FOR THE SEX SECTOR

A case of eastern European women in the EU[1]

Rutvica Andrijasevic

We will call them Olga and Natasha. Their story equals the stories of many other girls from the East who came to Italy blinded by a work promise, and then forced into prostitution by a pimp, a man of no scruples. As soon as they got off the bus that brought them illegally from Moldova to Italy, they were taken over by Rimi, an Albanian.[2]

This excerpt, taken from an Italian daily newspaper, is typical of many recent media accounts of trafficking from 'eastern' to 'western' Europe.[3] In analysing such representations, scholars have pointed out that – as in the above newspaper clip – trafficking is commonly represented along a victim–criminal binary, portraying traffickers as male criminals who coerce and deceive women into engaging in illegal migration and prostitution and the women themselves as innocent young victims (Berman, 2003; Doezema, 1999; Sharma, 2003; Stenvoll, 2002; Sutdhibhasilp, 2002). Taking the victim–criminal binary as its starting point, this chapter critically assesses current representations and understandings of 'trafficking' as a matter of organised crime and of the women involved as coerced and deceived victims. Accordingly, my interpretative approach does not focus on violence against women, a privileged topic among many feminist scholars and activists. Rather, by placing 'trafficking' in the context of European integration, I propose to shift the terms of analysis from violence and organised crime to those of migration and labour.[4]

In dominant discourse, the term trafficking is often used in ways that collapse a large span of operations. These involve, first, the recruitment and transportation of women from their departure to the destination country, and second, the living and working conditions upon arrival. As various scholars have argued (Anderson and O'Connell Davidson, 2003; Wijers and Lap-Chew, 1997), although a woman might find herself in slavery-like labour conditions (violence and/or threat of violence, confiscation of legal documents, no freedom of movement) as a consequence of having been transported to a foreign country, she might also be recruited without coercion and may or may not find herself in forced labour conditions. My analysis makes a distinction between these various operations, focusing on the recruitment and transportation phase of trafficking. This methodological approach joins recent scholarship on trafficking which questions the assumed correlation between trafficking and organised crime and proposes to investigate the ways in which border and migration regimes foster the legal, economic and physical vulnerability of migrant women (Berman, 2003; Sharma, 2003; Sutdhibhasilp, 2002).

This chapter is based on interviews held in Bologna between October 1999 and February 2000[5] with 25 women, aged 18 to 25 years. These women, all of them originating from eastern European non-EU candidate countries,[6] came to the EU via trafficking networks and subsequently worked as street prostitutes under various 'degrees of confinement' and under conditions of economic exploitation.[7] At the time of the interviews, all of them had stopped working as street prostitutes and were struggling with questions pertaining to their new living arrangements, such as whether to return home or stay in the EU. Their accounts reveal some of the intricate processes that constitute the conditions for trafficking.

Throughout this chapter, I cast the women's narratives against the backdrop of representations of women's trafficking found in the mass media,[8] as well as in feminist sources. By looking at processes of representation and how meanings are produced and allocated in public discourse, my analysis sheds light on different and often overlooked aspects of trafficking. I question the dominant discourses of trafficking and map out some of the central elements which converge with the EU political agenda, thus helping to legitimate policies geared at tightening border controls.

I shall begin my discussion of how women's narratives challenge accepted notions of victimhood by scrutinising their accounts of border crossings and how they entered trafficking systems. In tackling questions relative to the travel and recruitment process, my work brings to the fore the ways in which strictly controlled borders actually encourage trafficking. Consequently, as I argue in this chapter, visa and border controls form a crucial element that must be included in an analysis of trafficked women's accounts of their migration experiences. Finally, I shall discuss the current trend towards the criminalisation of irregular migration in the light of the respondents' own accounts of their engagement with immigration law. I shall argue that privileging the narrative of victimhood forecloses the possibility of identifying the motives that inform respondents' migratory project, thus seriously limiting scholarly understanding of trafficking as a migratory system.

Gendering the borders of enlarged Europe

During the past decade, various newspapers throughout western Europe have increasingly featured migration as an urgent threat, a crisis in need of containment (Dal Lago, 1999). In particular, the media portrayal of irregular migration – and specifically of trafficking – emphasises its magnitude. The newspaper clipping about Olga and Natasha quoted at the beginning of this chapter offers a good example. Next to portraying the two women's story in terms of deception into illegal migration and prostitution, it also places it alongside numerous other stories of the same kind. In doing so, it suggests a vast movement of east–west trafficking in Europe.

Such references to the magnitude of trafficking and an emphasis on the deceptive and coercive nature of the contracts between migrant women and third parties are not exclusively characteristic of the press. The tropes of 'waves' of trafficked women and of trafficked women as victims are deployed by a number of feminist scholars too. While Khalid Koser and Helma Lutz (1998: 3) stress the unavailability of reliable data on female migrants trafficked illegally for the purpose of prostitution, other scholars (Caldwell *et al.*, 1999; Lazaridis, 2001: 70) rely on questionable figures provided by governmental and non-governmental bodies, in which quoted numbers diverge by hundreds of thousands.[9] The vagueness and ambiguity of these figures foster accounts of trafficking from eastern Europe presented in terms of an 'explosive increase' (Molina and Janssen, 1998: 16) that has reached 'epidemic proportions' (UN in Pickup, 1998: 44). Such alarmist portrayals not only inflate the statistics to produce an imagery of invasion, but, as I argue below, deploy a particularly gendered image of migration which obscures the correlation between irregular migration and the juridico-material creation of borders in response to trafficking.

The governments of the EU member states, associating trafficking with 'illegal' migration from third countries and organised crime, have responded to the alleged magnitude of trafficking by a tightening of immigration laws (Wijers and Doorninck, 2002). In this respect, the implementation of the border protection scheme has been endorsed as a pivotal measure: 'Better management of the Union's external border controls will help in the fight against terrorism, illegal immigration networks and the trafficking in human beings' (European Council, 2001). The intensification of border controls, in particular at the external borders of the EU, has been seen as a necessary condition for the establishment of a free area of circulation within the EU (Turnbull, 1999).[10] This relocation of control to the EU's external borders has led to the creation of what has been dubbed 'fortress Europe' or, in Étienne Balibar's words, a 'double regime of the circulation of people' (Balibar in Simoncini, 2000: 32). It is designed to facilitate and encourage the labour mobility of EU citizens, while simultaneously restricting the mobility of 'third-country' nationals. The EU enlargement process has moreover transformed this double regime into multiple regimes of differentiated degrees of mobility between the EU, EU Candidates, and the non-Candidate states. As a condition for integration, the EU Candidate states are required to apply strict border and visa regulations with respect to non-Candidate states. In this way, the responsibility for border protection and for the interception of undocumented migration has been shifted from the EU to the Candidate states, turning the latter into a kind of 'buffer zone', the EU's new migration 'gatekeepers' (Andreas, 2000).

While some scholars prefer to downplay the importance of borders, since borders do not constitute an impenetrable barrier, nor can they be controlled comprehensively (Bigo, 2003; Andreas and Snyder, 2000), others talk of a 'war' to give expression to the conflict taking place at Europe's external borders and the human costs[11] it entails (Mezzadra and Rigo, 2003). Notwithstanding the different approaches, scholars concur in regarding the idea of fully policed borders, entertained as such by the sovereign states, as a 'myth' (Anderson, 2000: 25) and an 'illusion of control' (Bigo, 2003). However, borders and border-control have been described as playing an important psychological function in western European societies, namely providing a feeling of security and fostering citizens' sense of belonging to the political community (Bigo, 2000; Snyder, 2000). Moreover, borders are not simply static demarcations. The effects of borders extend not only outwards to sanction new partitions, they also extend inwards in the form of institutional practices and discourses, defining some people and nations as 'belonging' to the EU, and others as not. Borders' symbolic role is thus intrinsically connected to their practical role, for example that of filtering 'unwanted elements' out of the migratory flow (Andreas, 2000: 4). Within the discourse economy of illegal migration, the border serves as a site of crime. It is a locus where the law is broken and where the established order is violated by those trying to cross without the required documents.

In the visual media, the presented images of border-crossings are highly gendered. The absence of women in these depictions of border-crossing matches a discursive scenario in which migrant women do not figure as protagonists, but as characters endowed with little or no agency. While male migrants are presented as the characters of border-crossings, migrant women tend to disappear from view, reappearing only as war refugees and/or victims of trafficking (Andrijasevic, 2003).[12]

In their works on gender and migration, feminist migration scholars have accurately challenged mainstream migration theory based on the idea of the migrant family in which the man is perceived of as an economically motivated actor and the woman as his dependant, whether in an economic sense or in relation to the migratory project. In countering this mainstream fantasy, they have emphasised the role women play as 'active agents' in international migration (Anthias and Lazaridis, 2000; Kofman, 1999; Morokvašic, 1991). Yet, when it comes to trafficking, many feminist scholars remain uncritical in associating trafficking with forced migration and hence perpetuating a narrative of passive victimhood (Phizacklea, 1996; Kofman *et al.*, 2000). Annie Phizacklea, for example, writes that 'trafficked women are often deceived and coerced into illegal migration' (1998: 31), while Marina Orsini-Jones and Francesca Gattullo who have examined the issue of women's migration and trafficking in Italy and Bologna in particular, observe that migrant women 'are part of the very sad "slave trade" flourishing across Europe' (2000: 128).

These feminist scholars' characterisations of women within the trafficking networks are a far cry from portraying them as active agents. By incorporating certain aspects of the dominant discourse and portraying trafficking uncritically in terms of illegal migration and organised crime, these scholars ignore the multiplicity of women's motives and modes of entry into trafficking networks. But if we take the trouble to ask specific questions about migrant women's experiences, a different picture emerges. In which way and with whom did women cross the border and reach their destination? Were they undocumented or did they possess passports and visas? If they were in possession of a visa, how did they obtain it and for how long were those visas valid? By neglecting to pose such questions, feminist migration scholars also fail to question the ways in which the EU's border and visa regimes affect women's lives.

(Il)legality, borders and trafficking

In the respondents' accounts, having or not having a visa is linked to the ways in which they crossed the border and to the time it took to get across. The difference between documented and undocumented border-crossings is most apparent in the narratives of those women who were 'trafficked' to Italy twice: first on foot without a visa and a second time by bus with tourist visas purchased by a (travel) agent. When the respondents crossed the borders undocumented on foot, in a truck or by boat, descriptions of the journey constituted a central element of the migration narrative and included detailed descriptions of the events and actors involved. In her account, Oksana recalled the number and names of travellers, the weather conditions when crossing the Slovenian–Italian border, the vegetation of the landscape and even the state of the ground they walked on. When the same respondents returned to Italy for a second time with a valid visa, they travelled by plane or bus, crossing the international borders quickly and smoothly. In stark contrast to the first crossing narratives, accounts of the 'legal' crossing offer few details about the journey. We can attribute the disparity between descriptions of undocumented and documented forms of travel to differences in the degree of risk and danger involved. The fear of being caught by the border police during their undocumented crossings, of being sexually abused by traffickers, of contracting a disease or an illness during prolonged travel, of having little or no control over the terms of the travel and therefore being dependent on the traffickers, all of these produce a highly traumatic experience whose details are impressed in respondents' memories.[13]

Contrary to the idea that women are always forced or coerced by traffickers into illegal migration, some respondents tell how they were only able to realise their travel plans with the help of traffickers. A striking example comes from Liudmila, who hired an agency to buy her visa and organise her trip to Italy. But due to the instability in the region caused by NATO's bombing of Serbia, the agency in Moldova was unable to carry out this otherwise routine operation.[14] After months of waiting for the situation to improve, Liudmila finally decided to contact a trafficker who brought her to Italy in four days on condition that she worked as a prostitute.

Some respondents took longer to reach Italy because the border police intercepted the group they were travelling with. For example, Kateryna, ended up being deported from Austria. For Larisa, also apprehended by the border police, arrest meant permanent denial of admission to Hungary. A few weeks later, each of these respondents embarked upon another crossing via a different route. Larisa arrived in Italy from Albania by boat, while Kateryna crossed the Slovenian–Italian border on foot. Kateryna comments on her second journey: 'I was scared of being caught and sent back home. Because if they [the border police] would have caught me, I would have had to do it all over again.' Many narratives are punctuated by remarks that reveal the women's awareness of the necessity to cross the borders secretly. Kateryna continues: 'Some girls travel hidden in the back of a truck. They take sleeping pills in order not to do anything and not to eat at all. They take sleeping pills and sleep during the entire journey.'

Although such travel arrangements helped these women circumvent border controls, they also exposed them to the danger of abuse by third parties, or to detention and interrogation by the border police if captured during their border crossing. Having little or no control over the terms of the journey meant that the interests of third parties determined the women's travel routes and the length of travel (Koslowski, 2001). The proliferation of border controls and the introduction of new visa policies also raised the costs of travel.[15] Each border-crossing that a woman had to negotiate while travelling without documents from Moldova or Ukraine, for example, involved new expenses.[16] At times, women had to pay to be transferred from one agent to another, in order to be able to pay back the costs made during the previous segment of the journey and arrange for the next.

In other words, each segment of the journey was ascribed a monetary value which the respondents, having no financial means of their own, were obliged to pay off through sex-work performed at various locations during the journey. Hence, my research suggests that stricter immigration controls adopted to curb trafficking increase the costs of 'doing business' (Salt and Stein, 1997), raise the value of migrants as (labour) 'commodities' (Kyle and

Dale, 2001), and ultimately serve the economic interests of third parties. By extension, they increase the level of control third parties have over migrants, both during the journey and upon the arrival at their destinations (Anderson and O'Connell Davidson, 2003).[17] Quite paradoxically then, increased control over migrants' mobility is not likely to curb transnational crime, but rather to heighten its involvement in migration, due to the increased profits that accrue from trafficking activities (Finckenauer, 2001; Koslowski, 2001: 351).[18]

Not all respondents arrived in Italy undocumented; traffickers provided some women with the necessary travel documents. Realising that she would have to cross the border on foot because the third parties were initially unwilling to buy her a visa, Snežana refused to leave until she had successfully negotiated a visa and a bus ride to Italy. Another respondent, Tatiana, flew from Moscow to Rome on a 15-day tourist visa bought for her by two Russian women working as prostitutes in Italy. Oksana and Ioanna (the Olga and Natasha of the newspaper clipping at the start of this chapter) reached Italy in two days by bus. Contrary to what the newspaper claims, the two women did not enter Italy undocumented. Through an agency, they had bought short-term visas with money borrowed from a third party. This money covered the costs of the visa, the trip from Ukraine to Poland, a night in a hotel in Warsaw and a bus ticket to Bologna. Even though it is difficult, if not impossible, to travel through Europe on a regular bus without documents, the reporting newspaper described these two women as 'illegal'. This conflation of trafficking with undocumented migration sustains and strengthens the representation of trafficking as a form of illegal migration. It relies on an oversimplified distinction between 'illegal' and 'legal' migration. In my research, a number of respondents entered Italy with a valid visa but became undocumented after having overstayed the length of the granted visa.

Hence, trafficking might have legal elements such as legally obtained visas while legal migratory processes might involve illegal components, like requests for high fees advanced by the agencies or even illegal payments asked by Consulates. My data concur with other findings that no clear-cut separation can be made between legal and 'illegal' migration in relation to trafficking (Anderson and O'Connell Davidson, 2003; Maluccelli, 2001; McDonald et al., 2000; Sharma, 2003). Moreover, any attempt to endorse a model based on such a distinction is extremely problematic. Uncritical subsuming of trafficking under the category of 'illegal' migration masks the fact that tightened immigration controls have starkly reduced the number of legal channels available for migration, so that in contemporary times illegality has become a structural characteristic of migratory flows (Mezzadra, 2001: 78).

Deception and projects of migration

Media accounts offer little information on how women and traffickers get in touch with each other, except through kidnappings. An examination of respondents' life-stories reveals that in reality, trafficking systems are considerably more complex. In these accounts, third parties involved in organising the journey to the EU were many and carried out a variety of tasks. The initial contacts with individual recruiters or agencies are not described as abusive. This does not mean that the respondents were naïve when it came to third parties' economic interests. But neither did they underestimate the importance of third parties' involvement. In this sense, Oksana's account is typical: 'They help girls to find a job in a foreign country'. Some contacts through which women are offered employment and access to the EU, and for whom they subsequently work, seem to form part of larger criminal networks. Other trafficking systems, on the contrary, include a wide variety of people such as taxi drivers, housewives and restaurant owners who supplement their income by 'passing the word'. If, on the one hand, trafficking is a 'multi-billion dollar industry' (Ram, 2000: 1), on the other hand, it also forms an integral part of the local and informal economies of some eastern European countries. Indeed, in these countries, in a context of economic restructuring accompanied by high unemployment rates and the informalisation of labour, trafficking activities have come to form 'alternative ... circuits for making a living [and] earning a profit' (Sassen, 2000: 523). By identifying the various operations and actors involved at different stages in the trafficking process, respondents' accounts show that recruiting agents often had no interest in profiting from the exploitation of women's labour upon their arrival in the EU, but instead realised economic gain through their recruitment activities or the travel arrangements that they provided. My data problematise the interpretation that sees trafficking exclusively in terms of recruitment and transportation for the sole purpose of exploiting migrant women's labour in prostitution.

Furthermore, the media rarely provide information on the jobs advertised, thus perpetuating the idea that third parties inevitably deceive migrant women into prostitution. A number of studies show that a considerable percentage of women from eastern Europe who came to the EU, Canada or Turkey through trafficking systems agreed to work in the sex industry but were unaware of the living and working conditions awaiting them in their countries of destination (Gülçür and Ilkkaracan, 2002; Maluccelli, 2001; McDonald et al., 2000; Orfano, 2003; Wijers and Lap-Chew, 1997). While my findings point in the same direction, my data also suggest that when the emphasis is put on deception (or lack of it) as regards the type of work involved, then an analysis of the trafficking process remains caught in the web of moral arguments surrounding prostitution. Privileging the question of deceit in relation to prostitution tells us little about the terms of employment that the migrants have (or have not) themselves negotiated with third parties and deflects attention from women's migratory projects.

Migratory projects, whether inclusive of sex work or not, emerge as a central element in respondents' narratives of trafficking. For Ana, who 'just' wanted to 'get to Italy', entering the trafficking system and consenting to prostitution was merely a means to an end. For Ioanna, coming to Italy was linked to the lack of opportunities at home:

> I am 23 years old and now I am able to take care of the things on my own. I came to Italy because there was no job for me back home. Initially I said no, but if there was no other work, then going to Italy was the last chance to find a job.

While Ioanna left the Ukraine planning to improve her own and her family's situation, Kateryna left Romania in order to break out of a depression caused by humiliation in school and past violence at home: 'I wanted to start my life all over again in a place where no one knew me or things about me. I wanted to create a new image of myself.' For these women, migration to the EU forms part of a project designed to lead them out of poverty, lack of employment, lost self-esteem, family abuse, interrupted education, and a general sense of life stagnation. For the respondents then, entering the EU via trafficking systems was a means to travel and move on.

It is obvious that those respondents who were promised jobs as waitresses or domestic workers, and were then introduced into the sex industry, had not been informed about the terms of their employment in sex work. However, those respondents who did agree to a sex work contract were equally unknowing as to the details of that contract. We can look at the account of Kateryna for an illustration. Having accepted her boyfriend's offer to migrate from Romania to Italy and work there as a prostitute, Kateryna was not aware of the conditions under which she would be working. None of the specifics concerning working hours, the large number of clients and the constant control by a third party or by peers had been disclosed to her. Another respondent was told more precisely what would be expected of her. Oksana, who was about to return to Italy for a second time, had asked her friend Ioanna if she would like to join her and had described her previous experiences as a street prostitute (see the newspaper clip on Olga and Natasha at the opening of this chapter, which tells the story of the same respondents with emphasis on deception into prostitution). Ioanna states that she arrived in Italy fully prepared: 'I came to Italy and I knew all about it – what to tell to the clients, what to do, where to go – I knew it all.' However, examination of the verbal agreement between her and the third party reveals that she was not aware that she would be required to surrender most of her earnings and prostitute under conditions of confinement which made it difficult to get out of the contract.

My results confirm the conclusion also reached by other researchers that the term 'victim' is inadequate in depicting the condition of migrant women within trafficking systems (Maluccelli, 2001; Corso and Trifirò, 2003). This body of scholarship demonstrates that women are rarely kidnapped or coerced into migrating but that they rely on trafficking networks to realise their migration projects *whether geared towards sex work or some other type of work.*

While some degree of deception about the working conditions in the destination country characterised all of the respondents' accounts of how they entered trafficking networks, a narrow focus, typical of much feminist writing on trafficking, on the question as to whether or not women consented to prostitution, hinders our understanding of the exploitative labour relations in street sex work. Bridget Anderson and Julia O'Connell Davidson (2003) argue that the concept of deception, as put forth by the dominant definition of trafficking, begs the questions as to how extensive deception should be concerning job content, rates of pay, working practices, work rate, and length of the contract among others in order to qualify the woman as a 'victim of trafficking'. If, as in the UN Protocol to Prevent, Suppress and Punish Trafficking in Persons, the term trafficking refers to those situations in which a person has been recruited and transported, by means of deception, into exploitative working conditions by a third party intending to profit from that person's labour, then the ambiguity lies within the notion of deception itself.[19]

The vagueness of this notion, and its combination with the terms of force, coercion and exploitation as core components of the concept of trafficking, together establish an oversimplified and ultimately erroneous demarcation between voluntary and involuntary processes of migration. This is particularly important since violence, coercion, deception and exploitation occur also in voluntary and legally regulated systems of migration and employment. Moreover, the fact that the definition of trafficking presupposes an interrelation between deception and the subsequent exploitation of migrants on behalf of traffickers, conflates the range of interests that third parties might have in supplying migrant women with vague information concerning the working contract; it also ultimately criminalises a wide variety of actors who take part in different stages of the trafficking process.

Setting the crime scene

Both the media and feminist sources offer numerous portrayals of traffickers. For example, Emanuela Moroli and Roberta Sibona, two prominent feminists in Italy, describe traffickers in their book *Schiave d'occidente* as ferocious criminals who affirm their masculinity through physical abuse:

> There was no need of a valid reason to unleash Genti's rage. A mere pretext, invented on the spur of the moment, would do. Each time I

returned from working [on the street], he greeted me with a good beating . . . Of course, he also raped me in order to affirm his rights of ownership.

Moroli and Sibona, (1999: 39)

Throughout the book, the authors intervene in the text by combining their own views on trafficking with the direct quotes from women. This type of narrative is best illustrated by the last sentence in the above quote, where the teenage character's perspective filters the authors' view of prostitution as an expression of male sexuality based on the domination of women. This type of authorial manipulation of characters' perspectives produces a narrative which inscribes 'other' women as victims of violent men (usually from their own patriarchal culture).

In her reading of 'western feminism and third world prostitute' through the work of Wendy Brown, Jo Doezema points out that 'the desire for the protection of injured identities leads to collusion with, and intensification of disciplinary regimes of power' (Doezema, 2001: 33). Western feminist strategies, such as those in *Schiave d'occidente*, that aim at illustrating the horrendous 'reality' of trafficking by focusing exclusively on male violence and the exploitation of women, reinforce the idea of foreign women as powerless victims, and of foreign men as violent. Moreover, the authors do not question the role of the Italian state or immigration regulations as pivotal factors in sustaining migrants' social and political exclusion, and their vulnerability to violence. Instead, they look to the authorities in their effort to combat and suppress trafficking.

Newspapers often highlight that migrant women who wish to press charges against their traffickers may be intimidated with threats of violence: traffickers threaten women's families in their home countries, or the women themselves. Although the dangers of retaliation should certainly not be underestimated, again we must be wary of how, why and when narratives of violence are deployed. A respondent who tells *La Repubblica*[20] that she cannot return home because of the dangerous situation awaiting her there, gives another version of her story when interviewed by me. She explains that mentioning the threat of violence is part of a strategy to allow her to apply for a special residence permit; such permits are intended for those people who have been trafficked against their will and who risk serious violence if returned to their country of origin. This strategy was suggested to Oksana by the police officer responsible for her case. While there is insufficient space here to examine the ambiguous aspect of this police officer's position, I would like to stress that presenting oneself as a victim is indeed indispensable if an undocumented migrant woman wishes to use the legal immigration apparatus to her advantage and obtain the right to remain in Italy.[21]

I am not suggesting that episodes of violence do not occur. However, I am interested here in the rhetorical use of violence that creates a discursive space that can accommodate various narratives of violence. Although I have focused on women's experiences of migration as a way of countering dominant discourses and representations of trafficking, I am not arguing that women's narratives are not informed by established discourses, nor that they necessarily contradict them. However, at the same time, the topic of violence highlights the complexity of the victimhood narrative. Its plot lends itself to manipulation because it is already available within the mainstream discursive scenario on trafficking but, simultaneously, its appropriation feeds into and further sustains the dominant rendering of trafficking in terms of crime and violence.

Conclusion

The emphasis on the suffering of women involved in what goes by the name of 'trafficking' can be understood in the light of some of the empirical evidence that has been collected by various researchers. This frequently underscores the violence and hardship these women encounter in their quest for access to the European labour market. As such, it is both morally and humanely praiseworthy. My work does not aim either to deny or underplay the suffering and pain experienced by women involved in trafficking. My aim is rather to both broaden and deepen the framework of reference by which these elements of hardship can be understood and analysed. I argue that too strong an emphasis on prostitution per se – with the related attention to the standard repertoire of women's oppression, including the role of men's violence – presents serious political and theoretical limitations. Instead of privileging the issue of violence and/or exploitation exercised by third parties in the sex sector, this chapter proposes examining trafficking from the perspective of migration. From this viewpoint it becomes clear how, through a shared dependence on the categories of 'victim' and 'organised crime', various conceptualisations of trafficking merge to generate a mutually constitutive nexus that masks the complexities of the trafficking process.

A migration perspective extends the discussion of organised crime and victimisation so as to include an analysis of the role that the EU's migration policies play in creating and maintaining the conditions that lead to trafficking. My work shows that when formal avenues of migration become inaccessible, migrant women turn to irregular channels. Stricter border controls and more restrictive immigration regulations aimed at preventing trafficking do not protect women from abuse but, on the contrary, foster migrant women's vulnerability to violence and exploitation during travel and, paradoxically, leave ample space for profiteering and abuse. My data suggest that current EU mechanisms of migration control actually help to produce 'irregular' migration, channelling women into trafficking networks and consequently into prostitution. These considerations call for further analysis of how states increase migrants' vulnerability and dependence through a combination of restrictive residency and labour regulations, thus providing scope for relationships of enslavement and domination.

As discussed above, a number of feminist scholars who have investigated trafficking from the perspective of migration and/or globalisation, fall short of addressing the convergence, posited in dominant discourse, between trafficking, illegal migration and crime. A politically and theoretically informed feminist scholarship should, in my view, bring to the fore the material terrain of EU immigration regulations, and address the role that these regulations play in creating the conditions for the proliferation of trafficking. This reasoning would allow scholars to reallocate the responsibility for the persistence of trafficking from eastern Europe, now perceived of as the main producer of crime and trafficking, to the EU member states.

Shifting the terms of analysis of trafficking from violence and organised crime to migration creates another crucial theoretical opening. This opening allows for stories of women's migration to emerge. When trafficking is defined in terms of involuntary migration and organised crime, the implication is that 'trafficked' women are the victims of a non-consensual process of migration and that 'traffickers' are criminals who recruit and move their victims in order to profit from their labour in prostitution. This definition of trafficking relies on a vague notion of deception in order to indicate that the victim has been misled regarding the nature and terms of her 'contract' prior to migration. My analysis of respondents' narratives demonstrates that there is a direct relationship between women's entering into trafficking systems and their search for ways in which to realise their migratory projects. Women's migratory projects are best understood, I suggest, as an expression of their desire and demand for mobility. Informed by both economic and non-economic factors, women's migratory projects include trafficking as a means of achieving economic improvement and creating new life opportunities. Respondents' narratives of the recruitment and travel phase of trafficking reveal an urgent need to examine how trafficking is experienced and negotiated on the one hand, and represented and institutionalised on the other.

My data urge feminist (migration) scholars to take issue with the notions of coercion, deception and victimhood and to investigate the complexity of desires and projects that migrant women articulate in their attempt to achieve social and material mobility via trafficking systems. To consign the complexity of women's desires and projects to the category of the 'victim' amounts to denying their resistance to structural inequalities and their struggle to transform their lives. Finally, migrant women's life stories suggest that the category of 'trafficking' is inadequate as well as misleading when trying to grasp the complexity of current political subjectivities. These migrant women's narratives press scholars to come up with figurations other than 'organised crime' and 'victims' in order to account for socio-political transformations in today's Europe.

Notes

1 This is a revised version of an article that has appeared in French, under the title: 'La traite des femmes d'Europe de l'Est en Italie', *REMI* (2005) 21 (1). The author would like to thank Sarah van Walsum for the time and effort she put into editing this chapter.

2 *Il Resto del Carlino*, 18 July 1999. Author's translation.

3 I use the terms 'eastern' and 'western' Europe to indicate distinct geopolitical areas. I put them in inverted commas and do not capitalise the terms in order not to perpetuate images of two static blocs. In the post-1989 era, and especially at the moment of the European Union enlargement, this conceptualisation would be erroneous. From here on, west and east Europe will be used without inverted commas.

4 While people might be trafficked for purposes of domestic work, prostitution, entertainment industry, agriculture and construction work, this chapter is concerned exclusively with trafficking for prostitution. The inverted commas are used to indicate my criticism of the term 'trafficking', which I develop in the chapter. From this point onwards, trafficking for prostitution will appear simply as trafficking and without inverted commas.

5 Together with Belgium, Italy is the only EU state to include a specific clause in its immigration laws that allows for social protection and legalisation of trafficking victims. As a result, women can be more easily contacted in Italy than in most other EU countries. For over a decade, the city of Bologna has housed several innovative projects on trafficking, such as *Moonlight* working as an outreach street project, and *Progetto Delta* aiming at social protection and/or voluntary repatriation of trafficking victims. *Casa delle donne per non subire violenza* di Bologna – part of the latter project – is where I have conducted my fieldwork and a large number of interviews.

6 Namely, Romania, Ukraine, Moldova, Russia, Croatia and Serbia-Montenegro. Even though Romania is currently an EU candidate, at the time of the fieldwork it was considered to be lagging behind the other candidates and hence until recently (January 2002) its citizens needed a visa to enter Schengen territory.

7 I borrow the term 'conditions of confinement' from O'Connell Davidson. With this term she signifies 'conditions that prevent exit from prostitution through the use of physical restraint, physical violence or the threat thereof, or through the threat of other non-economic sanctions, such as imprisonment or deportation' (1998: 29).

8 The newspaper clippings have been collected between 1998 and 2000 from *La Repubblica*, a national daily, and *Il Resto del Carlino*, a Bologna local daily newspaper. These clippings are relevant not only for their portrayal of trafficking in general, but especially because they concern the very same women I interviewed.

9 The International Organisation for Migration (IOM) estimates that 700,000 women and children are trafficked per year across the globe, while United Nations (UN) sources oscillate between 2 million (IMADR in McDonald *et al.*, 2000: 1) and 4 million people (Ram, 2000: 2). As far as trafficking of women from eastern Europe into the EU is concerned, some EU sources report 500,000 women (Ram, 2000: 2) while others estimate between 200,000 and 500,000, a number that rounds up the presence of women from eastern Europe as well as Latin America, Africa and Asia (Molina and Janssen, 1998: 16).

10 The Schengen Treaty abolished internal borders between its member states, allowing for the free circulation of goods, capital, services and their citizens, yet it simultaneously reinforced EU external borders and set out to harmonise immigration and asylum policies. Today the Schengen area comprises Austria, Belgium,

Denmark, Finland, France, Germany, Greece, Iceland, Italy, Luxembourg, the Netherlands, Norway, Portugal, Spain and Sweden.

11 United for Intercultural Action, a Dutch-based European network against nationalism, racism and fascism, has counted 5,017 deaths of migrants that have resulted from border policing, detention and deportation policies, and carrier sanctions (UNITED, 2004). These numbers concern only those migrants who have been identified. Hence, the 'real' numbers are unknown.

12 Ursula Biemann has made similar observations concerning the Mexico–USA border (2000).

13 A study on the modes of entry of Filipina domestic workers into Italy presents quite similar results concerning the episodes of border crossing (Parreñas, 2001).

14 The respondents report that an agency charges between US$ 360 and 500, depending on the country of departure, for a visa and a bus ticket to Italy. Just for comparison, those respondents who worked as schoolteachers or secretaries in Moldova or Ukraine, earned between US$ 20 and 30 per month.

15 Rhacel Salazar Parreñas (2001) shows that the fee that agencies charged for assisting migrants with undocumented migration from the Philippines into Italy doubled to US$ 8,000 in the 1990s when Italy joined Schengen and strengthened the control at its external borders.

16 In the trafficking literature this operation is commonly referred to as being 'sold' (Global Survival Network, 1997; Kelly, 2002: 31–2).

17 A discussion on the conditions of confinement the respondents experienced in third-party controlled street prostitution is beyond the scope of this chapter. I have, however, addressed this issue in my PhD, especially in Chapter 3 (Andrijasevic, 2004).

18 Data indicate that organised criminal organisations were initially not involved with trafficking but that trafficking took place instead via the migrant network type of structure (IOM in Turnbull, 1999: 192).

19 See the UN Protocol to Prevent, Suppress and Punish Trafficking in Persons, adopted in November 2000, which defines trafficking in terms of forced transportation of deceived persons into exploitative and slavery-like conditions.

20 The exact date of the article is withheld for the safety of the informant.

21 For details on the specific regulations in Italy, see Isabel Crowhurst's contribution to this book, Chapter 13.

References

Anderson, Bridget and O'Connell Davidson, Julia (2003) *Needs and Desires: Is There a Demand for 'Trafficked' Persons?*, Geneva: IOM

Anderson, Malcolm (2000) 'The transformation of border controls: A European precedent?', in Andreas, Peter and Snyder, Timothy (eds), *The Wall around the West. State Borders and Immigration Controls in North America and Europe*, New York: Rowman & Littlefield, pp 15–30

Andreas, Peter (2000) 'Introduction: The wall after the wall', in Andreas, Peter and Snyder, Timothy (eds), *The Wall around the West. State Borders and Immigration Controls in North America and Europe*, New York: Rowman & Littlefield, pp 1–14

Andreas, Peter and Snyder, Timothy (eds) (2000) *The Wall around the West. State Borders and Immigration Controls in North America and Europe*, New York: Rowman & Littlefield

Andrijasevic, Rutvica (2003) 'The difference borders make: (Il)legality, migration and trafficking in Italy among eastern European women in prostitution', in Ahmed,

Sara, Castañeda, Claudia, Fortier, Anne-Marie and Sheller, Mimi (eds), *Uprootings/ Regroundings: Questions of Home and Migration*, Oxford: Berg, pp 251–72

Andrijasevic, Rutvica (2004) 'Trafficking in women and the politics of mobility in Europe', doctoral thesis defended at Utrecht University, The Netherlands

Anthias, Floya and Lazaridis, Gabriella (2000) 'Introduction: Women on the move in Southern Europe', in Anthias, Floya and Lazaridis, Gabriella (eds), *Gender and Migration in Southern Europe*, Oxford: Berg, pp 1–15

Berman, Jacqueline (2003) '(Un)Popular strangers and crisis (un)bounded: Discourses of sex-trafficking, the European political community and the pan-icked state of the modern state', *European Journal of International Relations* 9(1), pp 37–86

Biemann, Ursula (2000) 'Performing the border. Gender, transnational bodies and technology', in Biemann, Ursula, *Been There and Back to Nowhere: Gender in Transnational Spaces*, Berlin: b_books

Bigo, Didier (2003) 'Criminalization of "migrants": The side effect of the will to control the frontiers and the sovereign illusion'. Paper presented at Irregular Migration and Human Rights Conference, University of Leicester, 28–29 June

Caldwell, Gillian, Galster, Steve, Kanics, Jyothi and Steinzor, Nadia (1999) 'Capital-izing on global economies: The role of Russian Mafia in trafficking in women for forced prostitution', in Williams, Phil (ed), *Illegal Immigration and Commercial Sex*, London and Portland: Frank Cass, pp 42–73

Corso, Carla and Trifirò, Ada (2003) . . . *e Siamo Partite! Migrazione, Tratta a Prosti-tuzione Straniera in Italia*, Florence: Giunti

Dal Lago, Alessandro (1999) *Non-persone. L'Esclusione dei Migranti in una Società Globale*, Milan: Feltrinelli

Doezema, Jo (1999) *Loose Women or Lost Women? The Re-emergence of the Myth of 'White Slavery' in Contemporary Discourses of 'Trafficking in Women'*; accessed at: at http://www.walnet.org/csis/papers/doezema-loose.html

Doezema, Jo (2001) 'Ouch! Western feminists' "wounded attachments" to the "third world prostitute" ', *Feminist Review* 67, pp 16–38

European Council (2001) Presidency Conclusions Leaken, no. 42, 14/15 December

Finckenauer, James (2001) 'Russian transnational organized crime and human traf-ficking', in Kyle, David and Koslowski, Rey (eds), *Global Human Smuggling. Com-parative Perspectives*, Baltimore and London: The Johns Hopkins University Press, pp 166–86

Global Survival Network (1997) *Crime and Servitude. An Exposé of the Traffic in Women for Prostitution from the Newly Independent States*, Washington, DC: Global Survival Network

Gülçür, Leyla and Ilkkaracan, Pinar (2002) 'The "Natasha experience": Migrant sex workers from former Soviet Union and Eastern Europe in Turkey', *Women's Studies International Forum* 25(4), pp 411–21

Kelly, Liz (2002) 'The wrong debate: Reflections on why force is not the key issue with respect to trafficking in women for sexual exploitation', *Feminist Review* 73, pp 139–44

Kofman, Eleonore (1999) 'Female "birds of passage" a decade later: Gender and immigration in the European Union', *International Migration Review* 33(2), pp 269–99

Kofman, Eleonore, Phizaklea, Annie, Raghuram, Parvati and Sales, Rosemarie (2000)

Gender and International Migration in Europe, London and New York: Routledge

Koser, Khalid and Lutz, Helma (1998) *The New Migration in Europe: Social Constructions and Social Realities*, London: Macmillan

Koslowski, Rey (2001) 'Economic globalization, human smuggling, and global governance', in Kyle, David and Koslowski, Rey (eds), *Global Human Smuggling. Comparative Perspectives*, Baltimore and London: The Johns Hopkins University Press, pp 337–58

Kyle, David and Dale, John (2001) 'Smuggling the state back in: Agents of human smuggling reconsidered', in Kyle, David and Koslowski, Rey (eds), *Global Human Smuggling. Comparative Perspectives*, Baltimore and London: The Johns Hopkins University Press, pp 29–57

Lazaridis, Gabriella (2001) 'Trafficking and prostitution. The growing exploitation of migrant women in Greece', *The European Journal of Women's Studies* 8(1), pp 67–102

Maluccelli, Lorenza (2001) 'Tra schiavitù e servitù: biografie femminili in cerca di autonomia', in Candia, Giulianas et al. (eds) *Da Vittime a Cittadine. Percorsi di Uscita dalla Prostituzione e Buone Pratiche di Inserimento Sociale e Lavorativo*, Rome: Ediesse, pp 37–82

McDonald, Laura, Moore, Brooke and Timoshkina, Natalya (2000) *Migrant Sex Workers from Eastern Europe and the Former Soviet Union: The Canadian Case*, Ottava: Status of Women Canada

Mezzadra, Sandro (2001) *Diritto di Fuga. Migrazioni, Cittadinanza, Globalizzazione*, Verona: Ombre corte

Mezzadra, Sandro and Rigo, Enrica (2003) 'L'Europa dei migranti', in Bronzini, Giuseppe, Friese, H, Negri, Antonio and Wagner, Peter (eds), *Europa, Costituzione e Movimenti Sociali*, Rome: manifestolibri, pp 213–30

Molina, Fanny P and Janssen, Marie-Luise (1998) *I Never Thought This Would Happen to Me: Prostitution and Traffic in Latin American Women in the Netherlands*, Amsterdam: Foundation Esperanza

Morokvašic, Mirjana (1991) 'Fortress Europe and migrant women', *Feminist Review* 39, pp 69–84

Moroli, Emanuela and Sibona, Roberta (1999) *Schiave d'Occidente. Sulle Rotte dei Mercanti di Donne*, Milan: Mursia

O'Connell Davidson, Julia (1998) *Prostitution, Power and Freedom*, Ann Arbor: University of Michigan Press

Orfano, Isabella (2003) 'Country report Italy', in Payoke et al., *Research Based on Case Studies of Victims of Trafficking in Human Beings in Three EU Member States, i.e. Belgium, Italy and The Netherlands*, Commission of the European Communities, DG Justice & Home Affairs, Hippokrates JAI/2001/HIP/023

Orsini-Jones, Marina and Gatullo, Francesca (2000) 'Migrant women in Italy: National trends and local perspectives', in Anthias, Floya and Lazaridis, Gabriella (eds), *Gender and Migration in Southern Europe*, Oxford: Berg, pp 125–45

Parreñas, Rhacel S (2001) *Servants of Globalization. Women, Migration, and Domestic Work*, Stanford: Stanford University Press

Phizacklea, Annie (1996) 'Women, migration and the state', in Rai, Shirin and Lievesley, Geraldine (eds), *Women and the State: International Perspectives*, London: Taylor & Francis, pp 163–73

Phizacklea, Annie (1998) 'Migration and globalisation', in Koser, Khalid and Lutz,

102

Helma (eds), *The New Migration in Europe: Social Constructions and Social Realities*, London: Macmillan, pp 21–39

Pickup, Francine (1998) 'More words but no action? Forced migration and trafficking in women', *Gender and Development* 6(1), pp 44–51

Ram, Melanie (2000) 'Putting an end to the trafficking of women in the NIS and CEE', IREX Policy Paper; accessed at http://www.irex.org

Salt, John and Stein, Jeremy (1997) 'Migration as a business: The case of trafficking', *International Migration* 35(4), pp 467–91

Sassen, Saskia (1999) *Guests and Aliens*, New York: The New Press

Sassen, Saskia (2000) 'Women's burden: counter-geographies of globalization and the feminization of survival', *Journal of International Affairs* 53(2), pp 503–24

Sharma, Nandita (2003) 'Travel agency: A critique of anti-trafficking campaigns', *Refuge* 21(3), pp 53–65

Simoncini, Alessandro (2000) 'Migranti, frontiere, spazi di confine. I lavoratori migranti nell'ordine salariale', *Altreragioni* 10, pp 29–45

Snyder, Timothy (2000) 'Conclusions: The wall around the West', in Andreas, Peter and Snyder, Timothy (eds), *The Wall around the West. State Borders and Immigration Controls in North America and Europe*, New York: Rowman & Littlefield, pp 219–28

Stenvoll, Dag (2002) 'From Russia with love? Newspaper coverage of cross-border prostitution in northern Norway 1990–2001', *The European Journal of Women's Studies* 9(2), pp 143–62

Sutdhibhasilp, Noulmook (2002) 'Migrant sex workers in Canada', in Thorbek, Susanne and Pattanaik, Bandana (eds), *Transnational Prostitution. Changing Global Patterns*, London and New York: Zed Books, pp 173–93

Turnbull, Penelope (1999) 'The fusion of immigration and crime in the European Union: Problems of co-operation and the fight against the trafficking in women', in Williams, Phil (ed), *Illegal Immigration and Commercial Sex. The New Slave Trade*, London and Portland (OR): Frank Cass, pp 189–213

UNITED (2004) 'List of 5017 documented refugee deaths through Fortress Europe', 16 April 2004; accessed at: http://www.united.non-profit.nl

Wijers, Marjan and Lap-Chew, Lin (1997) *Trafficking in Women, Forced Labour and Slavery-like Practices in Marriage, Domestic Labour and Prostitution*, Utrecht: STV

Wijers, Marjan and van Doorninck, Marieke (2002) *Only Rights Can Stop Wrongs: A Critical Assessment of Anti-Trafficking Strategies*; accessed at: http://www.walnet.org/csis/papers/wijers-rights.html

6

A MIGRANT WORLD OF SERVICES[1]

Laura María Agustín

There is a strong demand for women's domestic, caring and sexual labour in Europe which promotes migrations from many parts of the world. This paper examines the history of concepts that marginalise these as unproductive services (and not really 'work') and questions why the west accepts the semi-feudal conditions and lack of regulations pertaining to this sector. The moral panic on 'trafficking' and the limited feminist debate on 'prostitution' contribute to a climate that ignores the social problems of the majority of women migrants.

In a variety of scenarios in different parts of Europe, non-Europeans are arriving with the intention to work; these are largely migrant women and transgender people[2] from the 'third world' or from Central and Eastern Europe and countries of the former Soviet Union. The jobs available to these women in the labour market are overwhelmingly limited to three basic types: domestic work (cleaning, cooking and general housekeeping), 'caring' for people in their homes (children, the elderly, the sick and disabled) and providing sexual experiences in a wide range of venues known as the sex industry. All these jobs are generally said to be services.

In the majority of press accounts, migrant women are presented as selling sex in the street, while in public forums and academic writing, they are constructed as 'victims of trafficking'. The obsession with 'trafficking' obliterates not only all the human agency necessary to undertake migrations but the experiences of migrants who do not engage in sex work. Many thousands of women who more or less choose to sell sex as well as all women working in domestic or caring service are 'disappeared' when moralistic and often sensationalistic topics are the only ones discussed. One of the many erased subjects concerns the labour market – the demand – for the services of all these women. The context to which migrants arrive is not less important than the context from which they leave, often carelessly described as 'poverty' or 'violence'. This article addresses the European context for women migrants' employment in these occupations. Though domestic and caring work are usually treated as two separate jobs, very often workers do both, and these jobs also often require sexual labour, though this is seldom recognised. All this confusion and ambiguity occurs within a frame that so far has escaped definition.

My treatment of these issues should be understood as part of a postcolonial project that problematises western endeavours to 'help' and 'save' migrant women. My research centred first in Latin America and then moved to Europe, where I have been in contact with migrants from every continent. My earlier theorising about 'race' has changed in the past few years, since the fastest-growing 'group' of migrants comes from Eastern Europe and the former Soviet Union – women usually considered 'white' and 'almost' European. The same jobs are open to them, and the same discourses of 'trafficking' and 'helping' apply. Thus, although 'exoticising' may well be taking place, 'race' is not a useful concept for analysis at this time.

A sector that cannot be defined

There is no general agreement about how to define services. Definitions from websites and books range from the very general, which includes everything but agriculture, mining and manufacturing, through one that includes transportation, finance, communications, real estate and trade, another that uses healthcare, advertising, computer programming and repair services, and one that refers to banking, insurance, health, education, sex, gambling, labour-hire, building contracting, food production, maintenance and repair, personal care, transportation, entertainment and retail. Attempting to arrive at a 'sector' that might help define the jobs offered to migrant women in Europe, one encounters the term 'personal/household services', but this lacks reference to health and to amusement and recreation.

Service jobs in the formal sector are varied enough; among possible jobs listed on one government website were: beauty therapist, cashier, computer salesperson, embalmer, florist, funeral director, grave digger, hairdresser, make-up artist, nail technician, newsagent, pharmacy assistant, retail buyer, retail manager, sales assistant, sales representative, service station attendant, ticket writer, video hire/sales. What do these jobs have in common, really? One might say that one individual pays another to help them get what they need, in some area, whether in person, over the phone or through correspondence. Service jobs in the so-called informal sector can be defined the same way, but notably these are *not* included among the potential 'job options' in the above list, nor are they offered to and found by migrant women all over the world.

In the general discourse about services, relationships between customer and employee may be conceptualised as dry and distant, but many involve considerable emotional or physical contact (for example, washing and cutting hair, massage therapy, counselling). The gamut of occupations sometimes considered as services is obviously too wide and complex to be contained reasonably with a discourse about an economic or labour 'sector'.

Behind this complexity lie the awkward economic concepts of 'productive' and 'unproductive' labour. An early essentialist definition by the eighteenth-century Physiocrats insisted that only agriculture was productive. Adam Smith suggested a new definition that called services 'unproductive', or not contributing to the accumulation of physical wealth. John Stuart Mill argued that some services contributed to economic growth, but the difficulty of defining these contributed to the shift of attention to another dichotomy, 'market' versus 'nonmarket' labour. So although by the twentieth century economists were agreeing that all paid services were 'productive', they only looked at market services; thus paid domestic workers were deemed product-ive but housewives were 'unproductive', 'unoccupied' or 'dependent' (Folbre, 1991; Folbre and Wagman 1993).

A slightly different kind of classification refers to 'reproductive' labour, which reproduces 'social life' by maintaining families and the houses they live in. This notion is also not clear-cut, entering into questions of what is 'necessary' and what is not.

> The reproduction of life melds into the reproduction of status . . . Nobody has to have stripped pine floorboards, handwash-only silk shirts, ornaments that gather dust. All these things create domestic work, but they also affirm the status of the household, its class, its access to resources of finance and personnel, and the adequacy of its manager, almost invariably a woman.
>
> (Anderson, 2000: 14)

In a discussion of how to 'measure' household activities, Anne Chadeau points to a similar problem: 'The changes some services bring about in household members through their emotional content have no market substi-tute, and therefore no market price' (Chadeau, 1985: 241). This becomes clear in the idealised discourse of the agent who is 'selling' domestic servants in the market:

> You have a 'wife' at home . . . [I]magine coming home at the end of a workday, and all the stress is off. The kids are happy, the laundry is washed and folded, you can smell the chicken cooking in the oven. The girls don't want to stick around with you and your husband at the end of their work day, so you have all the time alone you want . . . [T]hey leave to their room and you are home with your kids. It gives you peace of mind and it gives you your equilibrium.
>
> (Bakan and Stasilius, 1995: 325)

All jobs widely offered to migrant women today fall into these disputed categories, which can hardly be a matter of chance. While the categories cannot be defined and agreed to, the work goes on, uncounted, undervalued and subject to all manner of exploitation. For want of a better term, these jobs may as well be called services. As Saskia Sassen says, 'What emerges clearly is that a large share of women migrants constitute *a certain kind of labour* (1984: 1148, emphasis mine).[3] But what do the jobs actually have in common, and what makes them come to be 'work'?

> The *third-person* criterion has been used to draw the household product boundary between work and leisure . . . If a third person could be paid to do the unpaid activity of a household member, then it is 'work'; so clearly cooking, child care, laundry, cleaning and gardening are all work, as a household servant could be hired to perform these activities. On the other hand, it would not be sensible to hire someone to watch a movie, play tennis, read a book, or eat a meal for you, as the benefits of the activity would accrue to the servant, the third person, not the hirer.
>
> (Ironmonger, 1996: 39–40, emphasis in original)[4]

Duncan Ironmonger proposes classifying types of care and nurture 'as to whether they were care of the body or of the mind. The physical or bodily category includes meals, exercise, health, washing and sleep' (ibid.: 55). The tasks allotted to migrant domestic and caring workers would be covered (sex is not mentioned).

Diemut Bubeck, in an analysis of the gendered nature of caring work, focuses on its 'live' aspect:

> Caring for is the meeting of the needs of one person by another person where face-to-face interaction between carer and cared for is a crucial element of the overall activity and where the need is of such a nature that it cannot possibly be met by the person in need herself.
>
> (Bubeck, 1995: 129)

Her emphasis on the interactional quality means that it isn't enough to simply 'meet needs'; instead there must be a face-to-face relationship (or ear-to-ear or eye-to-eye, so that telephone calls and letters may be included).

Chadeau brings in the ambiguity over aspects of household work that are not strictly utilitarian, do not refer to actual biological needs, and can thus be called 'leisure'. She points out that the boundaries for these definitions are personal and depend on cultural contexts:

> Adults . . . usually perform these acts for themselves in western countries (washing, dressing, for example) but these acts could be delegated. The criterion on which the classification is based is then the social norm . . . [I]s washing and setting one's hair work (since this service can certainly be bought on the market), leisure for the direct

utility it produces or a biological need? It probably belongs, to a greater or lesser degree, to all three categories. Here again how great a part do social norms play in classification?

(Chadeau, 1985: 241)

Rhacel Parreñas, speaking of the domestic and caring work of Filipina migrant domestic workers, agrees that the labour of care varies according to different cultures:

There are three main forms of care expected to ensure the reproduction of the family: 1) moral care, meaning the provision of discipline and socialization to ensure that dependents are raised to be 'good' moral citizens of society; 2) emotional care, meaning the provision of emotional security through the expression of concern and feelings of warmth and affection, and 3) material care, meaning the provision of the physical needs of dependents, including food, clothing, and education or skills-training to guarantee that they become producers for the family.

(Parreñas, 2001: 117)

The search continues for ways to pin down acts of caring, with no agreement reached yet. Meanwhile, migrants are expected to accept such jobs, along with their lack of prestige, low pay and confusion as to what the work actually consists of and how it should be done.[5] Do different cultures clean and 'care' differently? According to many European employers of migrant women, they do (Colectivo Ioé, 2001; Anderson, 2000). In one popular stereotype that crosses borders, Latin American women are said to be good at childcare because they are 'affectionate' or 'sweet', while they are also accused of being sloppy cleaners. On bulletin boards accessible to migrants, in places like the lobbies of migrant organisations, clinics and NGOs, classes are commonly offered in 'Spanish cooking' or 'French cooking', as well as in how to be a domestic worker, in general. There is an odd irony here: women from the 'third world' are widely said to be more domestic and traditional than European ones, to be 'naturals' at cleaning and caring, but at the same time, they are found to need teaching in the up-to-date and particular ways of Europe.

The gender of 'a certain kind of labour'

But why should the demand be for *women*, particularly, to fulfil these roles? A migrant man presenting himself as a candidate for live-in domestic or caring work seems like an anomaly, though boarding a Filipino couple remains a status symbol in some elite circles, and once men were as common in domestic work as women (Oso, 1998). The literature on an 'ethics of care' and 'sociology of emotions' does not agree so far as to whether women are somehow inherently better at caring (Gilligan, 1982; Abel and Nelson, 1990). What is clear, however, is that societies widely *believe* that they are, across cultures; women are those who 'know how' to care.

> It may be that, in order for an ethic of care to develop, individuals need to experience caring for others and being cared for by others. From this perspective, the daily experience of caring provides [women and 'minority men'] with the opportunity to develop this moral sense. The dearth of caretaking experiences makes privileged males morally deprived.
>
> (Tronto, 1987: 652)

Being morally privileged, then, contradictorily leads to being apportioned some of the least well-paid work in the least controlled employment sector, where feudalism and exploitation are routinely accepted. In Joan Tronto's (1987) analysis, 'minority men' are also experienced in caring, yet in Europe they are rarely considered for these jobs. Arlie Hochschild (2000) addresses another moral consequence of the employment of migrant women as carers, the possibility that care is being imported from (and thus diminished in) 'third-world' countries to 'first' as though it were a simple resource. Migrant domestic workers indeed reveal pain at having left their own children behind, but at the same time, some start new families in their new country; some contract other women at home to take care of their children there, and so on. This complex issue crosses geographic and disciplinary borders, in which knowledge that one is supporting one's own family may palliate feelings of guilt, inadequacy or rage – or not (Parreñas, 2001).

The philosophising of economists as to what constitutes production and markets translates into government policies that affect national census-taking and calculations of economic growth through national income accounts. Christine Bose (1987) shows how ideological goals may enter into the exclusion of particular occupations, so that while in Britain in the late nineteenth century there were proposals to include housework in order 'to present a picture of Britain as a community of workers and a strong nation',

> [Australia] divided the whole population into breadwinners and dependents, the latter including women doing domestic work and unpaid workers in the home, as well as children and the infirm. The intent was to provide an image of a country where everyone did not need to work, and thus to appear to be a good place for British investment.
>
> (Bose, 1987: 101)

Many authors have shown how the majority of women's jobs inside houses are neither paid nor even considered 'work', and therefore don't 'count' in official government statistics (Benería, 1981; Waring, 1988). Housewives are counted neither among the 'employed' nor the 'unemployed'. Ruth Levitas gives a recent example from Great Britain:

In October 1997 the Office of National Statistics (ONS) published the first estimates of the extent and value of unpaid work in the British economy. If a monetary value were put on such work, at 1995 values it would have been at least equivalent to £341 billion, or more than the whole UK manufacturing sector, and perhaps as much as £739 billion, 120 per cent of gross domestic product. Among the reasons for this statistical development was the insensitivity of conventional national accounts to the movement of activities between market and non-market sectors. Yet despite this official endorsement, the dominant public and social-scientific understanding of 'work' remains paid work. Since the ONS figures confirmed that women do much more unpaid work than men, and that although men do more paid work, they also have more leisure, men's work is more acknowledged, as well as more highly rewarded, than women's work.

(Levitas, 1998: 8)

According to Levitas, this non-recognition of household and caring labour and the concomitant '[privileging] of market activity' (ibid.: 28) are factors that *construct* the discourse of social exclusion. And if work by women citizens is excluded, the same work done by women migrants is doubly or triply so (woman/migrant/illegal).

Journalist Peter Kellner demonstrates how growth of the economy itself is judged on very partial statistics, those deriving from 'tax returns, VAT records, payroll data and company records. Illegal activities, involving cash-only transactions hidden from the Inland Revenue and Customs and Excise, do not show up' (Kellner, 1999: 21). According to Kellner, *Economic Trends* valued such transactions at £700 million for stolen goods, £800 million for gambling, £9.9 billion for drug dealing and £1.2 billion for 'prostitution'. Since many of the myriad forms of trade found in the sex industry are usually not included under this term, it is likely that figures for commercial sex, including pornography, were much higher.

Introducing sex into the equation

The issue of sexual services needs to be treated apart because so far it has not been possible to integrate them into other service discourses. This separation forms part of the highly rigid manner in which migrant women workers are treated in Europe, by governments, feminists, NGOs and the press. The situation of women who do sex work on either a full- or part-time basis has so far been inextricable from the polemic on 'prostitution' and 'trafficking'. My concern is that while this is going on, the day-to-day situation of hundreds of thousands (millions, worldwide) of women is not being addressed in the pragmatic terms necessary to improve their living conditions.[6] Treating sex as a taboo contributes to the marginalisation not only of jobs in the sex industry but of domestic and caring tasks, since they often include sexual labour as well.

On the theoretical level – within the sociology of work, for example – most scholars are willing to consider carers and domestics together, and a few would include sex workers with them. In this analysis, there exists a continuum of commercial opportunities involving intimacy, including psychotherapy, therapeutic massage, bartending, hairstyling and escort work. Sex here is only another aspect of intimacy. Many discussions among those selling sex and some researchers do normalise the service aspect; Roberta Perkins, for example, refers to the 'personal services' offered by gays involving 'strippergrams, nude waitering for private parties, nude housecleaning' and so on (Perkins *et al.*, 1994: 190).

But many argue that sexual services cannot be considered 'work', whether they are paid occupations for millions of people or not, because sex should always be the expression of love (Barry, 1979; Dworkin, 1987). For Carole Pateman, sex is incomparable to other things, acts, situations:

> The services of the prostitute are related in a more intimate manner to her body than those of other professionals. Sexual services, that is to say, sex and sexuality, are constitutive of the body in a way in which the counseling skills of the social worker are not . . . [S]exuality and the body are, further, integrally connected to conceptions of femininity and masculinity, and all these are constitutive of our individuality, our sense of self-identify.
>
> (Pateman, 1988: 562)

A colleague who responded to researcher Lynn Chancer's hypothetical proposal to do participant observation in studies of sex-for-sale said: 'But you don't understand – prostitution is disgusting because what you're doing is so intimate. It's different . . . it just is' (Chancer, 1993: 145). Obviously, this concept of intimacy is widely held, although the western notion of 'self' and its assumed relationship to sexuality should not be universalised to non-western cultures. But why should these intimate acts be excluded from theorising on commercial services? Barbara Sullivan notes that:

> the retailing of intimacy is a common feature of modern life and of other paid work like therapy and massage. In the case of both therapy and massage, equality and reciprocity are not usually features of

the professional relationship. Moreover, it is only in the last few decades that these values have been seen as desirable in 'normal' intimate relations. It is clear, too, that the enormous differences between men and women, particularly in terms of economic, social and political resources, means that equality and reciprocity are rarely real features of contemporary relationships between adult men and women.

(Sullivan, 1995: 184)

One thing is clear: it is *only* possible to isolate sex from other personal services if sexual contact is accepted as utterly different from all other kinds and in that sense both sanctified and stigmatised, and if intimacy is constructed as occurring in particular ways, its definition based on particular 'acts' (Vance, 1984; Johnson, 2002). My own contribution to this debate is to point out that the isolation of paid sex from other services assumes that the *only* thing that happens in a sexual service is a sexual act. The relationship between customer and service-provider is thus reduced to overt and specified physical contacts with particular points of the human body known as erogenous zones, and everything else that goes on is excluded. For 'anti-prostitution' theorists, if sex is there, then that is the only thing that has to be looked at, and if any other kind of intimacy is present, then it is intimacy gone wrong. But much research demonstrates that there is a lot more than sex going on in the long evenings spent in bars, clubs, driving around and other social activities that may or may not end in paid sex (Allison, 1994; Leonini, 1999; Frank, 2002).

Wendy Chapkis (1997) supports her argument that sex is work with Arlie Hochschild's study of the emotional labour of flight attendants, which concluded that the most telling issue may be their 'control over the conditions and terms of the exploitation of [their] emotional resources'.[7] Faked orgasms have been offered as a clear-cut example of emotional labour performed by sex workers for clients who feel more excited and gratified if they believe workers are (Lever and Dolnick, 2000). In this sense, those selling sex without themselves feeling sexual interest are presumably engaging in emotional labour simply by making the effort to appear excited. There is no reason to limit this 'faking' to those selling sex, however: babysitters and carers of grannies may pretend to care, too, by smiling on demand, listening to boring stories or doling out caresses without feeling affection.

The 'prostitution' concept erases the diversity of the sex industry, which includes phenomena as disparate as erotic telephone conversations, accompaniment of businessmen to elegant parties, brief acts such as 'hand relief', dancing or shows in bars, sex shops, soapbubble massages – the list goes on and on (Agustín, 2000). Suffice it to say that in these activities, too, definitions and perceptions of 'service' vary not only according to the kind of acts involved but also according to subjective perceptions of pleasure. How

112

can we define 'good sex'? What makes a client feel fulfilled? How does one project or perform sensuality, lust, receptivity, sexual caring? Each of the many activities now included in the industry is open to clients' differing subjective judgements about whether they are carried out satisfactorily or not, and few limit definitions of satisfaction to the purely physical (see the World Sex Guide website, http://worldsexguide.com, where clients describe their experiences). The value of a service depends on the customer's personal perception of it. Moreover, a desire for satisfaction should not be limited to the receiving end of the service: purveyors also have ways of feeling satisfied by their work. No one would deny that job satisfaction can occur in nail salons or among shoeshine boys and street sweepers, other tasks viewed as low-skill and low-prestige, so why deny it to people selling sex?

Beyond moralising discourses, where it is possible to talk about a sex industry, there is a tug of war between the rationalised discourse of health, safety and professionalism at one extreme (related to concepts of 'sex worker rights' and in state regulatory projects) and, at the other, the 'irrational' discourse of tenderness, flexibility and non-professionalisation (in western clients' testimonies as well as those of some sex workers). In this way, sex-service discourse is no different from discourses on housework and caring work, all sharing a tendency to define tasks that can be bought and sold as well as assert the particular, special, indefinable human extra necessary to do the job well. Paid activities in these domains may include feelings of intimacy and reciprocity, whether the individuals involved intend them or not, and despite the overall structures involved being patriarchal and unjust. The ability to maintain emotional distance turns out to be an aspect of the work which only some workers master (Hochschild, 1983; Wouters, 1989; Chapkis, 1997). And there is a further problem, that emotional involvement may occur on the part of the *buyer* of services as well: employers who demand acts of pointless servitude from domestic workers or unreasonable educational skills from ill-paid nannies; clients who become dependent on particular sex workers; elderly people who manipulate their carers.

The demand for services

Western societies have long employed people outside the family to help with housework and home nursing, and sex has been paid for outside the home as far back as historians have been able to go. What is notable now is the lack of progress or rationalising among these chores concomitant with other kinds of changes in society. The domestic and caring sector is often referred to as feudal, involving servitude or servility. How is it that these social phenomena are looked on so uncritically within western societies? I have identified three areas of life that appear to be involved – family, sex and consumption – but since boundaries between them cannot be maintained I shall treat them generally, beginning with the concept of family.

In some parts of Europe, middle- and upper-class families still prefer to hire live-in maids, servants who are present from morning to night to perform a wide range of tasks, some considered personal and even taboo (preparing and serving food, cleaning bathrooms, washing undergarments, for example). When the employee is a carer, she may have charge of the most personal and delicate of bodily tasks, and even the maid or babysitter who comes in for a few hours and then leaves is privy to intimate family details. In some places, more commonly in Mediterranean countries, this willingness may not represent a change so much as a holdover: in these societies an acceptance of social hierarchy means that families may decide to forego some intimacy in exchange for having a servant available at all times (Oso, 1998; King and Zontini, 2000). On the other hand, *all* societies in which both partners in a family relationship leave the house to work generate a need for outsiders to be brought in to care for children and the elderly, unless a complete array of state services exists. As extended families are reduced to their nuclei, there are no extra aunts and grandmothers willing to take on these tasks, and daughters are growing up in societies where women's independence from the family is now promoted.

At the same time, western gender politics are changing the shape of the nuclear family or committed couple. The most obvious outcomes of the movement toward 'gender equity' since the 1960s have been women's entry into many labour markets once closed to them and acceptance of the idea that women have the right to work outside the home. Nancy Folbre and Julie Nelson refer to the results of this change in a discussion of concepts of 'public and private':

> While some of women's tasks were largely instrumental – cleaning and cooking, for example – many tasks contained more personalised and emotional components. Women were in charge of children, elderly, and the ill; maintaining personal relationships; offering emotional support, personal attention, and listening; embodying (or so it was understood) sexuality. This social contract is changing. As women move increasingly into the world of paid work, many of these traditional intimate tasks are being performed in relationships that include the explicit movement of money. Paid child care, nursing homes for the elderly, talk therapy and phone sex are just a few examples.
>
> (Folbre and Nelson, 2000: 1)

The point is that while women have moved significantly into the public sphere, men have moved to a much lesser degree into the private. This means, assuming the demand remains steady for cleanliness and order inside the house, that either women who work outside it do double labour, or someone is hired to do the housework and caring. 'Equal' gender relations between the members of the western couple therefore may crucially rely on the employment of a third person. Women, not illogically, are those hired to do this traditional women's work.

Traditionally, the family was assumed to be the site of love and commitment and sex to be properly located only there, as Rayna Rapp *et al.* explain:

> In the family history literature, family usually means a grouping of kinsfolk minus servants, boarders, etc., who *should* be living together inside of households. I want to argue that we need to focus on the 'should' portion of that definition (i.e., the idea of kin-based families as normative) in order to reveal a key structure crucial for the understanding of ideology. It is through their commitment to the concept of family that people are recruited to the material relations of households. Because people accept the meaningfulness of family, they enter into relations of production, reproduction, and consumption with one another . . .
>
> (Rapp *et al.*, 1983: 235)

Nowadays, however, more *kinds* of relationships are accepted as meaningful, or, indeed, as 'familial' (Davidoff and Hall, 1987; Silva and Smart, 1999). Though these changes are not universal and vary by generation, class and ethnicity, it is fair to say that in Europe many concepts of family now extend beyond the walls of houses (living together not being a requirement) and increasingly include non-blood or formal marriage relationships. This means that the commitments Rapp refers to are also made outside 'home' environments, and, therefore, family homes that bring in an outsider do not strike such a dissonant note.

This loosening up or broadening of the field of 'significant' relationships may help explain some of the demand for sexual services, as well. Anthony Giddens has pointed out how present-day western societies idealise relationships considered sexually and emotionally 'free' and 'equal', supposedly formed without 'interests' and which continue only as long as the two people involved (they are always two) feel satisfied. Part of the freedom experienced within this structure is ascribed to a sexuality now not tied to reproduction (Giddens, 1992). In some parts of the west – again variable according to generation – it is common nowadays to speak of relationships and partners, rather than marriage. Discourses of gender equality and individuality encourage heterosexuals to look for relationships that suit their own personal emotional needs (Nelson and Robinson, 1994). In the literature on non-heterosexuality, there are emphases on the right to form family-like arrangements as well as the right not to (Weston, 1997). For many people, the romantic ideal has not been achieved, or is not sought, or has failed, which means they may not be part of a couple but still want intimacy and sex. In this context, paying for it occasionally looks less important.

Families, even those that appear conventional from the outside (married woman and man with children all living together), are not impermeable sites. As hundreds of AIDS studies have shown, loving a wife or husband does not impede having sex with, or loving, all kinds of other people. When someone else comes to live in the house as a maid, in conditions of intimacy, they may be told to feel they are 'one of the family'. Sex occurs within families, but there is public outrage if it becomes known that a family member has sex with a domestic worker – this seems to constitute a contemporary taboo, despite a wealth of literature demonstrating the historically strong erotic association between maids and sex in European societies (Stallybrass and White, 1986; McClintock, 1995). The contradictions are rife. This said, I now move on to changes in the domain of sex that affect the market for services.

The ideal of sexual 'liberation' has now been active in the west for four decades and has evolved to include specific ideals of liberation for women, gays and lesbians, bisexuals, trans/intergender people, disabled people, children and other identity groups. The liberation concept follows the classic 'hydraulic' model of drives and repressions that must be set free (Gagnon and Simon, 1974; Weeks, 1982). Accordingly, every human being ought and has the right to know him or herself intimately, both physically and emotionally, in order to arrive at a sexual 'identity'. The link made between personal identity and sex and the construction of a new category, 'sexuality', was a central theme of Michel Foucault's *History of Sexuality* (1978, 1985, 1986). The many paradoxes of the search for sexual identity – its possibilities for limiting as well as expanding personal possibilities – have been the subject of much theorising since; however, the attainment of self-knowledge and discovery is still considered desirable.

> Self-identity, at the heart of which is sexual identity, is not something that is given as a result of the continuities of an individual's life or of the fixity and force of his or her desires. It is something that has to be worked on, invented and reinvented in accord with the changing rhythms, demands, opportunities and closures of a complex world.
>
> (Weeks, 1995: 38)

For RW Connell, social practice, the individual's personal narrative, is what makes a sexual persona (1987). Thus the search, with its experimentations, is constructed as necessary, and since such experimentation is considered perverse and criminal when it occurs inside western families (as incest or abuse), it is outside the family that it must take place. So in many contexts, the desire to leave home and family and relate to other people in the world in intimate situations is seen as positive. If there were no hegemonic condemnations of promiscuity, infidelity and paid sex, there would be no contradictions here, but these are still common. The result is that those who buy sexual services rarely speak about it in public, while speaking about it to peers in private may be actually constitutive of a heterosexual masculine identity (Allison, 1994; Bird, 1996; Leonini, 1999).

These changes in attitudes to sexual behaviour, so notable at the discursive level, look different through the lens of gender. There, the denunciation of promiscuity is almost universally levelled at girls, not boys (apart from some more generally anti-sex pronouncements from fundamentalist religious leaders and the Vatican). There is also resistance to the idea that women might want to watch others have sex, have multiple sexual partners, engage in public sex, pay for sex or be paid to have sex, the last inevitable given much of the 'prostitution' discourse, which insists that it is a form of exploitation *by* men *of* women. There is now a significant literature on western women as purchasers of sex on holiday (see, for example, Pruitt and LaFont, 1995; Phillip, 1999; O'Connell Davidson and Sanchez Taylor, 1999), but it remains to be seen whether this documentation will help expand our understanding of the search for identity and personal services or will only be treated within the 'prostitution debate', where it is condemned.

The 'drive' model of sexuality mentioned above has been the subject of much debunking, particularly in relation to a 'hegemonic masculinity' (Connell, 1987). Male sexual 'needs', which have justified much gender oppression, are criticised as not real but cultural constructions (McIntosh, 1978; O'Connell Davidson, 2001). Nevertheless, the liberation model is still going strong, and the proliferation of sexual images and opportunities is usually related to a 'de-repressing' of the population.

According to Jeffrey Weeks, 'choice of lifestyles is central to radical sexual politics; choice to realise our sexual desire, choice in the pattern of sexual relationships, choice in our general ways of life' (Weeks, 1995: 45). Can this affirmation made on behalf of sexual identities apply to commercial sex? Is being a 'client', 'prostitute' or 'sex worker' an analogous identity to those apparently based on sexual 'orientation'? If identities are multiple, shifting and temporary, perhaps so. For in the 'free markets' of advanced capitalism, objects, experiences and services that not long ago were not commercially available now seem to proliferate before our very eyes. Possible spaces to go to (in order to experience or flee from life, rest, relax, hide, learn) have burgeoned, and as for travel, at present almost no site is too far away for consideration, even for working-class people (and if only 'once in a lifetime'). A wide range of activities have become potential consumer products so that purchasable experiences continuously multiply.

Thus the proliferation of sexually oriented shows and services on offer is not surprising, since the same has occurred with products in most commercial domains. John Urry (1990) divides touristic gazing possibilities into 'collective', in which the presence of other people adds to the experience, and 'romantic', in which privacy is important. Both kinds of experiences are available in the sex industry, whose sites are used by clients to drink, eat, take drugs, get together with friends, do business, impress partners, watch films, travel, be with a variety of sexual partners and pay for a gamut of services. The sexual moment need not occupy a central place within the whole experience; for many, drinking and socialising in the presence of symbolic, decorative women or men may be more important (Allison, 1994; Leonini, 1999; Frank, 2002).

The price of wealth and progress

The social changes sketched produce a demand that draws women migrants towards the west. At the same time, changes to the world economy, including manufacturing's move out of the west and 'structural adjustment' policies of the International Monetary Fund, armed conflicts, natural disasters and poverty help draw them away from home. But human character is at work, as well. Media images of travel reach everywhere, the desire to see the world is not limited to richer travellers and tourists, and some people seek adventure more than others. To pay attention only to the jobs migrants do is to essentialise them as workers and deny the diversity of their hopes and experiences (Agustín, 2002a). When they arrive in the west, few of the jobs available to them are located in the formal sector, many pay miserably, and working conditions are often semi-feudal. Clandestinity and lack of labour regulation leave the field open to abuses of all kinds, but to totalise all women's migrations as 'trafficking' is to deny them the capacity to make decisions and take risks (Agustín, 2002b, 2003). And labelling them without listening to their own testimonies about what they are doing means theorising (and fantasising) without considering a good part of the data (Agustín, 2005).

There is no mystery about why migrations take place, and little about the demand for migrant women's services. What cannot be explained easily is why western governments have failed for so very long to value women's service jobs and apply to them normal regulatory codes and rights. For some time the conditions discussed in this essay have been accepted: women work more than men, housework exists in economic limbo, housewives aren't thought to be 'employed', 'caring' is supposed to be its own reward, and the exchange of sex for money isn't considered 'work'. The refusal to normalise traditional women's services reproduces negative ideas about women's worth and colonises women from poorer countries as in the days of overt empire. Service jobs per se are not looked down on: the waiter, the physiotherapist and the hairdresser are examples of jobs involving some degree of physical and/or personal intimacy that are perceived as normal. Yet rather than examining this imperialist remnant, reactions often make the leap to saying European borders should be closed and women not allowed to migrate to do these jobs. This 'solution' constructs non-western women as better off staying home and negates the fact that the salaries offered are seen as positive opportunities that justify risk. The moral panic on 'trafficking' conveniently feeds these isolationist proposals, keeping the social gaze fixed on extreme cases while neglecting the more prosaic needs of the majority of migrant women. Proposals to stem migration also fail to consider the European social context, with its changing needs and desires. The world of services in which migrant women live, and the European social context, could be ameliorated considerably by the adjustment of long-pending gender inequalities in the consideration of what is 'work', along with a willingness to reflect on desires that seem to be the 'price' of wealth and progress.

Notes

1 First published as: Agustín, Laura (2004) 'A migrant world of services', *Social Politics* 10(3), pp 377–96. Reprinted by permission of Oxford University Press.
2 Transgender is the more encompassing term, gender rather than physical attributes being the overriding issue. Part-time and occasional transvestites, pre-op and post-op transsexuals, people identifying as 'in between' and as a 'third sex', are all included. In this study, transsexuals working in service sectors are included as 'women' because they usually present as women while working.
3 '[E]mployers often openly stipulate that they want a particular type of *person*, justifying this demand on the grounds that they will be working in the home . . . [She] should be 'affectionate', 'like old people' or 'be good with children'. The worker wants to earn as much money as she can with reasonable conditions, but the employer's wants are rather more complicated' (Anderson, 2000: 114, emphasis in original).
4 Ironmonger (1996: 61, n 4) notes not understanding why the term is *third* person rather than *second* or *other*.
5 These issues have been found to be similar in other parts of the world; see, for example, Hondagneu-Sotelo, 2001.
6 Another recent collection, Ehrenreich and Hochschild, 2003, has a similar focus.
7 Hochschild explains:

> While some [flight attendants] distance themselves from the job by defining it as 'not serious', others distance themselves from it in another way . . . They use their faces as masks against the world; they refuse to act. Most of those who 'go into robot' describe it as a defense, but they acknowledge that it is inadequate: their withdrawal often irritates passengers, and when it does they are forced to withdraw even further in order to defend themselves against that irritation.
>
> (Hochschild, 1983: 135)

References

Abel, Emily K and Nelson, Margaret K (1990) *Circles of Care: Work and Identity in Women's Lives*, Albany: State University of New York Press

Agustín, Laura (2000) 'Working in the sex industry', *OFRIM*, 6 (June), pp 155–72; available at: http://www.swimw.org/engver.html

Agustín, Laura (2002a) 'Challenging place: Leaving home for sex', *Development* 45(1) pp 110–16

Agustín, Laura (2002b) 'The (crying) need for different kinds of research', *Research for Sex Work* 5 (June), pp 30–2

Agustín, Laura (2003) 'Sex, gender and migrations: Facing up to ambiguous realities' *Soundings* 23, pp 84–98

Agustín, Laura (2005) 'Migrants in the mistress's house: Other voices in the "trafficking" debate', *Social Politics*, 12(1) pp 96–117

Allison, Anne (1994) *Nightwork: Sexuality, Pleasure and Corporate Masculinity in a Tokyo Hostess Club*, Chicago: University of Chicago Press

Anderson, Bridget (2000) *Doing the Dirty Work: The Global Politics of Domestic Labour*, London: Zed Books

Bakan, Abigail and Stasiulis, Daiva (1995) 'Making the match: Domestic placement agencies and the racialization of women's household work', *Signs* 20(2) pp 303–35

Barry, Kathleen (1979) *Female Sexual Slavery*, Englewood Cliffs, NJ: Prentice-Hall

Benería, Lourdes (1981) 'Conceptualising the labour force: The underestimation of women's economic activities', *Journal of Development Studies* 17, pp 10–28

Bird, Sharon R (1996) 'Welcome to the Men's Club: Homosociality and the maintenance of hegemonic masculinity', *Gender & Society* 10(2) pp 120–32

Bose, Christine E (1987) 'Devaluing women's work: The undercount of women's employment in 1900 and 1980' in Bose, Christine, Feldberg, Rorslyn, and Sokoloff, Natalie (eds) *Hidden Aspects of Women's Work*, New York: Praeger

Bubeck, Diemut E (1995) *Care, Gender and Justice*, Oxford: Clarendon Press

Chadeau, Ann (1985) 'Measuring household activities: Some international comparisons', *Review of Income and Wealth* 31, pp 237–53

Chancer, Lynn S (1993) 'Prostitution, feminist theory, and ambivalence: Notes from the sociological underground', *Social Text* 37, pp 143–71

Chapkis, Wendy (1997) *Live Sex Acts*, New York: Routledge

Colectivo, Ioé with Agustín, Laura (2001) *Mujer, Inmigración y Trabajo* [Women, Immigration and Work], Madrid: IMSERSO

Connell, Robert W (1987) *Gender and Power: Society, the Person and Sexual Politics*, Stanford: Stanford University Press

Cutrufelli, Maria R (1988) 'La demanda de prostitución', *Debats* 24, pp 23–30

Davidoff, Leonore and Hall, Catherine (1987) *Family Fortunes: Men and Women of the English Middle Class, 1780–1850*, London: Hutchinson

Dworkin, Andrea (1987) *Intercourse*, New York: Free Press

Ehrenreich, Barbara and Hochschild, Arlie (eds) (2003) *Global Woman: Nannies, Maids, and Sex Workers in the New Economy*, New York: Metropolitan Books

Folbre, Nancy (1991) 'The unproductive housewife: Her evolution in nineteenth-century economic thought', *Signs* 16(3) pp 463–84

Folbre, Nancy and Nelson, Julie (2000) 'For love or money – or both?', *Journal of Economic Perspectives* 14(4), pp 123–40

Folbre, Nancy and Wagman, Barnet (1993) 'Counting housework: New estimates of real product in the United States, 1800–1860', *Journal of Economic History* 53(2), pp 275–88

Foucault, Michel (1978, 1985, 1986) *History of Sexuality Vols I–III*, New York: Pantheon

Frank, Katherine (2002) *G-Strings and Sympathy*, Durham, NC: Duke University Press

Gagnon, John H and Simon, William (1974) *Sexual Conduct*, London: Hutchinson

Giddens, Anthony (1992) *The Transformation of Intimacy: Sexuality, Love and Eroticism in Modern Societies*, Stanford: Stanford University Press

Gilligan, Carol (1982) *In a Different Voice: Psychological Theory and Women's Development*, Cambridge, MA: Harvard University Press

Hochschild, Arlie R (1983) *The Managed Heart: Commercialization of Human Feeling*, Berkeley: University of California Press

Hochschild, Arlie R (2000) 'Global care chains and emotional surplus value', in Hutton, Will and Giddens, Anthony (eds) *On the Edge: Living with Global Capitalism*, London: Jonathan Cape, pp 130–46

Hondagneu-Sotelo, Pierrette (2001) *Doméstica: Immigrant Workers Cleaning and Caring in the Shadows of Affluence*, Berkeley: University of California Press

Ironmonger, Duncan (1996) 'Counting outputs, capital inputs and caring labour: Estimating gross household product', *Feminist Economics* 2(3), pp 37–64

Johnson, Lisa (ed) (2002) *Jane Sexes It Up: True Confessions of Feminist Desire*, New York: Four Walls Eight Windows

Kellner, Peter (1999) 'We are richer than you think', *New Statesman*, 19 February, pp 21–2

King, Russel and Zontini, Elisabetta (2000) 'The role of gender in the South European immigration model', *Papers* 60, pp 35–52

Leonini, Luisa (ed) (1999) *Sesso in Acquisto: Una Ricerca sui Clienti della Prostituzione*, Milan: Edizioni Unicopli

Lever, Janet and Dolnick, Deanne (2000) 'Clients and call girls: Seeking sex and intimacy', in Weitzer, Ronald (ed) *Sex for Sale*, New York: Routledge, pp 85–99

Levitas, Ruth (1998) *The Inclusive Society? Social Exclusion and New Labour*, London: Macmillan

McClintock, Anne (1995) *Imperial Leather: Race, Gender and Sexuality in the Colonial Contest*, New York: Routledge

McIntosh, Mary (1978) 'Who needs prostitutes? The ideology of male sexual needs', in Smart, Carol and Smart, Barry (eds), *Women, Sexuality and Social Control*, London: Routledge & Kegan Paul, pp 53–64

Nelson, Adie and Robinson, Barrie (1994) *Gigolos and Madames Bountiful: Illusions of Gender, Power, and Intimacy*, Buffalo: Toronto University Press

O'Connell Davidson, Julia (2001) 'The rights and wrongs of prostitution', *Hypatia* 17(2), pp 84–98

O'Connell Davidson, Julia and Sanchez Taylor, Jacqueline (1999) 'Fantasy islands: Exploring the demand for sex tourism', in Kempadoo, Kamala (ed) *Sun, Sex and Gold*, Lanham, MD: Rowman & Littlefield, pp 37–54

Oso, Laura (1998) *La migración hacia España de mujeres jefas de hogar*, Madrid: Instituto de la Mujer

Parreñas, Rhacel (2001) *Servants of Globalization: Women, Migration and Domestic Work*, Stanford: Stanford University Press

Pateman, Carole (1988) *The Sexual Contract*, Stanford: Stanford University Press

Perkins, Roberta *et al.* (1994) *Sex Work and Sex Workers in Australia*, Sydney: University of New South Wales Press

Phillip, Joan (1999) 'Tourist-oriented prostitution in Barbados: The case of the beach boy and the white female tourist', in Kempadoo, Kamala (ed) *Sun, Sex and Gold*, Lanham, MD: Rowman & Littlefield, pp 183–200

Pruitt, Deborah and LaFont, Suzanne (1995) 'For love and money: Romance tourism in Jamaica', *Annals of Tourism Research* 22(2), pp 422–40

Rapp, Rayna, Ross, Ellen and Bridenthal, Renate (1983) 'Examining family history', in Newton, Judith L, Ryan, Mary P and Walkowitz, Judith R (eds) *Sex and Class in Women's History*, London: Routledge & Kegan Paul, pp 232–58

Sassen-Koob, Saskia (1984) 'From household to workplace: Theories and survey research on migrant women in the labour market', *International Migration Review* 18(4), pp 1144–67

Silva, Elizabeth B and Smart, Carol (eds) (1999) *The New Family?*, London: Sage

Stallybrass, Peter and White, Allon (1986) *The Politics and Poetics of Transgression*, Ithaca, NY: Cornell University Press

Sullivan, Barbara (1995) 'Rethinking prostitution', in Caine, Barbara and Pringle, Rosemary (eds), *Transitions: New Australian Feminisms*, New York: St Martin's Press, pp 184–97

Tronto, Joan (1987) 'Beyond gender difference to a theory of care', *Signs* 12(4), pp 644–63

Urry, John (1990) *The Tourist Gaze: Leisure and Travel in Contemporary Societies*, London: Sage

Vance, Carol (ed) (1984) *Pleasure and Danger: Exploring Female Sexuality*, London: Routledge and Kegan Paul

Waring, Marilyn (1988) *If Women Counted*, San Francisco: Harper & Row

Weeks, Jeffrey (1982) 'The development of sexual theory and sexual politics', in Brake, M (ed) *Human Sexual Relations*, Harmondsworth: Penguin, pp 293–309

Weeks, Jeffrey (1995) 'Desire and identities', in Parker, Richard and Gagnon, John (eds) *Conceiving Sexuality*, New York: Routledge, pp 33–50

Weston, Kath (1997) *Families We Choose: Lesbians, Gays, Kinship*, New York: Columbia University Press

World Sex Guide, http://worldsexguide.com

Wouters, Cas (1989) 'The sociology of emotions and flight attendants: Hochschild's *Managed Heart*', *Theory, Culture and Society* 6, pp 95–123

7

GENDER, MIGRATION AND CLASS

Why are 'live-in' domestic workers not compensated for overtime?[1]

Guy Mundlak

An introduction just on time

In Lars von Trier's film *Dogville* (2003), the drama unfolds on a naked black stage with simple lines drawn on the floor, depicting a map of a small town, which serves as a metaphor for real and complex communities. A foreign woman seeks refuge and is invited into the community, but is asked to pay a price in the form of service. This is not really waged work because she receives a home instead. The community does not know exactly what kind of work they can give her: 'There is really nothing to be done'. Yet, once she is there, they don't know how they could manage without her. Every hour, on the clock, she would move from one family to another. She cleaned in the house, worked in the field, watched after the children, listened to life-stories, and was even used for sex. For each and every person in the community the foreign woman offered, for one hour a day, something they thought no one else could offer. When the community decided that the price for staying in the community must be raised, they oddly required her to move from one household to another every half an hour. They benefited from her service twice a day, and gained a better control over her time and mind. After formal hours, she was tied down to a heavy iron device to prevent her escaping, making sure she would be available the next day. She was also expected to be appreciative; after all, she was a guest of the family.

Being a foreigner, being a woman, being a labourer: the three are tied together, managed and regulated by time. The community's norms determine her allocation of time. Time is a commodity to pay for the invitation. When necessary, time is blurred. Time of labour, time of care, time of 'leisure' – are all one and the same. After all, she was never 'asked to work' and 'there is really nothing that needs to be done'. It was merely an intimate token of appreciation that was expected of a foreigner seeking a home. Other times, time is strongly regulated. When prices need to be clear, an hour is traded for

123

two periods of half an hour, just like two part-time workers who do more than the job of one full-time worker. Time is a method of subtle regulation that can trumpet possibilities of accommodation or exploitation at work. Regulating time is technically complicated and relatively concealed, and therefore better than meddling with 'bottom line' wages which are clear and easy to understand and compare. It is also better than discipline and punishment, which are difficult to administer when care, compassion and trust are expected from the labourer.

This chapter looks at the reality of migrant women who are invited to become part of the family and to work around the clock, through the odd perspective of overtime regulation. The first section contrasts the centrality of time in the live-in's relationship with the household where she works, and the typical exemption of live-ins from time regulation. The second section refutes the simple legalistic explanations for this exemption, and suggests instead that the overtime exemption is a reflection of the live-in being, typically, a migrant, a woman and poor. The third section extends the argument to account for the social implications of this arrangement. The overtime exemption raises awareness of the problematics of employment, gender and immigration regulation. It is therefore hardly a technical adjustment in labour law as is often suggested, but rather an essential component in separate regulatory spheres that intersect around the rather extreme nature of the live-in relationship.

The move from the minute details of law to the systemic logic of current trends in the labour market and the welfare state must remind us, again, that law does not constitute relationships only through highly visible statutes or adjudication in the Supreme Court. The seemingly mundane details that govern the day-to-day interactions are highly useful devices for social engineering. Just like the symbolic simple white lines drawn on von Trier's stage, the regulation of time draws technical lines that demarcate work and 'leisure', insiders and outsiders, public and private, labourers and employers; it also ties all distinctions together and fits them into one coherent whole.

Live-in workers: time and time-exempt

Live-ins are engaged in domestic and care work, and their tasks usually include either cleaning and serving, or care for children, disabled and elderly family members, or both. The phenomenon of live-in workers is not new. The contemporary practice of employing live-ins is a variation of the common law servant, but live-in arrangements can also be traced back to earlier feudal practices (Graunke, 2002: 136–50). Whereas there was a move away from live-in arrangements during most of the twentieth century, towards the end of the century the live-in arrangement began gaining in popularity as the result of two complementary processes. On the demand side, as the number of dual-career families increases, there is a growing demand for live-ins who can take full responsibility for all household and care tasks. On the supply side, globalization processes that reduce the transaction costs of transborder migration increase the numbers of live-ins who seek work in more prosperous economies. As the employment of live-ins in the developed countries has increased, it is no longer restricted to wealthy manor owners, but extends to the homes of young dual-career professionals (Sassen, 1988; Hochschild, 2002).

The growing reliance of families on live-ins entails their engagement as the only household employee. This distinguishes them from the servants of the manor, who were part of a team in which there was a highly structured hierarchy and a division of labour. The modern live-in represents the epitome of multi-tasking (Parreñas, 2000; Sotelo, 2001; Romero, 2002). She is secluded from fellow workers, and her employment as a live-in is expressly designed to eliminate any artificial divisions of labour. If she can physically complete a task, it is part of her job definition. Being the multi-tasker she is, the live-in worker is also secluded from other employees who are similarly situated. Moreover, as many live-ins are migrant workers, they are also removed from their natural community and surroundings to begin with. They are in touch with their community only on their days off, or only with those who are employed in the same neighbourhood, through daily encounters in the park, shopping centres and the like.

From the live-in's point of view, her company, her employer, her home and her work are all one and the same. The nature of the work performed by the live-in, complemented by the multiple dimensions of seclusion, suggests that being a live-in worker is more than a job. It is a way of life, temporary perhaps, but not necessarily short-term. It assumes that the place, task and time are all detached from labour market and other social norms. Unlike the traditional worker, the live-in does not provide the employer a definite period of time in which the worker's services are for the employer to use, but is viewed as someone whose time is at the disposal of the employer almost wholesale.

Peggie Smith nicely demonstrates the strong roots of timelessness, multi-tasking and solitude that characterise live-ins, in reference to a study by Emily Blackwell, conducted in 1883:[2]

> She abandons family life, having no daily intercourse with her rela-
> tives as do out-door workers living in their own homes. She loses
> her personal freedom, for she is always under the authority of the
> employer. She can never leave the house without permission; there is
> no hour of the day in which she is not at the bidding of her mistress;
> there is no time in her life, except [a] few . . . seasons of absence, for
> which she may not be called to account.
>
> (Smith, 1999: 871)

Yet the basic structure (or 'structurelessness') of this particular employment relationship remains even today. Live-ins also describe their work in terms of a continuous time commitment:

> I begin at seven in the morning. I change her, feed her. Give her all the injections and medication. Then I clean the apartment. When you take care of an elder, the first thing that you need is patience. For example, when you feed her it can take up to an hour . . . I wake up at four in the morning just to check that the woman is alive.
>
> (Parreñas 2000: 159)

Daily schedules are also related to the duration of placement:

> Then there's the problem of hours which seem to get more flexible (that is, longer) the longer you work for the family. There's also the problem of being asked to do work – dog walking, ironing, serving at dinner parties – that was not part of the job description and was not included in the original salary. And if the job can be flexible, the salary is often inflexible . . . Then there is the problem of summers. Many families offer nannies a Hobson's choice: either go away with them and be trapped in some all-white resort, or take token wages while they're gone . . . Basically I am on call around the clock. I feel like my life isn't mine even when I am home.
>
> (Cheever, 2002: 35)

Time is also an issue in formal contracts and rules, as described in a handbook issued by a Hong Kong employment agency:

> Learn to CLOCK WATCH. Schedule your time and work . . . During your FREE TIME, REST IF YOU MUST, BUT BE READY TO ANSWER THE DOOR OR TELEPHONE. Sew clothes or other special chores like re-potting some plants and cleaning kitchen cupboards.
>
> (Constable, 2002: 121)

While the double-bind that has been highlighted over the years has been that which requires a difficult juggling act between work outside and inside the home (Hochschild, 1997), the live-in experiences a double-bind of her own. If she works too fast, she will be asked to do more. If she works too slowly, she will be reprimanded for not working hard enough. It is precisely because she has nowhere else to go that she is not expected to schedule her time. Any scheduling and planning is considered as undermining the nature of her work.

Similar descriptions appear in numerous ethnographic studies of domestic care and live-in arrangements. Common to all of them are the descriptions of a boundaryless relationship. The live-in is conveniently (to the employer) internalised into the household and no longer viewed as an external agent. There are no clear boundaries between working time and 'leisure' time. There is no clear demarcation of the tasks to be performed. A central tenet that surfaces time and time again in interviews worldwide is the 'you are part of the family' claim (Bakan and Stasiulis, 1997; Gregson and Lowe, 1994). The employee is claimed to be part of the family rather than an arm's-length contractual agent, and her work is therefore considered as part of the ongoing family routine. However, the 'you are part of the family' shibboleth does not capture the reality in which the mutual emotional attachment and moral responsibilities that bind the family together are wholly absent from the relationship between the live-in and the family.

The exemption of live-ins from time regulation

The boundaryless relationship between the live-in and her employer undoubtedly results in friction, and the relatively common abuse of rights. A similar abuse of rights is typically encountered by migrant workers in various occupations, as well as by women employed in hierarchical situations and peripheral workers in general. Yet, the boundaryless relationship amplifies the problems. The employee cannot easily retreat from her work. As a migrant worker she fears deportation. As a woman she fears abuse. As a peripheral worker she cannot easily access the courts or other venues to claim her rights, nor are her alternatives in the labour market good enough to merit taking action and helping herself. In addition to these three characteristic weaknesses, the live-in does not have an alternative home; there is no place to which she can escape. This is not to say that live-ins should only be perceived as helpless victims. They develop entrepreneurial strategies to make the best of this difficult arrangement. However, the inherent features of the live-in arrangement render their starting point particularly difficult.

How does the law perceive the live-in relationship? Comparative studies demonstrate the many similarities across legal regimes, despite institutional differences (Mundlak, 2005; Blackette, 1998). Sometimes the law constructs a status of au-pair, a term that usually designates a person who stays with a family as part of a cultural exchange programme. Although the cultural experience is sometimes tainted by a hierarchical exchange of work for housing, food and pocket money – which overall very much resembles the employment relationship, the law holds that this is an intimate form of co-habitation and not a common commercial exchange. Consequently, au-pairs are typically exempted from the coverage of employment law. Other than au-pairs, live-ins are generally recognised to be employees. Some legal systems may seek to deny their rights when they are undocumented workers, but in most situations, there is no a priori exception to the coverage of employment law to live-in workers, nor even to undocumented workers. The simple statement of the law would therefore be that, generally, live-ins are formally entitled to rights of other employees.

While there are differences across countries with regard to the coverage of labour law, one area in which the outcome is almost universal is the exemption of live-ins and their employers from time regulation in general, and to overtime rules in particular. The exemption from overtime is sometimes stated explicitly and tailored only to live-ins. Yet, in most cases the overtime exception is concealed. Sometimes it is the result of applying general exceptions, such as the withdrawal of time regulation from workers in establishments with a small number of workers, from domestic work generally, from workers who are engaged in work that requires 'special trust', or from workers whose worktime cannot be measured. Sometimes, worktime regulation is applied but not the rules on overtime. Sometimes the number of hours permitted to employ overtime is applicable, but overtime is not compensated. Other times it is compensated but not as much as for overtime in other occupations.[3] Sometimes it can even be compensated but the worker must meet the burden of proof to demonstrate that she worked overtime. But when work is done in the intimate space of the household, such a burden of proof can be detrimental to the lawsuit. Finally, even when time regulation is applied, as are the rules on compensating workers for overtime, the law tends to be generous to the employers in splitting the day between the employer's use of the live-in's time, and the live-in's time for herself. Being on call, short and unscheduled tasks, or just being present while a child is asleep, are easily dismissed as off-worktime.

Legal justifications and alternative explanations for the time exemption

Traditionally, the overtime exception was part of a broader approach that withheld employment regulation from live-in arrangements. The relationship between the live-in and the family for which she works – so the argument went – cannot be captured in conventional terms of 'employer' and 'employee'. The high level of intimacy and the sanctity of privacy distinguish it from other employment situations. This argument has been refined and gradually employment standards have been applied to the live-in. There is currently a need for a more particular explanation to the overtime exception.

One justification holds that while the live-in is an employee, a special state of trust obtains between the parties. It would therefore not be appropriate to count the hours of work, as is the practice in, for example, industrial manufacturing. A second justification holds that it is impossible to measure the amount of time worked by the live-in. The boundaryless relationship, in which working time and leisure time are not neatly demarcated, denies the existence of measurable time that lies at the basis of overtime arrangements. The difference between these two justifications is that the former holds that it is *inappropriate* to require overtime payment, while the latter holds that it is *not feasible* to measure working time in such a relationship. Both justifications can account for the general applicability of employment standards on the one hand, nevertheless exempting live-in workers from overtime payment, on the other. This exception is not because live-ins are not employees. Nor is it because they are not as deserving as other employees. They are. It is merely a 'technical adjustment' to the law of minimum employment standards which stems from the particular problem of regulating time in this work relationship.

The two justifications for the overtime exemption are not particularly convincing. First, the high-trust relationship draws on exemptions that are generally applied to high-ranking, salaried officials. These are workers who, despite their formal status as 'employees', have interests that are closer to those of the shareholders than to those of other employees. The juxtaposition of high-ranking managers, engineers engaged in Research and Development and domestic live-ins is an odd one. The second justification for the exemption is equally problematic. This type of exemption may be suitable for travelling sales agents whose whereabouts throughout the day are unknown. But the working time of the live-in is easily gauged. The work is performed within the 'establishment' and is highly visible. It is true that some employers do not want to deal with measuring and recording working time. However, this is also true of employers in industry, who prefer to forgo the use of the classic time clock because it clashes with the organisational culture the employer wants to promote. Just because the employer forgoes the measurement of time does not justify a blanket exemption of live-in workers from overtime arrangements.

The weakness common to both justifications is indicative of the basic fallacy that underlies them. Both justifications *assume* a boundaryless workplace. The first assumes there are no clear boundaries between the employer and the employee, who are in fact viewed as inseparable and symbiotically linked. The second assumes there are no boundaries between working time and leisure time. However, these assumptions do not reflect any intrinsic truth regarding the relationship between the live-in and her employer. The high-trust argument is based on the 'we are all a family' fallacy, which has been used to deny the live-in her privacy and her autonomy. It is a clear example of demarcating the household as a private sphere to deny the public protection that is typical to labour law (Olsen, 1983; Ehrenreich, 2002). Similarly, the absence of supervision justification adopts a view benefiting the employer, who is always in favour of greater flexibility and less precision in defining the employment contract (Offe, 1985: 14). The reason there are no boundaries between work and leisure time is because the law does not require them, and the contract-maker (the employer in these situations) seeks to avoid them. If the live-ins were to be replaced by two or three live-out domestic workers working several hours a day, there would be no problem measuring the work performed in hourly units. While arguably complicated managerial tasks cannot be broken up into units of time, cleaning and care work can be scheduled easily. The problem is that such scheduling would undermine the live-in's economic advantage to the employer.

The overtime exemption therefore is not an obvious legal response to an objective problem. The proposed justifications emphasise administrative problems and conceal a more fundamental prejudice (Smith, 2000). Arguably, the real reasons must be sought in the live-in's gender, foreignness and class, and how these features interact (Macklin, 1992; Fitzpatrick and Kelly, 1998; Banks, 1999). These explanations also account for the absence of solidarity, and the 'divide-and-conquer' effects of this legislative arrangement which guarantee their perpetuation over time.

Live-ins are women

What seems to be a better explanation for the overtime exception is that most live-ins are women. The gendered composition of live-ins affects their employment standards in various ways. Live-ins perform the tasks that are stereotypically considered either part of women's innate nature or the result of social indoctrination. The live-in's occupation is the clearest example of 'women's work' done for money. Women who perform 'women's work' as labour – as a paying job, rather than as unpaid work within the home – receive relatively low market wages. Yet when they are live-ins, they are not even considered to be fully marketing their work, because they have moved their home along with their work. Consequently, the work they do is not perceived as a 'job'. This in large part explains the high-trust justification. Live-ins are not doing a 'job' because they have a high-trust, intimate relationship with their employers. This intimacy belongs to the sphere of relationships between a woman and her family (spouse, children and parents).

To be clear, there is nothing about work at home, care work or any other occupation for that matter, which is innately a women's job. Nor is there is anything intrinsic in the work itself that explains why women do it much more than men. Social constructs could be much different, but the point is that they are not, and as will be argued hereafter, the overtime exception for live-ins is merely one more statutory instrument that is being used to preserve the status quo rather than question it.

The gender argument in itself is not sufficient. There are live-ins, most of them women as well, who are highly paid and can bargain for their rights and secure their 'private time'. These are the high-wage 'nannies' (Romero, 2003). They are employed to do care work, and they too perform 'women's work'. This is a separate niche within the live-in labour market, and the problems of other live-ins are not necessarily alien to them either. They, too, have to cope with solitude, the awkward balancing of intimacy and the work relationship, and employers' intrinsic desire to make the work schedule and work definition more flexible. But the mental and tangible resources they have to cope with these pressures are relatively high, because these nannies are neither foreign nor poor. Further layers are therefore needed to explain the exemption from time regulation.

Live-ins are foreigners

Domestic workers who work on an hourly basis do not live-in. They come and go at fixed times as contractually negotiated. It is the employment relationship that brings them and their employers together; the rest of the time they are apart. When off the job, the domestic employees resort to their own world. When on the job, the parties' relationship is 'professional'. The parties agree to a general time frame. Within that time frame, the use of the employee's time is determined on the parties' implicit and explicit agreements regarding the positive and negative incentives to elicit work (for example, bonuses and monitoring devices).

By contrast, live-ins generally do not hail from the neighbouring town. They prefer a live-in arrangement because they do not have an alternative home in the vicinity. Sometimes they want a live-in arrangement to save on the costs of housing. At other times they must accept a live-in arrangement because that is what employers demand. In some countries, the live-in arrangement is even required by the state as part of the immigration requirements. In the case of undocumented migrants, a live-in arrangement is also an asylum of sorts, albeit a fragile one, from the immigration authorities. Given their distance from their own community, the employer is their only home.

Ironically, employers who are concerned with their privacy display a preference for foreign live-ins, because they do not intrude as much as local workers. They are always there, but the common metaphor used for such workers is that they are 'invisible' (Rivas, 2002). This may be because they do not speak the language. Or it may be because their personal problems and lives are supposedly 'left behind' and their presence is dedicated only for the purpose of live-in work. Their invisibility is also ascribed to be a cultural matter that the live-ins bring with them from a far and exotic culture. The preference for a foreigner also helps to mediate the seemingly conflicting virtues of invisibility and 'being part of the family'. Common then among these reasons is that their foreignness is a fundamental reason for the employers' preferences as well as for the employees' assent to the boundaryless live-in arrangement.

Live-ins as an issue of class

The live-in's gender and foreignness also interact to construct yet a third important explanation for the overtime exemption. Live-ins are generally poor, if not in dire need, and they are willing to compromise over wages that are at the legal minimum (and often even below that). Alienage also creates a wage gap between the prevailing wage in the country of origin and the country of work. This is the gap that makes statutory manipulation possible.

The implication of the overtime exception is that it pushes down the minimum wage. Minimum wage arrangements commonly (but not universally) apply to migrant workers (and obviously apply to women). However, a minimum wage is usually determined either by the number of hours worked or on the basis of a monthly salary. If workers are not entitled to overtime, this means that hourly compensation is directly tied to the *number* of hours worked, but with no extra per-hour compensation for the hours worked over and above the regular working day or working week. If the workers receive a monthly salary, this salary will have been calculated for a 'normal' working week worker. But for live-ins the same salary is actually provided for a greater number of hours, thus reducing the wage per hour. Consequently, some countries maintain a contradictory position. On the one hand, they apply the minimum wage laws to live-ins, but at the same time they exempt their employers from overtime payment and reduce the minimum wage. A standard argument in support of the payment of the minimum wage to foreign workers is that sub-minimum wages would lead to the preference of migrant workers over local workers, but this is generally not a problem with regard to live-ins. Domestic (that is, not migrant) workers usually prefer a work-out to a live-in arrangement anyway. Instead, it seems that the overtime exception makes it possible to maintain a façade of equal treatment with regard to minimum wages, while allowing a real distinction on the basis of the method the wage is calculated.

Gender, alienage and class: who can voice the live-ins' interests?

The intertwining features of gender, class and alienage make live-ins exceptionally vulnerable in the labour market. Arguably, though, labour law is well versed in aiding the weaker populations. This is particularly evident with regard to the growing body of anti-discrimination law and minimum labour standards, of which time regulation is an integral part. Why then does the protective mission of labour law so universally cease when live-ins' time is concerned?

Politically, this arrangement seems to be very convenient for many, and thus relatively secure from change. If live-ins have one characteristic which can potentially be used to promote their rights, it is the fact that they are women. Clearly, the other two axes that prescribe their position in the labour market do not have the same potential, because other poor and migrant workers are not a major source of political power. Women, on the other hand, have gained more influence in the political sphere and can be assumed to promote the live-ins' interests in solidarity. Solidarity, however, is rare. Live-ins secure the traditional division of labour within the household but eliminate its disadvantage to women. Given the minor role of men in household chores and family care work to begin with, the live-ins are viewed by the household and by society as predominantly an aid to the women who employ them. Most commonly, it is women who recruit, instruct and 'manage' the live-ins.

Dual-career families are those in which both partners have a career outside the home. Compared to the traditional division of labour in the household, the exceptional feature of dual-career families is that the woman engages in a dual career of her own – both within and outside the household (Hertz, 1986). Consequently, society perceives live-ins as a means to relieve the *woman* of her dual role. The major advantage of live-ins to the families that employ them is around-the-clock availability; counting their hours would eliminate this advantage. Of course, there are other ways to perceive, encourage and aid dual-career families. Somewhat too obvious even to mention, the male partner could assume a greater role within the household. Yet very little is done fundamentally to move the dual-career family away from the traditional gender division of labour (Shelton and John, 1996). Some think the matter is not appropriate for social intervention; others suggest that there are no practical ways to compel a different division of labour.

Limiting the social response to the traditional division of labour to cost-saving methods, such as the overtime exception, frames the problem in a manner that sets poor and rich women against each other. It allows women, as employers, to develop a greater capacity to overcome the 'double-bind' that disadvantages them as employees (Williams, 2000). The live-ins therefore serve multiple, class-related objectives. To the household they designate the social status of their employers like other prized commodities such as luxury cars and gadgets. But more particularly, they also have been commonly described as the servants that relieve the 'lady of the house' from the menial tasks (Macklin, 1992: n 307 ff; Smith, 1999). Consequently, they relieve the household from reconsidering the division of labour within it, and maintain the social status quo. Any effort at solidarity among women on these two sides of the live-in relationship risks the token arrangement that society and the law have crafted to relieve the gender tension, and could result in bringing back the traditional status quo. Career women may not be able to afford this, while men, because they are not involved, may not sufficiently care. Traditional or modern, the division of labour is structured as the internal affair of women, ignoring the benefits men and employers alike derive from it. Otherwise stated, the overtime exception distances men from the problem and puts in place a divide-and-conquer strategy that undermines the potential for solidarity,

The overtime exemption: de-commodification and re-commodification of time

The overtime exception makes time a commodity (Polanyi, 1944). The day is composed of 24 hours, all equal, and all of which can be negotiated in contract. College graduate nannies and migrant live-ins must arrange in contract their working schedule, and the division between 'work' and 'leisure' is governed by the market. The overtime exception withdraws the objective of time legislation, which is essentially to de-commodify time. Time regulation holds some hours to be qualitatively different from others and removes (at least in part) the governance of time from the marketplace.

The de-commodification of time can be seen as an integration of two interrelated statutory projects. The first is that of labour law, which de-commodifies various experiences and dimensions of the employment relationship and isolates them from market forces. Not only time, but such rights as health, safety, privacy and equality have also been removed from the marketplace. These dimensions of the employment relationship are characterised as being more than just economic rights, but also as a matter of human dignity. An 18-hour working day, just like toiling in a sweatshop without proper ventilation, is not only a matter of inequality in economic bargaining, it is also dehumanising. Laws regulating working time partially de-commodify time-units (Radin, 1996: 102–14). This does not mean they take away time's economic value. Things that are not commodities may have an economic value, but that is not their only value. The law tags some hours as working time, and others as leisure time. There are limits to the extent of overtime a worker may perform, and some hours of the day are slotted in a totally non-commodified manner as inalienable leisure time.

Second, the de-commodification of time is also an essential component of the welfare state, which partially isolates human experience and opportunities from the functioning of the market (Esping Andersen, 1990). The allegedly meritocratic regime governed by the market gives place to a regime based on principles of democratic participation and social integration. A disabled person who receives aid in kind, or in the form of an allowance or reimbursement from the state, is 'deserving' and entitled because she complies with the social criteria defined by the community, and not because society is engaged in charity or mercy. One's economic and social position is therefore determined not only by markets, but also on the basis of one's attachment to the distributing community.

The welfare state project is therefore closely tied to the labour law project. The de-commodification of time provides a qualitative guarantee of individual well-being, civic engagement, political participation and social interaction, all of which are integral to social citizenship. The achievement of statutory time regulation and the broader impact of the overtime exception should therefore be assessed in relation to these two projects of de-commodification.

The overtime exception for live-ins: labour market regulation and the exclusion of women

The simple assessment is that time regulation in general, and overtime regulation in particular, have benefited workers. The industrial norms of the past have been outlawed and the workday is more humane and more compatible with human dignity. Together with minimum wage provisions, on the one hand, and welfare benefits, on the other, dignity is also complemented by adequate income. Despite the generally positive assessment, the regulation of time also demonstrates the intrinsic difficulty in advancing the interests of labour. The traditional gender-based critique of time regulation argues that it is founded on the male, factory worker model. It assumes two types of time – 'work' and 'leisure' – thus ignoring the fact that there are at least three types of time, one of which applies to women in a predominant manner yet remains invisible in statutory time-regulation: 'house and care time'. When a person is not at work he is assumed to be at 'leisure', but for many women, 'leisure' is essentially non-paid work at home (Williams, 2000). Moreover, the particular arrangements associated with time regulation, such as the right to fringe benefits or the use of working time to determine entitlement to unemployment funds, welfare and the like, have often been geared to exclude women from the primary labour market and squeeze them out to its periphery.

The problems are generally slanted in two complementary directions. First, labour law is interested in employment issues, and women who work at home are assumed to be outside the employment sphere. Otherwise stated, if the role of labour law is to de-commodify certain dimensions of work, then women's work at home is not commodified to begin with and employment law is therefore irrelevant. Second, employment law often takes the convenient, full-time (and indefinite) model of employment, which is disproportionately male, and arranges for its partial de-commodification. For example, in most countries overtime is differentiated from extra-time (EIRO, 2003). An employee who has a part-time contract (for example, 20 hours a week) and works extra hours is not entitled to overtime or to any other legal protection. Legal protection is extended only to those employed over and above the maximum number of hours prescribed by law. Because more women than men are employed only part-time, time regulation is commonly a means for exclusion.

If the problem is identified as women's economically and legally unrecognised work, some have suggested that women's work at home must be commodified (Silbaugh, 1997; Ertman, 1998; Cahn, 2001). The argument here is that the only way to achieve recognition of household work is to value it in market terms. The social realisation that women have a job at home, as well as outside it, would shape the way the law looks at part-time arrangements and extra work, in which women are over-represented but which fall short of current overtime arrangements. The meaning of commodification of women's work is difficult to pinpoint, but if the de-commodification of time by means of regulation is part of the disadvantage law has imposed on women in the labour market, then it is appealing to think that re-commodification may be the most appropriate response. However, the over-time exception of live-ins from time regulation demonstrates the weakness of such a response. The exception makes overtime a matter for contractual negotiation and removes public constraints from the contractual definition of the live-in's tasks and time commitment.

The live-in arrangement is an extreme example of the commodification of women's work. If, as a result of re-commodification, live-ins are placed at a serious disadvantage, this should also serve as a warning to those who believe that the simple solution to women's unrecognised contribution at home is to translate it into market value. There is no reason to assume that if women's household work (when done in their own household) is commodified, that women's bargaining power will immediately improve. The commodification of live-ins suggests that the market valuation of women's work does not capture the true value of their work. Consequently, the devaluation of women's work is one and the same, regardless of whether women's work is relegated to the market, the public sphere or the family. Shifting the work from one sphere to another does not resolve the problem of devaluation itself.

Not only does the re-commodification of time prove to be a hollow promise for live-ins, but the losses extend beyond the live-ins themselves. In the process of shifting time from the family to the market sphere, the fundamental problem is ignored. For example, if the problem is identified as women's (and men's) lack of control over their life's schedules, then live-ins merely augment the problem. They free the wealthier workers to surrender to the market's work schedules, suggesting that around-the-clock work is the labour market norm. The fact that some women can accommodate such demands is also used to argue that there is nothing gendered or discriminatory in such schedules. Consequently, it is legitimate to require all women to accommodate such schedules. The norm, made possible by live-ins' work, is applied to production workers, secretarial staff and single mothers who are expected to take care of themselves, avoid welfare and conform to prevailing norms of work. Yet it is these workers who cannot roll the costs of the norms over to others.

The live-ins' overtime dilemma is indicative of the basic problem in time regulation and in labour regulation more generally. Whether time is de-commodified or re-commodified, there are some women who pay the price. The re-commodification of time by means of the overtime exemption plays off women as employers against women as labourers. Women's need to adapt to the increasingly flexible demands of market-compensated labour and 'leisure', and to squeeze in unrecognised care time between the statutory types of time, requires finding a means of escaping the overly simplified construction of time. The overtime exception of live-ins provides exactly this flexibility. Flexibility is only made possible by the multi-tasking, full-time, present but invisible live-in, whose time has been re-commodified so as to fit into the schedules and meet the needs of all others.

The question is therefore *not* 'commodification or not', but rather who pays the price, and how the social and legal precepts of time allocate resources to the labour market participants (as well as to those excluded from the market). It seems that the two versions of time regulation illustrated here both fail to address the fundamental social, economic and legal institutions that determine the allocation of household work to women. Live-ins allow the maintenance of household work as women's work, avoiding the need to bring men into the supply pool of household labourers. The overtime exception further applies a divide-and-conquer strategy among women, undermining gender-based solidarity. Hence, it utilises age-old mechanisms of discrimination but does not respond to them.

The overtime exception for live-ins: welfare state institutions and the exclusion of migrants

An alternative to the commodification of household labour discussed earlier is the feminist argument that paid work in the labour market is the only promising strategy (Shultz, 2000). Under this agenda, it is suggested that turning household work into paid work performed by others who are not members of the household is better, because society only values waged work in the labour market. Women will not advance their interests unless they conform to these social values, instead of trying to obtain recognition for household work as if it were work in the labour market. The problem with this prescription is that the retrenched welfare state is more reluctant to sponsor childcare, expand the care for the elderly, or intervene in the internal division of labour within the family. Thus, to encourage greater entry of women into the labour market, live-ins are admitted with the permission of the state (or with partial acceptance of undocumented work). Yet these women who are also engaging in waged labour cannot rely on the traditional methods of labour market empowerment. Union organising, lobbying, solidarity and asserting rights in courts are not readily available or accessible to live-ins. Facing a non-organised workforce, the state can provide the overtime exception and continue to ensure that women's time will be cheap. Live-ins' function in the welfare state is therefore best captured by an insiders–outsiders schema.

The shifting of time serves important functions in the welfare state and therefore accommodates the welfare state's objectives (Walzer, 1983: 56–61). It has been noted that – like labour law – welfare state institutions are gendered and patriarchal in nature (Pateman, 1988). In the past, women were encouraged to marry and remain at home. Now the agenda is changing in two complementary ways. The good wife is expected to work as well. Moreover, a growing number of single mothers, who previously relied on welfare, are being required to work. Live-ins are scarcely of any assistance to the second category, but they are an important part of making the first one possible. The overtime exception makes live-ins less expensive. It also has the market effect of reducing the costs of care even in homes that do not employ a live-in. This allows the welfare state to pay less in aid to families that need to care for their children or their aging parents. It can also promote non-economic aspects of dignity, such as the dignity of people with disabilities, by allowing them to remain at home with a live-in who constantly cares for them, rather than having to be taken to an institution for similar care.

The problem that the overtime exception poses to the de-commodification proposed by the welfare state institutions is therefore similar to the one in labour law – it does not *solve* the problem, but merely *shifts* it. Live-ins allow women to take part in waged work, civic life and politics. These are necessary steps for social inclusion and citizenship. It is the exclusion of live-ins on the basis of alienage that makes all this politically and socially possible. They are not deemed to be deserving as citizens or residents (just as women were denied from the democratic process in the past) and the project of social inclusion displays less (or no) concern for their inclusion.

Moreover, while it is sometimes assumed that migrant workers are 'outsiders' who make cohesion among the 'insiders' easier, the growing reliance on live-in arrangements actually segments the insiders and makes social transformation more difficult to achieve. Live-ins provide a convenient solution for dual-career families that are well compensated in the labour market. The poorer segment of the workforce must cope with an increasingly time-demanding market, which is based on schedules of women who can afford highly time-flexible help. It is the lesser-waged families and single mothers, then, for whom the need for day-care arrangements becomes a struggle. This can give rise to two-tiered social provision, as is commonly observed in other welfare state institutions such as healthcare and pensions. Making the live-ins more 'affordable' broadens the segment of the population that seeks privately negotiated solutions, instead of prompting public pressure for universal solutions to one of the most significant barriers to social inclusion. The time exception therefore directly devalues the live-in's work, but also indirectly devalues the welfare state's institutions for social provision.

Populist arguments are often made about the costs of extending social citizenship rights to migrants and the fear of human-dumping on the welfare state. But the overtime exception suggests that in the political calculations, the economic benefits of live-ins are discounted, just as the political economy makes invisible all the benefits of domestic work performed by women without pay. The live-ins are therefore not a threat to the welfare state, instead they make its more contemporary practices possible.

Conclusion: To everything there is a season and a time to every purpose under heaven[4]

Why should the matter of overtime be of particular interest? Clearly, the problems live-in workers encounter go far beyond this seemingly minor matter. Physical and mental abuse, even employers' power to withhold pay, would seem to merit more attention. These are all serious problems. However, the issue of overtime merits attention beyond its practical significance.

Even as law becomes more progressive and aware of women's issues, the fundamental structures of exclusion remain. Law shifts the burden of women's time from some women to others. Regulating time, or deregulating it, has done little to address the broader patterns that have a disparate impact on women: growing pressure in the workplace for employer-managed time flexibility; extensive hours; the stagnating distribution of care time between men and women; and the availability of quality day-care facilities. The state avoids a right to better compensation for overtime and abstains from guaranteeing a universal right to work part-time. It accepts time arrangements as well as social arrangements as given, and merely seeks to find a cheap way to accommodate the existing arrangements. Absent a response to these problems, women's time remains qualitatively distinct and undervalued.

The live-ins' gender and position in society as migrants are complementary components that explain the overtime exception. Gender, alienage and class shape an exceptionally vulnerable position in the social hierarchy and in domestic labour markets (Sotelo, 1996). The law constitutes the class of migrants who remain poor because their whole day, and hence all their market power, are compensated by one lump sum. Rather than guaranteeing migrants social rights of housing, adequate subsistence and dignified work opportunities, the time exception aids in tucking them into the private household, away from the public effort to de-commodify individuals' time and status.

The overtime exception for live-ins has little to do with the alleged justifications that the law provides for the exception – such as that their work cannot, or should not, be measured. Its function and purpose only make sense when viewed as a means to ensure the smooth functioning of the family, the market and the welfare state and to avoid the questions necessary to assess how these could be made more inclusive.

Notes

1 This article is an abridged and revised version of Mundlak, 2005; reprinted by permission of Oxford University Press.
2 Blackwell, E, 'The Industrial Position of Women', *Popular Science Monthly* 23 (1883), p 380.
3 Cf Council Directive 93/104/EC of 23 November 1993 concerning certain aspects of the organisation of working time, Article 17(1) (exemption of 'family-worker' from time regulation, because their 'duration of the working time is not measured and/or predetermined or can be determined by the workers themselves'). In the United States, The Federal Labor Standards Act (FLSA) 29 USC s 213(b)(21)(1994). (Act covers domestic workers (but not all care-workers) for the purpose of minimum wage, but only live-outs are covered with regard to overtime.) There are very different methods of exclusion at the states' level, e.g., Delaware excludes live-ins from the category of 'employees' [19 Del C Sec 901]

and California allows a greater degree of 'flexibility' in contractual arrangements negotiated with domestic workers [Cal Lab Code Sec 511]. In the United Kingdom, while overtime is mostly a matter of contractual arrangements, rather than regulation, the discounting of overtime can be observed in decisions regarding the calculation of minimum wage, e.g. *Walton v Independent Living Organization*, [2003] EWCA Civ 199. Finally – in Canada variations can be observed across provinces. While some grant equal rights regarding overtime, others demonstrate the various types of exclusion. For example, in Quebec, The Act Respecting Labor Standards, RSQ c N-1.1 entitles live-ins to a lower minimum wage and prescribes a longer working week for them compared to other caregivers. Hence, while overtime arrangements apply, their economic value is smaller than that of other employees.

4   Ecclesiastes 3: 1.

References

Bakan, Abigail and Stasiulis, Daiva (eds) (1997) *Not One of the Family: Foreign Domestic Workers in Canada*, Toronto: Toronto University Press

Banks, Taunya (1999) 'Toward a global critical feminist vision: Domestic work and the nanny tax debate', *Journal of Race and Justice* 3, p 1

Blackett, Adelle (1998) *Making Domestic Workers Visible: The Case for Specific Regulation*, Geneva: ILO

Cahn, Naomi (2001) 'The coin of the realm: Poverty and the commodification of gendered labour', *Journal of Gender, Race and Justice* 5, pp 1–30

Cheever, Susan (2002), 'The nanny dilemma', in Ehrenreich, Barbara and Hochschild, Arlie (eds), *Global Woman: Nannies, Maids and Sex Workers in the New Economy*, New York: Metropolitan Books, pp 31–8

Constable, N (2002) 'Filipina workers in Hong Kong homes: household rules and relations', in Ehrenreich, Barbara and Hochschild, Arlie (eds), *Global Woman: Nannies, Maids and Sex Workers in the New Economy*, New York: Metropolitan Books, pp 115–41

Ehrenreich, Barbara (2002) 'Maid to order' in Ehrenreich, Barbara and Hochschild, Arlie (eds), *Global Woman: Nannies, Maids and Sex Workers in the New Economy*, New York: Metropolitan Books, pp 85–103

EIRO (2003) *Overtime in Europe*; accessed at: http://www.eiro.eurofound.eu.int/2003/02/study/

Ertman, Martha (1998) 'Commercializing marriage: A proposal for valuing women's work through premarital security agreements', *Texas Law Review* 77, pp 17–112

Esping-Andersen, Gosta (1990) *The Three Worlds of Welfare Capitalism*, Princeton: Princeton University Press

Fitzpatrick, Joan and Kelly, Katrina (1998) 'Gendered aspects of migration: law and the female migrant', *Hastings International & Comparative Law Review*, 22, pp 47–112

Graunke, Kristi (2002) ' "Just like one of the family": Domestic violence paradigms and combating on-the-job violence against household workers in the United States', *Michigan Journal of Gender & Law* 9, pp 131–205

Gregson, Nicky and Lowe, Michelle (1994) *Servicing the Middle Classes: Class, Gender and Waged Domestic Labour in Contemporary Britain*, New York: Routledge

Hertz, Rosanna (1986) *More Equal than Others: Women and Men in Dual-Career Marriages*, Berkeley: University of California Press

Hochschild, Arlie R (1997) *The Time Bind: When Work Becomes Home and Home Becomes Work*, New York: Metropolitan Books

Hochschild, Arlie (2002) 'Love and gold', in Ehrenreich, Barbara and Hochschild, Arlie (eds), *Global Woman: Nannies, Maids and Sex Workers in the New Economy*, New York: Metropolitan Books, pp 15–30

Macklin, Audrey (1992) 'Foreign domestic workers: Surrogate housewife or mail order servant?', *McGill Law Journal* 27, pp 681–760

Mundlak, Guy (2005) 'Re-commodifying time: working hours of "live-in" domestic workers', in Conaghan, Joanne and Rittich, Kerry (eds), *Labour Law, Work and Family*, Oxford: Oxford University Press

Offe, Claus (1985) *Disorganized Capitalism*, Cambridge, MA: MIT University Press

Olsen, Frances (1983) 'The family and the market: A study of ideology and legal reform', *Harvard Law Review* 96, pp 1497–578

Parreñas, Rhacel S (2000) *Servants of Globalization*, Stanford: Stanford University Press

Pateman, Carol (1988), 'The patriarchal welfare state' in Gutmann, Amy (ed), *Democracy and the Welfare State*, Princeton: Princeton University Press, pp 231–60

Polanyi, Karl (1944) *The Great Transformation*, Boston: Beacon Press

Radin, Margaret-Jane (1996) *Contested Commodities*, Cambridge, MA: Harvard University Press

Rivas, Lynn M (2002) 'Invisible labours: Caring for the independent person', in Ehrenreich, Barbara and Hochschild, Arlie (eds), *Global Woman: Nannies, Maids and Sex Workers in the New Economy*, New York: Metropolitan Books, pp 70–84

Romero, Mary (2002) *Maid in the USA*, New York: Routledge

Romero, Mary (2003) 'Nanny diaries and other stories: Imagining immigrant women's labour in the social reproduction of American families', *De Paul Law Review* 52, pp 809–47

Sassen, Saskia (1988) *The Mobility of Labour and Capital: A Study in International Investment and Labour*, New York: Cambridge University Press

Shelton, Beth A and John, Daphne (1996) 'The division of household labour', *Annual Review of Sociology* 22, pp 299–322

Shultz, Vicky (2000) 'Life's work', *Columbia Law Review* 100, pp 1881–963

Silbaugh, Katharine (1997) 'Commodification and women's household labour', *Yale Journal of Law & Feminism* 9, pp 81–121.

Smith, Peggie R (1999) 'Regulating paid household work: Class, gender race and agendas of reform', *American University Law Review* 48, pp 851–924

Smith, Peggie R (2000) 'Organizing the unorganizable: Private paid household workers and approaches to employment representation', *North Carolina Law Review* 79, pp 45–110

Sotelo, Pierrette H (2001) *Domestica: Immigrant Workers Cleaning and Caring in the Shadow of Affluence*, Berkeley: University of California Press

Walzer, Michael (1983) *Spheres of Justice*, New York: Basic Books

Williams, Joan (2000) *Unbending Gender: Why Family and Work Conflict and What to Do About it?*, Oxford: Oxford University Press

8

THE RIGHT TO DOMICILE OF WOMEN WITH A MIGRANT PARTNER IN EUROPEAN IMMIGRATION LAW

Betty de Hart

In the landmark case *Boultif*, decided in 2001 by the European Court of Human Rights (ECHR), the Algerian national Mr Boultif was under threat of expulsion by Switzerland because of criminal offences. In this case, the European Court set up guidelines for deciding cases of public order. This chapter addresses the meaning of the Court's decision for the position of the female partner, the Swiss Mrs Boultif. The issue at stake is the right of women (migrant women and female citizens) to establish their family life with a migrant partner in their country of permanent residence, or citizenship. More specifically, I am interested in the ways implicit, gendered norms determine and limit women's right to establish their family life. I shall confine myself to three kinds of implicit norms and their role in the case law of the European Court of Human Rights and the European Court of Justice (ECJ). The three norms under discussion are cultural ties, parenthood and love.

Although I discuss case law, I will not present a legal analysis, nor an extensive overview of the relevant European case law. I merely want to highlight some landmark cases, as examples of how implicit norms work, reading them as texts that construct meanings of gender and ethnicity (Smart, 1991; Frug, 1992). In the conclusions, I shall present 'the right of domicile' as an alternative strategy to review the position of women with migrant partners. The right of domicile would mean that anyone with citizenship or permanent residence in a country has a right to choose domicile in that country, which includes the right to establish family life with foreign family members.

First norm: cultural ties

Boultif[1]

The Algerian national Mr Boultif entered Switzerland in 1992. Shortly after, he married his Swiss wife. The couple had no children. In 1995, he was convicted to 18 months' imprisonment because of several criminal acts. The Court of Appeal increased the sentence to two years. Mr Boultif was released from prison early on grounds of good behaviour. After having served his prison sentence, he worked as a gardener and electrician. In May 1998 the immigration authorities refused the renewal of his residence permit.

The Swiss Federal Court found the refusal to renew the residence permit justified, not in violation of Article 8 of the European Convention on Human Rights (ECRM) and necessary in the interests of public order and safety. The applicant had lived in Algeria most of his life and had not demonstrated particularly close ties to Switzerland. While it would not be easy for Mrs Boultif to follow him to Algeria, it was not completely impossible. She spoke French and had had telephone contact with her mother-in-law. Because Mrs Boultif had worked most of her life, she was not economically dependent on her husband. The couple could also establish their family life in Italy, where the applicant had lived lawfully for several years before coming to Switzerland.

The European Court saw the refusal to renew the residence permit as interference in Boultif's right to respect for family life. The Court subsequently set out to determine whether this refusal reflected a fair balance between the applicant's right to respect for his family life and the state's interests in preventing disorder and crime. To this end, the Court set out the following guiding principles: the nature and seriousness of the offence; the duration of the residence; the period since the offence; the nationalities of the parties concerned; the family situation – including the duration of the marriage and children; whether the spouse knew about the offence; and whether the spouse could be expected to follow. Relevant also were the difficulties that the spouse would meet in the country of origin of the applicant, although the mere fact of these difficulties could not prevent expulsion. In applying these guidelines to this specific case, the Court seems to have given considerable weight to the Swiss nationality of Boultif's spouse. The Court also took into consideration the fact that the offence had been committed in 1994, and that until his departure to Italy in 2000, Mr Boultif had committed no further offence. Therefore, the Court found the danger for the future mitigated. Finally, the couple's possibility to live elsewhere was considered.

The Court noted that the Swiss Mrs Boultif could not be expected to follow her husband, because she had never lived in Algeria, had no other connections to that country, did not speak Arabic and did not know her family-in-law. It had not been established that the couple could reside lawfully in Italy. The Court considered that the applicant had been subjected to a serious impediment to establish family life, since it was practically impossible for him to establish his family life outside Switzerland, while on the other hand, at the moment that the Swiss authorities decided to refuse his continued stay in Switzerland, the applicant only presented a comparatively limited danger to public order. The Court was thus of the opinion that the interference was not proportionate to the aim pursued. There had accordingly been a violation of Article 8 of the Convention.

In discussing this case, I wish to focus on Mrs Boultif and her right to establish her family life in Switzerland. The question is as follows: under what circumstances does a woman have the right to establish and maintain family life with a migrant husband in her country of citizenship? In the search for an answer to this question, the importance of the case can hardly be underestimated. It sets guidelines for expulsion in public order cases and includes the interests of family members in such cases. However, if we place the *Boultif* case within its historical context, we may also see it in another light. I shall place this case against the historical background of Dutch immigration law, assuming that in other European countries, developments may be more or less comparable.

The historical context

What if the same case had occurred in the Netherlands in 1960? At that time, a Dutch Mrs Boultif would have automatically lost her Dutch nationality upon marrying a foreigner. Hence, she could be expelled together with her husband. Policy in the 1950s stipulated that if a foreign husband was expelled, his wife and children were to be expelled along with him.[2] Mrs Boultif would not have been given a choice. As a woman, her place was with her husband. Expelling the wife together with her husband preserved the unity of the family.

After the law was reformed in 1964, Dutch women no longer lost their Dutch nationality upon marrying a foreign husband. Mrs Boultif, still a Dutch citizen, could no longer be expelled together with her husband. She would have the 'choice' of following her expelled husband or staying behind in the Netherlands, separated from her husband. Dutch case law of this period shows several cases of expulsion of migrant men married to Dutch women, while none of migrant women married to Dutch men.[3]

One might assume that this could be explained by the lower criminal behaviour of women as compared to men. However, two other factors should be mentioned. First, until 1985, foreign women married to Dutch men could opt for Dutch nationality. They could acquire Dutch nationality through a simple declaration, free of charge, without further requirements. If a foreign woman, married to a Dutch national, was threatened with

144

expulsion, she could easily avoid expulsion by opting for Dutch nationality. If she did not want to acquire Dutch nationality, she was still protected from expulsion after one year of marriage. At that point, she automatically acquired the so-called 'blue card' status, a status meant to protect the unity of the family.[4] This protection did not extend to the families of Dutch women since this status was not granted to their foreign husbands. So, while foreign women with a Dutch husband were protected against expulsion, foreign husbands married to Dutch women could be expelled at any time in the event of criminal conviction. Case law shows that, as before 1964, the Dutch woman was expected to follow her husband. Although laws had changed, the underlying ideology had not.

In 1976, the Dutch Secretary of Justice, responsible for immigration law, promised in a media interview that migrant men married to Dutch women would be allowed to stay in the Netherlands after detention. The resulting Dutch case law shows that the courts did not welcome the Secretary's sugges-tion. One court decided that this new policy did not include the 'more serious cases'. In the same verdict, the court rejected the plaintiff's claim that Dutch women were discriminated against, because it 'was not impossible that a non-Dutch woman married to a Dutchman would be expelled in spite of her marriage'.[5] However, this was highly unlikely since, as we have already seen, she could either opt for Dutch nationality or claim the blue card status.

This blue card status was granted to the migrant husbands of Dutch wives after 1977, following questions raised in parliament concerning the dis-criminatory character of the blue card policy. Soon after the blue card status had been granted to foreign men in 1977, this status as such became a topic for debate. It was abolished in 1994, without much ado. At the time, the Secretary of Justice claimed that the aim was not to worsen the position of family members, but to allow for expulsion in case of marriages of convenience and in the event of criminal acts.[6]

The Dutch policy of the so-called 'sliding scale', introduced in 1990, limits the possibilities for expulsion.[7] The question of whether a person can be expelled or not depends on the duration of legal residence in the country and the severity of the sentence applied. After 20 years of legal residence in the Netherlands, expulsion is no longer allowed. Since its introduction, the slid-ing scale has become stricter and recently, the Minister of Integration and Immigration announced her intention to review it once again.[8]

Since the blue card was abolished in 1994, Dutch case law shows an increase in the number of expulsions, almost exclusively involving migrant men and not migrant women. Again, one might suggest that migrant men are more criminal than migrant women. However, another explanation is that it is still women and not men who are expected to follow their partners in the case of expulsion. A Dutch legal scholar drew this conclusion in 1990 when reviewing the European Court's case law. In all the cases that had been dealt with by the Court, it was a woman's foreign partner who was refused residence, and it was the woman who was expected to follow her partner to his country of origin (Swart, 1990: 188).

The development of public order policy and national and European case law since 1960 shows that not much has changed. Reasoning from the perspective of the citizen or permanent residence partners, it is still women, more often than men, who are faced with the dilemma of having to choose between following their spouses or staying behind alone. How the Court proposes to deal with the question of when a woman is expected to follow, becomes clearer through a discussion of a second European Court case, *Amrollahi*.

Amrollahi v Denmark[9]

In *Amrollahi*, an Iranian national applied for asylum in Denmark in 1989. He had deserted the Iranian army in 1987. He was granted a residence and work permit in 1990, and in 1994 his residence permit became permanent. In 1992, he met a Danish woman. They lived together and they had a daughter in 1996. They married in 1997 and had a son, born in 2001. The woman also had a daughter from a previous relationship, who lived with the couple. At first, Amrollahi earned his living as owner of a pizzeria. Since 2000 he had been on welfare and underwent job training while his wife held a job. In 1997, Amrollahi was charged with drugs trafficking, sentenced to three years' imprisonment and expelled from the country for life.

The Danish government claimed that there had been no violation of Article 8 ECRM. Given the seriousness of the crime, expulsion was deemed necessary in a democratic society. Amrollahi was assumed to have strong ties with his country of origin, since he had reached adulthood by the time of his departure and had had his school education there. He was not considered to have strong ties with Denmark, as he had been resident for only eight years at the time of the expulsion order. There was no evidence to prove that his spouse and children would not be able to accompany him to Iran.

The European Court held that the expulsion was in accordance with the law and pursued a legitimate aim. The question of whether the interference with family life was necessary in a democratic society was answered by ascertaining whether the decision to expel struck a fair balance between the interests of the state and the applicant's right to respect for family life. With reference to the *Boultif* case, the Court applied the same criteria.

The European Court took into consideration that drugs trafficking was a serious offence. Amrollahi's connections with his country of origin were considered existing, but not strong, since he had lost contact with his family in 1987 because of his desertion. The ties with Denmark, on the other hand, were strong. These ties included his wife and children, who were all Danish citizens.

The next question was whether the family could establish family life in

Iran. Concerning this question, the Court stated that the wife had never been to Iran, did not speak Farsi and was not a Muslim. Besides her marriage to an Iranian husband, she had no ties with the country. Living in Iran would cause obvious and serious difficulties. The daughter of the previous relationship refused to move to Iran. The Court found that the wife could not be expected to follow the applicant to Iran. Although the applicant had stayed in Turkey and Greece before coming to Denmark, his residence there had been illegal and in the Court's opinion there was no indication that the couple could obtain authorisation to reside lawfully in one of those countries, or in any other country but Iran. Since it was de facto impossible to continue their family life outside Denmark, the expulsion was in violation of § ECRM.

Discussion of *Boultif* and **Amrollahi**

The *Boultif* and *Amrollahi* cases are important, because of the weight attached to the interests of women as citizens. An expulsion order can be in violation of Article 8 ECRM if the event of that expulsion will lead to serious difficulties for the citizen spouse. It should be noted, however, that the mere fact of such difficulties is not sufficient. Second, it is significant that in the *Boultif* case the criterion of threat to the public order is applied in the sense of 'actual threat'. This brings the judgment closer to EC law. Finally, *Boultif* has had an important impact on Dutch case law, where judges deciding on the expulsion of migrants have used the list of guiding principles. This jurisprudence has ensured that in cases of expulsion, the interests of family members are taken into account. However, in other respects it raises several questions, particularly concerning implicit assumptions regarding gender and culture.

In both cases, the women not only had the nationality of the country of residence, they were 'ethnically' Swiss and Danish. Hence, the first question to address is: what if Mrs Boultif had not been a Swiss national by birth, or a white woman? What if she had been a second-generation Algerian woman, born in Switzerland and naturalised at a later age?

More recent case law provides an answer to this question. In the *Yildiz* case, a Turkish man was expelled from Austria because of several thefts and traffic offences. He was married to a woman with Turkish nationality, born in Austria. They had a child, also born in Austria. The European Court considered that although the woman was Turkish, she had been born in Austria. The Austrian authorities had failed to establish whether or not she could be expected to follow her husband to Turkey, in particular whether or not she spoke Turkish and had maintained any links, other than nationality, with that country.[10]

This case seems to imply that there is no difference in the evaluation of the ties between a woman born in Austria of Turkish descent and nationality, and a woman born in Austria, of Austrian descent and nationality. However, the way the ties are evaluated may well to lead to such differences. A closer look at the factors the Court found relevant may clarify this. In *Boultif*, the Court mentions the following factors as relevant.

- Mrs Boultif never lived in the countries of origin of her husband.
- She had no other ties to the country of origin of the husband.
- She did not speak Arabic.
- She did not know her family in law.

The *Amrollahi* case adds the factor:

- She was not a Muslim.

Although it might seem logical to look at the ties with Algeria or Iran when expulsion is considered, the implications for mixed families are problematic. It leads, in fact, to an evaluation of the cultural make-up of the family.

I can explain this by using information provided by NGOs of mixed families. Such NGOs present the mixing of cultures and interculturality as the ideal model for mixed families. The German NGO IAF, for example, speaks of the 'principle of equality' of cultures within a family and encourages the acceptance of cultural differences (IAF, 1989: 123). The Dutch organisation LAWINE focuses on the creation of a bicultural identity, that is, the process by which a person engages in intensive contact with two or more cultures and integrates essential elements of these cultures into his or her personality. LAWINE also contends that every bicultural couple has ties with two countries: the country of residence and the migrant partner's country of origin (LAWINE, 2001: 29, 33).

Had she lived up to such a model, as many Dutch and German women in mixed families try to do, Mrs Boultif would at least have visited Algeria several times, if not lived there for some time.[11] She would have met her family-in-law; she would have spoken some Arabic. She might or might not have converted to Islam, or she would have studied some of the underlying thoughts of Islam. Had she and Mr Boultif had children, these children would have been brought up biculturally and bilingually, and they would also have visited the country of their father, of their Algerian grandparents. In short, Algeria would not have been a strange, foreign country to Mrs Boultif. She would have had ties to both countries.

However, living up to this bicultural ideal could have cost Mr and Mrs Boultif dearly. The implication of *Boultif* is that in such a case, Mrs Boultif could have been expected to follow her husband to his country of origin. Here, again, I would suggest that not that much has changed since the 1960s. One of the most important arguments for taking away the nationality of women who married a foreign husband was their supposed cultural and social alienation. The woman was no longer assumed to belong to her own society, but was supposed to become part of her husband's cultural and social group. Hence, she could and should follow him to his country of origin (De Hart, 2005).

Furthermore, if we see how ties with the husband's country of origin are evaluated, the differences between the Swiss Mrs Boultif and the Turkish Mrs Yildiz become evident. The European Court judged that the Austrian authorities failed to establish whether Mrs Yildiz could follow her husband to Turkey. They failed to establish if she spoke Turkish and if she had ties to the country, other than nationality. The question is how such an evaluation would have worked out. The case does not indicate that Mrs Yildiz spoke Turkish. However, she had visited Turkey several times, she had lived there for a while, and had left her child with relatives there. She had ties with both countries. One might suggest that this happens more often and is more self-evident in the case of second-generation migrant women. The logic followed by the Court suggests that migrant women like Mrs Yildiz can more readily be expected to follow their husbands than white women like Mrs Boultif. In a case concerning a Moroccan father with a wife and children in the Netherlands – which was declared inadmissible – the European Court explicitly considered that the wife 'is of Moroccan origin and that she has both Netherlands and Moroccan nationality'.[12]

Similar differences occur in Dutch public order cases. In a decision of the Council of State, Administrative Jurisdiction Division, it was decided that a wife and children of Turkish descent could be expected to follow their Turkish husband and father to Turkey after his expulsion, although the wife and children had all been born in the Netherlands. The factors taken into account were the guiding principles of *Boultif*: the wife and children spoke Turkish, the wife visited Turkey regularly, her family (not she herself) had ties with the country, and she and the children had both Turkish and Dutch nationality. The conclusion of the Court was that they could not be put on a par with someone who had no ties with the country other than by marriage or family.[13] The cultural make-up of the family was more decisive than the fact that the woman and the children had been born in the Netherlands and had been living there all their lives. The conclusion is that the *Boultif* case is not only about the cultural make-up of a family, but also about ethnicity.

We have now sufficiently addressed our first question, namely: What if Mrs Boultif had had ties with Algeria? The next question is: What if Mr Boultif had been an American national? What if his country of origin had not been Algeria, but the United States? How would the European Court then have evaluated the 'seriousness of the difficulties that the spouse is likely to encounter in the country of origin'? Although this has not been made explicit, it seems relevant that the countries of origin in all of these cases were non-western, Islamic countries. Especially in the *Amrollahi* case, the implicit assumption seems to be that a western woman cannot be expected to live in an Islamic country like Iran.

Several authors have established that, in terms of national law in any case, the husband's country of origin does matter. Bhabha and Shutter (1994: 58), for example, have concluded that in British law a woman is more likely to be expected to follow her husband if he comes from a western country than if he comes from a non-western country. Similarly, Van Blokland *et al.* (1999: 112) have concluded that, in the Netherlands, women with an Islamic background have a better chance of getting a residence permit after divorce than women of non-Islamic background. Judges seem inclined to protect women from circumstances in such non-western, Islamic countries.

Of course, it is favourable that a court takes the position of women in a certain country into account in its decisions. However, this is not without problems. The first problem is that the European court case law is in danger of reproducing the image of barbaric, Islamic countries from which we need to protect 'our', and may be even 'their' women. What is more, it suggests that there is no problem in a woman having to follow her husband to the United States.

A further implication is that women's problems arise from the circumstances in their husbands' Islamic countries of origin, rather than from national immigration regimes that force them to follow their husbands. In such reasoning, it is Islamic law, not our liberated European law, that is causing women these problems. From this perspective, the European Court proves to be a 'colonial feminist'. Colonial feminism refers to a way of speaking and writing about women and Islam that reproduces the image of Islam as oppressor and of the west as liberator. It legitimises the western position of power. In this manner, the debate on the position of women is caught up in a struggle about culture (Ahmed, 1992). This is exactly what happened in the cases *Boultif* and *Amrollahi*.

Second norm: parenthood

Berrehab [14]

Berrehab was a Moroccan father. Shortly after his divorce from a Dutch woman, their daughter Rebecca was born. Because of the divorce, Berrehab was threatened with expulsion. He saw his daughter four times a week for several hours at a time. After his expulsion to Morocco, he applied for a new residence permit. This was refused, as was his application for a short-term visa.

The European Court stressed the fact that the case of *Berrehab* did not concern a first admission, but a person who already held legal residence in the Netherlands, who had a house and a job and had family ties there. The Court specifically addressed the interests of the daughter Rebecca. Intense and frequent contact with her father was especially relevant for her, given her young age. It was clear that she could not follow her father to Morocco. It was also clear that exercising visiting rights from Morocco was not a realistic alternative. Hence, there was a violation of Article 8, the right to respect for family life.

Berrehab turned out to be a groundbreaking case for Dutch immigration law. It led to an amendment of policy, making visiting rights with a child in the Netherlands a ground for granting a residence permit.[15]

In principle, this case would affect policies in two situations. In the first, as in *Berrehab*, the migrant father's residence permit might be withdrawn after divorce; he would then be allowed to stay in order to protect the family life between himself and the child.

In the alternative situation, a migrant mother's residence permit would be withdrawn following divorce; she could then be allowed to remain in the Netherlands in order to protect the family life between the Dutch father and the child, which would be violated if she were to take the child with her. Here, the family life between the father and child, not that between the mother and child, would be at stake (assuming that the child is being taken care of by the mother and would leave with her in the event of expulsion). In the alternative situation, however, the impact of *Berrehab* on Dutch policy and case law turned out to be disappointing. A residence permit was only granted if visiting rights had been determined by court order, if they took place on a regular basis, and if the father paid alimony.[16]

The effect of *Berrehab*, and its impact on Dutch practice, was to make migrant parents dependent on the behaviour of Dutch parents. If visiting rights were not being effected, either because the Dutch father was not interested or the Dutch mother refused to co-operate, there would be no grounds for prolonging residence after divorce. Moreover, the fact that since 1998, parental custody remains with both parents after divorce, did not lead to any changes in Dutch immigration policy. A custodial parent with a child in the Netherlands could still be expelled.

In short, extending residence after divorce in the interest of family life with a child depended on so many factors and so many requirements, that critics spoke of a discrepancy between immigration law and family law. While in family law the principle that family life between parent and child should be protected had gained in importance, in immigration policy this principle became reduced to a bare minimum (Van Blokland, 1997; Van Walsum, 2000).

In the *Ciliz* case,[17] the European Court also drew attention to this discrepancy between family and immigration law. More particularly, it showed how decisions in immigration law could prevent access to family law procedures. Ciliz was expelled in the midst of pending procedures in which the family court and the Council for Child Protection were trying to mediate between a mother and a father involved in a conflict over visiting rights. After Ciliz had been expelled, he was not allowed to return on a short-term visa to take part in further proceedings.

In *Ciliz*, the Court made clear that family life is not a static, but a dynamic concept and that the migrant father should be allowed to develop family life with his child. The Dutch courts soon took up this conclusion and Dutch immigration policy was amended accordingly. It now includes attempts of the migrant parent to have a family life, such as trial visiting rights. However, this policy also states that the violation of family life may be justified in the situation where the family law procedure concerning visiting rights has been started in order to acquire residence rights.[18]

The *Ciliz* case brings the norms of parenthood in family law and immigration law closer together. The European Court acknowledged that 'the relationship between the parents following the separation was not as harmonious with respect to the father's access to his child as in the case of *Berrehab*. Neither can it be said that the applicant demonstrated at all times to what extent he valued meetings with his son.' In other words, although Ciliz was clearly not the model-father that Berrehab was, he still had a right to family life.

The result of *Ciliz* is that decisions taken within the context of immigration law should take into account decisions taken in family law. The flipside, however, is that immigration issues now enter into the family courts. Increasingly, family courts deciding on custody and visiting rights anticipate immigration law decisions. Since immigration decisions are often negative, this development may seriously harm the migrant parents' chances of obtaining custody or visiting rights.

An example is *Rodrigues Da Silva and Hoogkamer v The Netherlands*, now pending before the European Court.[19] In this case, the Dutch Council for Child Protection advised to grant sole custody to the Dutch father, because the residence status of the Brazilian mother, who was an illegal resident in the Netherlands, was very insecure. The Council wanted to ensure that the mother could not take the Dutch child with her in the event that she had to return to Brazil. The family court decided accordingly.

It is possible that the Court was working on the assumption that removing the mother's custody might improve her chances of being allowed to remain in the Netherlands, since expulsion would put her family life with the child at risk. The question is whether this assumption was correct. It was equally conceivable that, once the mother no longer held custody, her chance of getting a residence permit would diminish because, as we have seen, the chances of a migrant mother being granted a residence permit are greatest when the family life of the child and the Dutch father is at risk. Although the case reads like a deliberate attempt by mother and father to solve their immigration law problems, in fact the course they chose was a risky one. Being granted full custody, the father's family life with the child was assured. In effect, the family court set the mother aside.

It might also have made it easier for the immigration authorities to expel the mother.

In spite of *Berrehab* and *Ciliz*, the interests of immigration law are still decisive, and are starting to infiltrate family law. As demonstrated, the position of migrant parents after divorce is still precarious. However, immigration law also affects the citizen or permanently resident (ex) partner's possibilities to share the care for their children with their ex-partner. The *Berrehab* case is not only about a migrant father's right to enjoy family life with his daughter, but also about the former Mrs Berrehab's right to share custody arrangements and visiting rights with her ex-husband. It is about her right to respect for family life as well.

Third norm: love

Akrich[20]

The last case was decided by the European Court of Justice, and concerns the freedom of movement and the right to respect for family life of a British woman and her Moroccan husband, Akrich.

Akrich married his British wife in 1996 after having tried in vain to enter Britain on a false French passport. By June 1997, however, it became clear that Akrich would not be admitted in spite of this marriage. His wife subsequently moved to Ireland with the intention of having her husband join her there. At his own request, the British authorities brought him to Ireland. Both of the partners worked in Ireland. Mrs Akrich clearly stated her intentions to move there: she knew that a stay of about six months would give her the right to return to the United Kingdom with her husband, because then she would have made use of her right of free movement as an EU-citizen. Before their return to the UK, Mrs Akrich found a job and they settled their living arrangements. Again, the British authorities denied Mr Akrich access. In their view, this couple had intentionally abused Community law in order to circumvent national immigration law.

Because of the right of free movement within the EU, EU-citizens can choose for themselves the country to which they wish to emigrate within the EU, together with their partner and children. As a consequence, in some countries the immigration regime is more favourable for EU-citizens than for their own citizens. This is known as the problem of 'reversed discrimination'. In the Netherlands, a British woman with a Moroccan husband has a better legal position than a Dutch woman with a Moroccan husband.

In an earlier decision, the European Court of Justice determined that after a citizen woman had worked in another EU country, and taken her husband with her, she could return to her country of citizenship with her husband under the conditions of the more favourable EU-law, because she now counted as an EU-citizen. Otherwise, her right of free movement as an EU-citizen would be limited.[21]

In *Akrich*, the Court introduced the new condition that the third-country partner, who is married to an EU-citizen, has to be lawfully resident in the country before he leaves for another EU-country with an EU-husband or wife. Since Akrich had no lawful residence in the UK, the couple could not return to Britain.

The *Akrich* case ended the practice of the so-called 'EU-turn', which is exactly what Mr and Mrs Akrich did: couples who met with insurmountable hindrances in national immigration law left for another EU-country to live and work there for a limited period of time (one year), with the aim of returning to the country of origin under the EU-law regime. Following the *Akrich* decision, this EU-turn would no longer be an option in many cases.

For the aim of this chapter, another aspect of the case is just as relevant. Apparently, the marriage of Akrich and his wife was suspected of being a marriage of convenience, although it had existed for four years at the time the pre-judicial questions were brought before the European Court, and Mrs Akrich was willing to move abroad for a year in order to be able to live with her husband in Britain. It was decided that the principle of free movement is not applicable when the national of a Member State and the national of a non-Member State have entered into a marriage of convenience in order to circumvent the provisions relating to entry and residence of nationals of non-Member States.

Thus, the intentions of the partners become relevant, although the Court does not state how these intentions should be determined. In his conclusion to *Akrich*, the Attorney General Geelhoed referred to the Resolution of the Council of 1997 on the subject of combating marriages of convenience.[22] The EU Directive on family reunification also mentions marriages of convenience as marriage concluded with the sole aim of circumventing the rules on entry and residence.[23]

With the introduction of the marriage of convenience in EU-law, love has become decisive for the freedom of movement. Because that is what the marriage of convenience is about: in their examination of suspected marriages of convenience, immigration officials do not question whether the aim of the marriage was solely entry or residence, but question whether there was love between the partners. This makes immigration officials into the 'moral gatekeepers' of the European Union; moral gatekeepers, because they give their subjective judgement on the cultural and social desirability of the marriage (Wray, 2004).

It is no coincidence that Mr Akrich was Moroccan and male, and his wife British. The precarious residence status of Mr Akrich alone cannot sufficiently explain the British authorities' suspicion.

Dutch immigration practice shows that it is specifically Dutch white women with husbands from Islamic countries who are suspected of having entered into marriages of convenience, because these marriages deviate from the norm of a romantic love marriage (De Hart, 2001). The construction of the marriage of convenience is strongly connected to more general social attitudes towards mixed marriages which, overall, are not positive, especially where mixed marriages of Dutch women with foreign men are concerned. In the construction of the marriage of convenience and in the general social attitude towards mixed marriages, assumptions about women are similar. Women are viewed as 'foolhardy' (Ware, 1992: 231–2). Foolhardiness is one of the most important characteristics of white women in Orientalist discourse. It is the white, western woman who by her behaviour endangers both herself and her society. She has some emancipated inclinations, which are part of her unwillingness to conform. It is her fate to dabble in things she knows nothing about. Choosing an Islamic husband is typical behaviour for a foolhardy woman. It is not a conscious choice, since a truly liberated western woman would never do it. By marrying an Islamic husband, a woman proves her irrationality and powerlessness. She is not aware that, first, he is only marrying her because of the residence permit and, second, that in marrying him, she is giving up her liberties as a western woman. This discourse also casts the migrant man in the negative role of oppressor and user of women, as the eternal perpetrator.

The *Akrich* case shows that the construction of the marriage of convenience and the negative stereotypes that it contains, do not solely affect couples in the same situation as Akrich. The marriage of convenience has become an argument for limiting the freedom of movement of all EU-citizens, men or women, with a partner who is a third-country national, Moroccan or American. It is one of the reasons why it is so important to critically examine the implicit norms in immigration law: they affect everyone.

Conclusions

I conclude this chapter with some theoretical and methodical implications for studying the gendered effects of immigration law.

First, it is striking that in each of the cases under discussion, *Boultif*, *Amrollahi*, *Berrehab*, *Ciliz* and *Akrich*, men and not women were the partners with a dependent residence permit based on marriage. We should read the Court's case law not only in terms of its implications for the rights of migrant men, but also as being about the rights of women, white women and migrant women, citizens and permanent residents. Hence, studying the gendered implications of immigration law means not only looking at women as the dependent partners. It has never been the case that only men 'import' their brides; women 'import' grooms too (Kofman, 1999: 272). Solely focusing on wives as dependent partners in family reunification limits our view of the much more varied and complicated ways in which women's lives and relationships are affected by immigration law. What is at stake here is women's right to choose their partners, and to establish family life in their country of residence and citizenship. The gendered effects of immigration law are that women, maybe not formally but in any case effectively, have less rights to establish their family life in their country of citizenship or residence than men have.

Second, our discussion of European court case law implies that we cannot study gender adequately without including other factors, such as ethnicity and culture. We must adopt an 'intersectional approach' when studying the gendered effects of immigration law (Crenshaw, 1990). Gender and ethnicity are closely connected and cannot be studied separately. Men and women in one group are constructed differently from men and women in another group. Gender has ethnic aspects and ethnicity is always gendered (Wekker, 1998: 51).

Third, a study of gender and immigration law should include males. As demonstrated, a woman's right to respect for family life is affected as much by the images of women as it is by the images of men. Ratna Kapur (2002) addresses the problems of migrant women as a result of being represented as the eternal victims. If women are the eternal victims, then migrant men are the eternal perpetrators. We cannot effectively combat the image of women as eternal victims without combating the image of migrant men as the eternal perpetrators. Gender is not only about women, it is also about men.

Finally, the question is: What is the alternative? In a case like that of *Boultif*, how could one avoid the problems indicated? Is it, in fact, not the case that a woman with no ties at all with Algeria, would experience far more difficulties in following her husband than a woman who is familiar with the country and the language? Is an alternative argument possible?

I suggest centring the 'right of domicile' as an effective strategy. In 1985, in the *Abdulaziz* case, the European Court of Human Rights decided that states did not have to respect a couple's choice of domicile. Thus, a state is not obligated to admit the foreign partner of a citizen or of a permanent resident.[24] In *Akrich*, the European Court of Justice decided that the right to family life (Article 8 ECHR) should be taken into account in case of admission of the third-country national spouse into a Member State.

However, citizenship or permanent residence loses its meaning if it does not include the right to establish a family in the country where one is living (Boeles, 2000: 186–7). The consequence of centring the right of domicile is that the deciding factor is the family and the private life that has been established in the country of residence. This family life cannot be crossed out against ties with the country of origin of the migrant partner. The domicile is where one is at home. Having a domicile in one place does not exclude having activities or ties in another place. Ties in another country do not erase the domicile in the country of residence, nor could they provide grounds for expulsion.

The right of domicile would mean that anyone with citizenship or permanent residence in a country would have the right to chose domicile in that country, and thus, a right to establish family life there with foreign family members. Although in this chapter only the position of the right of domicile for women with a migrant partner has been addressed, a right of domicile would include anyone with citizenship or a permanent residence status for that country, including children (Bhabha, 2004).

I am aware that the right of domicile offers no solution for several issues addressed in other contributions to this volume, such as undocumented migrants or trafficked women. The right of domicile should be understood as a minimum standard: the least that citizenship and permanent immigrant status should entail is the right of domicile. It is a start.

However, as we have already seen, the European Court of Human Rights maintains that states do not have to respect a couple's choice of domicile. Against the background of current immigration law, the right of domicile may seem a radical suggestion, but it is not. In fact, the right of domicile was the starting point of immigration law in times of formal gender discrimination. At the time, the right of domicile of men was acknowledged in immigration law and citizenship law in most countries of the world. Female partners were granted either the husband's citizenship or a secured residence status. This norm was in the minds of the drafting committee that prepared Article 8 of the European Convention on Human Rights in the 1950s. They thought that the father, as head of the family, could not be an independent citizen, could not feel free in his own country, if he was menaced in his own home, and if, every day, the state could steal from his soul or the conscience of his children (quoted in Knop, 2001).

It seems this line of thinking has been left together with the patriarchal structure of immigration law (Knop, 2001). But maybe we should not leave it, but uphold it in a non-patriarchal and modernised form, in order to make sure that Mrs Boultif, Mrs Berrehab, Mrs Yildiz and Mrs Akrich can feel themselves independent, free citizens, with their souls and consciences unthreatened.

Notes

1 ECHR, *Boultif v Swizerland*, 2 August 2001, Appl No 54273/00.
2 Aliens Circular (Vreemdelingencirculaire) of 1954, date of commencement 1-4-1955.
3 E.g. Koninklijk Besluit, 15 March 1975, *Rechtspraak Vreemdelingenrecht* 1975, 8.
4 Article 10(2), Dutch Aliens Act 1965.
5 President rechtbank's Gravenhage, 14 January 1977, *Rechtspraak Vreemdelingenrecht* 1997, 1.
6 Nota van Toelichting bij de wijziging van het Vreemdelingenbesluit, Staatsblad 1994, 8, p 17. Answer to the letter of Nederlands Centrum Buitenlanders, *Migrantenrecht* 1994, p 75. See also Groenendijk and Barzilay, 2001: 24–7.

7 Vreemdelingencirculaire 1994, A4 4.3.2.2, date of commencement 20 February 1990, bijlage bij de wijziging van de vreemdelingencirculaire 7287/90/DVZ (TBV 33), p 1.

8 TBV 2002/34, 30 July 2002. Verslag notaoverleg Illegalennota, 21 June 2004, 29 537, No 15.

9 ECHR, *Amrollahi v Denmark*, 11 July 2002, Appl No 56811/00.

10 ECHR, *Yildiz v Austria*, 31 October 2002, Appl No 37295/97.

11 For argument's sake, I ignore the fact that at the time it was very dangerous for western women to live in Algeria because of the political situation, a fact brought forward by the Boultifs, but ignored by the Court.

12 ECHR, *Amara v The Netherlands*, 5 October 2004, Appl No 6914/02. It should be noted that the fact that the wife has dual nationality is caused by Morocco's refusal to allow renunciation of nationality.

13 Afdeling Bestuursrechtspraak van de Raad van State, 25 September 2003, *Jurisprudentie Vreemdelingenrecht* 2003, 503. See also Afdeling Bestuursrechtspraak van de Raad van State, 2 February 2005, *Jurisprudentie Vreemdelingenrecht* 2005, 130.

14 ECHR, *Berrehab v Netherlands*, 21 June 1988, Appl No 3/1987/126/177.

15 Vreemdelingencirculaire 2000, B 2/13.2.4.

16 Boeles in annotation of *Ciliz, Jurisprudentie Vreemdelingenrecht* 2000/187.

17 ECHR, *Ciliz v Netherlands*, 11 July 2000, Appl No. 29192/95.

18 Vreemdelingencirculaire 2000, B 2/13.2.4.

19 ECHR, *Rodrigues Da Silva and Rachal Hoogkamer v The Netherlands*, 14 September 2004, decision of admissibility, Appl No 50435/99.

20 ECJ, 23 September 2003, C–109/01 (*Akrich*).

21 ECJ, 7 July 1992, C370/90 (*Singh*).

22 Council Resolution on Measures to be Adopted on the Combating of Marriages of Convenience, 97/C 382/01, adopted 4 December 1997.

23 Article 16 (2)(b). EC Council Directive 2003/86/EC of 22 September 2003 on the right to family reunification; OJ L251, 03.10.2003, p.0012–0018.

24 ECHR, *Abdulaziz v United Kingdom*, 28 May 1985, 9214/80, 9473/81, 9474/81.

References

Ahmed, Leila (1992) *Women and Gender in Islam: Historical Roots of a Modern Debate*, New Haven: Yale University Press

Bhabha, Jacqueline (2004) 'The "mere fortuity" of birth? Are children citizens?', *Differences* 15(2), pp 91–117

Bhabha, Jacqueline and Shutter, Sue (1994) *Women's Movement, Women under Immigration, Nationality and Refugee Law*, Stoke-on-Trent: Trentham Books

Boeles, Pieter (2000) 'Nederland en toekomstig Europees gezinsherenigingsrecht', *Migrantenrecht*, pp 178–87

Crenshaw, Kimberle (1990) 'A black feminist critique of anti-discrimination law and politics', in Kairys, David (ed), *The Politics of Law. A Progressive Critique*, New York: Pantheon, pp 195–218

De Hart, Betty (2001) 'Der herzensgute Kerl und die unbesonnene Frau', in IAF (ed), *Abschlussbericht Fabienne, Strategien gegen Diskriminierung*, Frankfurt: IAF, pp 18–27

De Hart, Betty (2006) 'The morality of Maria Toet. Gender, citizenship and the construction of the nation-state', *Journal of Ethnic and Migration Studies* 32(1), pp 49–68

Frug, Mary J (1992) *Postmodern Legal Feminism*, London and New York: Routledge

Groenendijk, Kees and Barzilay, Robin (2001) *De Verzwakking van de Rechtspositie van Toegelaten Vreemdelingen (1990–2000)*, Utrecht: Forum

IAF (1989) 'Jede Blume duftet anders', *Bereicherungen und mögliche Konfliktursachen in bi-nationalen Families und Partnerschaften*, Frankfurt: IAF

Kapur, Ratna (2002) 'The tragedy of victimization rhetoric: Resurrecting the "native" subject in international/post-colonial feminist legal politics', *Harvard Human Rights Journal* 15 (Spring), pp 1–37

Knop, Karen (2001) 'Relational nationality', in Aleinikoff, Thomas A and Klusmeyer, Douglas (eds), *Citizenship Today: On Gender and Nationality in International Law*, Washington, DC: Carnegie Endowment, pp 89–126

Kofman, Eleonore (1999) 'Female "birds of passage" a decade later: Gender and immigration in the European Union', *International Migration Review* 33(2), pp 269–99

LAWINE, Stichting (2001) *Biculturele Relaties in Nederland*, Amsterdam: LAWINE

Smart, Carol (1991) 'De vrouw in het juridische vertoog', *Tijdschrift voor Genderstudies* 12(4), pp 499–514

Swart, Albertus HJ (1990) 'Artikel 8 van het Europees Verdrag tot bescherming van de rechten van de mens', *Handelingen Nederlandse Juristenvereniging* 120(1), Zwolle: WEJ Tjeenk Willink

Van Blokland, Els (1997) 'Zorg, gezag en ouderschap', *Nemesis* 13(3), pp 85–7

Van Blokland, Els, Jansen, Sabine and Vegter, Marlies (1999) *Onzekere Rechten. Onderzoek naar de Rechtspositie van Vrouwen met een Afhankelijke Verblijfsvergunning Na Scheiding*, Nijmegen: Ars Aequi/ Clara Wichmanninstituut

Van Walsum, Sarah (2000) 'Het ene gezin is het andere niet; gezinsnormen en (on)gelijkheid in het Nederlandse immigratiebeleid', in Holtmaat, Hendrika MT (ed), *De Toekomst van Gelijkheid. De Juridische en Maastchappelijke Inbedding van de Gelijkebehandelingsnorm*, Utrecht: Commissie Gelijke Behandeling, pp 45–60

Ware, Vron (1992) *Beyond the Pale: White Women, Racism and History*, London: Verso

Wekker, Gloria (1998) 'Gender, identiteitsvorming en multiculturalisme: Notities over de Nederlandse multiculturele samenleving', in Geuijen, Catharina HM (ed), *Multiculturalisme*, Utrecht: Lemma, pp 39–53

Wray, Helena (2004) 'Hidden purpose: Ethnic minority international marriages and "intention to live together" ', unpublished paper presented at Hart Legal Workshop, London

Part III

NATIONAL CASE STUDIES

9

TRANSNATIONAL CONTINGENCY

The domestic work of migrant
women in Austria

Bettina Haidinger

This chapter will explore the social, economic and legal-political conditions that have led to the establishment of an informal labour market for domestic services, in which predominantly female migrants are employed. In the first section I shall outline some recent developments in the field of domestic work. Next I shall describe the concrete working conditions of (migrant) women employed in private households in Austria. Finally, I shall explore to what extent existing socio-economic structures may help explain why specifically migrant women are currently being employed in Austria as domestic workers.

Housework commodified

The organisation of housework is a broadly experienced social problem, which receives very little public attention. The regulation of housework and care in the current socio-demographic context has been left to the workings of the existent structures of the welfare state, the migration regime and the gendered division of labour. Solutions are sought on an individual, household-internal basis. A common strategy is to employ a paid domestic worker, with the result that housework is being commodified. Tensions surrounding the performance of housework are thus resolved by outsourcing the work involved from the nuclear family to someone from outside. The requisite skills and responsibilities, however, remain with women: women act both as employers and as employees in this sector. To that extent, the chosen strategy for reconciling paid work with family responsibilities has left the gendered division of labour intact. Female employers may have won quality time for their families and/or their careers; the task of running the household remains in the hands of women.

Employing domestic workers can only work as a viable option as long as the workers' earnings remain considerably lower than those of their employers. The purchasing power of (dual-earner) families in the higher income bracket meets the supply of low-cost labour in the service sector. Such a supply exists thanks to the emergence of a specific class of women with no access to alternative sources of income. This development in the labour market has been the result of both structural forms of exclusion and sexist and racist discrimination in the labour market (Ehrenreich, 2003: 95).

Ethnicity and domestic work

In Austria, restrictive immigration laws (Law on Aliens) and the Austrian Alien Employment Law impose important limits on migrant women's options, which I shall elaborate on further in this chapter. These laws, which regulate access to the labour market according to nationality, resonate with a parallel development towards the segmentation of the labour market along the lines of ethnicity, thus helping to reshape the hierarchy of the labour market. The result has been an ideological revaluation of migrant women's work as that of servants.

The employment of migrant women as domestic workers is then, in part at least, an expression of their ideological position within Austrian society. It is not only because of their low wages that these women are hired as domestic workers. In Austria, migrant women are often perceived of as representing underdeveloped societies and traditional ways of life (see Caixeta *et al.*, 2004). As such, they represent attributes that their employers wish to dissociate from their own emancipated lifestyle, and which they project onto their 'exotic' employees: caring, self-sacrificing, motherly, submissive, tidy. The conjunction of nationality (ethnicity, culture, race) with gender has thus generated a new category of women that can be subordinated to the category of emancipated Austrian women (Anderson, 2000: 152; Cruz Roja, 2004; Haidinger, 2004b: 73).

The new dynamics of the Austrian labour market have also found expression in the allocation of migrant workers – both men and women – to the informal labour market. Migrant women who work as domestics within this shadow economy, in which labour relations are not legally regulated, are very dependent on their employers' good graces and may be subjected to arbitrary uses of power. The unregulated nature of their position is often compounded by the lack of a valid residence permit and/or valid work permit. Thus both in discursive terms and in practice, an 'other' woman is being imagined, created and distinguished from the social reality of the native woman.

In the process, both the value of housework and the nature of the public/private divide are being redefined, bringing a new class of workers into being, employed in a service sector that is largely hidden from view, and introducing a new type of power relationship within the private household. Brigitte

Young (2000) has compared the relationship between employers and employees in the private household to the feudal relations between a lady and her maid. In such relations, formal individual rights do not play a significant role. Rather, these relations are characterised by a highly personalised and hierarchical bond between employer and employee. The husband/male partner remains distant from this constellation. He continues to leave the organisation of his private life to women. In the private sphere he only consumes without having to participate in domestic work, thus remaining free to deploy all his energy in the public sphere.

It is important to note that for the migrant women themselves, paid labour in private households normally serves as a transitional strategy on their way towards building up a future in Austria or elsewhere. For undocumented women, in particular, it represents one of the few ways to secure an income. Domestic work is by no means their preferred job. That they do this work is the result of various circumstances, including extreme hardship. Jobs in this sector typically figure as temporary solutions often correlating with the conditions and circumstances that govern women's lives (Höglinger and Berka, 1994: 57).

Working conditions in private homes

In this section I shall describe some of the characteristics of paid domestic work and the conditions under which migrant women employed in this sector must work, paying particular attention to the situation in Austria.[1]

The employer–employee relationship in private households is characterised by its personal nature and the emotions associated with such an arrangement (see Cruz Roja, 2004; Haidinger, 2004b: 70). The private household forms a very intimate environment, to which labour inspection authorities have no legal access. As a result, they are unable to control labour conditions.[2] Symptomatic of this type of employment is the total lack of enforceable employee rights and the resultant insecurity regarding the duration and regularity of work, as well as the lack of insurance in the event of accident or illness. Only in very few instances is a contract drawn up. In the majority of cases, informal employment is the dominant form.

The Vienna Chamber of Labour consultation services report that the most frequently registered complaints concern wages that have been withheld,[3] working conditions that fail to meet legally prescribed standards, irregular employment of workers via the employer's own company,[4] and excessive working hours. Other complaints refer to employers taking advantage of their employees' lack of language skills or their social isolation (Arbeiterkammer Wien, 2000). Full payment of salaries, payment of agreed bonuses, paid vacation,[5] pay for overtime, supplementary payments, regular breaks during working hours, social insurance benefits and time off are the exception.

The reality is that employers can and do take advantage of the fact that their domestic workers lack a residence permit. In the worst-case scenario, these workers may be deported, but there are no legal repercussions, as a rule, for their employers. Although legal minimum standards like the Austrian Law on Domestic Help and Domestic Workers (*Hausgehilfen- und Hausangestelltengesetz*) or the minimum wage tariff agreed upon by the social partners can, in theory, be applied and sued for in these cases, standing up for their rights involves a high risk for the women involved. Moreover, it is often impossible to supply the evidence required, given the reluctance of witnesses (employer, neighbours, other domestic workers) to co-operate.

Modes of employment: live-in, au-pair or live-out

A live-in not only works within her employer's household but also resides in her home. Living space and workplace are one and the same. Bridget Anderson argues that live-in domestic work can be a rational choice for recently arrived migrant women (Anderson, 2000: 39). The problems of housing and work are solved in one blow. The woman can minimise her expenditures and get accustomed to the new language and living circumstances. Moreover, this option not only provides her with a roof over her head, it also keeps her out of sight of the authorities, an important point of consideration for women without a residence permit. She can live inconspicuously in her employer's home, where she works and spends most of her time. At the same time, however, the live-in arrangement makes her very dependent on her employer. Her work, her housing and her chances of being able to remain in the country are all primarily enabled and determined by the co-operation and good graces of her employer, who has the power to bring everything to a sudden end. Moreover, in the long run, live-in domestic work does not provide sufficient financial security for the women involved. The provision of room and board helps justify their extremely low wages, thus keeping them financially dependent on their employers. In this position of compounded dependency, it is difficult for these women to resist abuses of power.

On the whole, this mode of employment is not very common in Austria, but the number of au-pairs working in Austrian households is rising. Au-pair arrangements form a specific type of live-in employment which is common throughout Europe and which has recently experienced a significant increase in popularity in Austria. An au-pair agreement in Austria involves the engagement of a young woman (men rarely participate in these arrangements) aged between 18 and 28, for the undertaking of some domestic work and babysitting in exchange for a small allowance and room and board. These young women are also supposed to take advantage of the opportunity to learn more about the language, culture and society of the host country.

On 1 April 2001, an amendment to the Austrian Law on Alien Employment, introduced by the Ministry of Economy and Labour, came into effect, exempting au-pairs from non-EEA countries from the quotas imposed on migrant labour.[6] As a result, employers presently need only register their request for an au-pair with the regional Labour Market Service (AMS).

> The federal Minister of Economy and Labour, Dr Martin Barten-stein, sees this measure as offering an opportunity to young people while providing support to young families. Given that the number of au-pair agreements in Austria has been reduced to nearly nil during the past few years, this amendment opens up the possibility for young families in Austria to take in young people aged between 18 and 28 years, originating from either Central and Eastern Europe or countries overseas, for a maximum period of one year, so that they can perform light household tasks as well as mind the children.
>
> (Press release, Federal Ministry of Economy and Labour, 1 April 2001)

This facilitation of au-pair employment should not be viewed solely in terms of labour migration regulation, but also as an aspect of welfare state reform. Within the parameters set by the prevailing trends to restrict labour migration and cut down on social services, this amendment provides for jobs for migrants that can help to resolve tensions created by these very same policy developments. By exempting au-pairs from the strict quota for work-ers from non-EEA countries, it has made it possible to employ de facto workers in private households. Au-pairs are not registered as workers, so their contracts are not subject to industrial law. Their low wages have now become officially justified on the grounds that they are receiving room and board along with the opportunity to accumulate social and cultural capital through their stay in Austria (Hess, 2002: 107). Austrian families are now officially allowed to take on a domestic worker to carry out housekeeping and childcare duties for 25 hours a week, at a rate of €2 per hour. Since it is unlikely that the guest families will keep to the stipulated working hours for au-pairs, these women will most likely face the same problems that confront the live-in domestic workers described above: unpaid overtime; the obliga-tion to perform tasks they weren't hired to do; degrading treatment – such as not being allowed to share in the family meals; and various forms of humili-ation ranging from racial discrimination to threats and sexual abuse (Hess, 2002: 106).

Different circumstances characterise the working conditions of the so-called live-outs. These domestic workers do not live in their employer's home. Their working place is therefore separate from their living space. This is the pre-dominant form of employment in France, Germany (Anderson, 2000: 69) and Austria. The work itself is characterised by irregular working hours spread over a number of households. It requires flexibility, mobility, and a tight and well-planned working schedule (Gather and Meissner, 2002: 130). Steady, full-time employment is the exception; work is usually negotiated on an hourly, weekly or monthly basis (Haidinger, 2004b: 71). The fact that these jobs are contracted on an hourly basis does not mean that they are insignificant. Migrant women in particular can average up to 60 to 70 hours per week, spread over up to ten households (Höglinger and Berka, 1994: 37).

The relative importance of formal and informal labour in the domestic service sector

According to the Austrian Social Security Agency (ASSA), in 2004, 6,950 persons formally employed in private households were engaged in so-called minor employment, that is with a minimum insurance covering accidents only. Some 6,239 of these workers were women. From 1996 to 2004 the number of people working in this sector in minor employment, measured in absolute terms, more than doubled. At the same time, the number of full-time or part-time employees with full insurance coverage (covering the risks of old age, medical costs and unemployment as well as accidents) dropped from 4,680 to 3,377 (ASSA, 2005). Table 9.1 gives an overview of the employment trends in the entire private household sector. The percentage of those engaged in minor employment increased from 39 per cent in 1996 to 67 per cent in 2004.

In 2004, foreign workers made up 18.1 per cent of all those formally employed in private homes, while they only accounted for 12 per cent of the total working population in Austria. Still, the number of foreign workers officially noted as employed in private households remains low: 612 in 2004, only 0.2 per cent of the total number of foreign employees in Austria (Biffl, 2004: 54). But while these official employment statistics reveal only small numbers, ASSA estimates that the total number of domestic workers (with or without Austrian nationality) employed in the informal sector stood at about 100,000. How do we account for this discrepancy?

Where direct statistical evidence is lacking, economists have developed

Table 9.1 Employees in the economic sector 'private households,' 1996–2004

	Persons in minor employment	*Insured persons*	*Total number of persons in full-, part-time and minor employment*	*% of persons in minor employment from total employees*
1996	2,978	4,680	7,658	39%
1998	3,707	4,519	8,226	45%
2000	5,331	4,004	9,335	57%
2002	6,620	3,683	10,303	64%
2004	6,950	3,377	10,327	67%

Source: ASSA, 2005.

models for estimating the amount of money circulating in the shadow economy, based on figures extrapolated from related sources (Kassberger and Schwarzl, 2000). Thus ASSA data on income from employment in private households, which was €74 million in 2003, have been compared to the actual expenditures made by households on domestic help. These expenditures are calculated on the basis of a consumer survey held in 1993–94 (Statistik Austria, 2004).

As indicated in Table 9.1, approximately 10,300 persons were formally employed as domestic workers in 2003, receiving a total of €74 million for their services. The average salary of a domestic worker therefore amounted to €581 per month. According to the estimates within the National Accounts (Statistik Austria, 2004), private households spent €432 million on domestic services in that same year, enough to pay for 60,000 employees in the informal sector. Assuming people working in the informal sector are paid less and/or work fewer hours than their formal counterparts, the number of informally employed domestic workers may in fact be considerably more.

Domestic workers' income

Salaries paid to employees in private households, as published by Statistik Austria (2005), are lower than in any other economic sector. The median gross income for employees with social insurance working in private households in 2003 was €907 per month for men and €888 for women. By way of comparison, the median income for all economic sectors in 2004 was €1,944 (Statistik Austria, 2005: 222). Of course, the fact that the median income of domestic workers is so much lower than the average wage can be partly explained by the high proportion of part-time employment in this sector. However, even if we take this factor into account, the earnings in this sector remain relatively low.

As of 1 January 2003, the minimum wage for live-in domestic workers ranged from €531.30 (for a household help without kitchen duties with one to five years of experience) to €1,490.70 (for nurses and tutors with 11 years of experience or more) gross income, calculated over 238 hours per month. This amounts to an hourly wage of between €2.23 euro and €6.26 (excluding additional earnings such as overtime pay).

Domestic workers who do not receive room and board are entitled to a minimum ranging from €5.48 to €10.52 (gross) per hour. Although the law governing domestic help and employees (*Hausgehilfinnen- und Hausangestelltengesetz*) defines numerous occupations (domestic help, housekeepers, household managers, etc.) and sets differentiated guidelines for minimum wages for each occupational group, such as household help with or without kitchen duties, nurses, tutors, etc., these rules and regulations hardly have any impact on the actual labour market (Höglinger and Berka, 1994: 35). Since hardly any households can afford to invest in several domestic workers for different household jobs, most households pay one person to perform a variety of tasks. Consequently, the distinct occupational fields tend to merge together into one profession, that of the maid of all work.

A qualitative study examining the working conditions of migrant women in private households in Austria in 2004 reports a current fluctuation in hourly wages between €7 and €9, on the basis of interviews held with the migrant women themselves (Caixeta *et al.*, 2004). It seems that an average amount of pay has been established in the informal sector that lies above the current net to minimum wage. This may further increase the tendency towards informal employment in this sector since workers may well prefer the higher earnings it offers rather than regular employment with its accompanying deductions for taxes and insurance. For their part, employers still pay less than they would if they paid regular wages. In the end, they benefit most, since only employees stand to benefit from employers' contribution to social insurances and taxes. At the same time, according to Höglinger and Berka, the legally prescribed minimum wage serves the interests of employers in the sense that they can use it as an argument to resist raising wages any higher.

Women's work, migration and the Austrian welfare state

This section will deal with the relevance of socio-economic and political structures in Austria for the development of a labour market for domestic services, organised along gendered and ethnic hierarchies. I shall first describe the prevailing conditions under which the female majority population[7] works as well those pertaining to migrant women on the labour market. I shall pay particular attention to the legal limits imposed on migrant women's right to reside in Austria, their access to the labour market and their claims to social benefits. By way of conclusion, I shall reflect on the place that has been allotted to women within the Austrian welfare state.

Women's participation in the Austrian labour market

Although Austrian women's participation in paid labour has increased steadily over the past decades, they continue to bear the primary responsibility for childcare and housework.[8] Moreover, they continue to perform this work free of charge, regardless of whether they have a paid job or not. In a survey of Statistik Austria on 'family – care – domestic work – childcare' the following results were presented: 'Family life and children are of great importance to most Austrians. However, most men still leave housekeeping, childcare and care for relatives to women' (Statistik Austria, 2003). Economically active women work an average of 35 hours per week at paid labour. They spend 18 hours a week on housework and 11 hours on childcare. In total they average 64 hours a week. The total workload of economically active men is 48 hours: 41 hours of this total is devoted to paid labour, four hours to housework and three hours to childcare. The workload of working mothers with a husband/ partner is the heaviest. On average, they work 32 hours at paid employment and 40 hours in the home, totalling 72 hours per week. It is interesting to note that the total number of hours worked by single mothers is actually less, that is, 68.5 hours a week. They spend more time in paid employment (34.5 hours) than on childcare and housework (34 hours). The presence of a husband/male partner in the home not only increases the amount of unpaid work to be done by women, it also seems to hinder their participation in paid labour (see Table 9.2) (Federal Ministry of Social Security, Generations and Consumer Protection, 2003: 21).

While the number of women in paid employment has increased over the past decades, it is important to note that this has been largely due to an increase in part-time work. Since 1991, the number of women in part-time employment has increased by 62 per cent. In contrast, the number of women in full-time jobs has declined by 1.5 per cent (Bauer and Eichwalder, 2003: 512). Including minor employment, the number of women working part-time in Austria represents 31.3 per cent of all employed women (Bauer and Eichwalder 2003: 517). The highest proportion of part-time workers, over 50 per cent, consists of wives and women with a partner and children (Federal Ministry for Social Security, Generations and Consumer Protection, 2002: 51).

Statistics on women's economic activity suggest that the growth in part-time employment for women may actually form part of a (political) strategy to reconcile the conflicting demands of family and wage labour.[9] In any event, the most frequently cited reasons given by women for working part-time are their caring responsibilities or other family-related reasons (Federal Ministry for Social Security, Generations and Consumer Protection, 2003: 42).

In analysing the gendered employment structure, it is necessary to differentiate between Austrian and migrant women.[10] In both cases, the pattern of employment is characterised by a high concentration of women in specific professions, migrant women being particularly overrepresented in certain segments of the service sector such as hotels, restaurants and the cleaning

Table 9.2 Average working hours of women and men, 2002

	Domestic work	Childcare	Gainful employment	Total amount
Economically active women	18	11	35.0	64.0
Economically active men	4	3	41.0	48.0
Economically active single mothers	18	16	34.5	68.5
Economically active mothers with husband/partner	24	16	32.0	72.0

Source: Federal Ministry of Social Security, Generations and Consumer Protection, 2003: 21.

industry (Federal Ministry for Social Security, Generations and Consumer Protection, 2002: 155). The majority of migrant women work in jobs located in the lowest wage bracket. Their wages are lower than those of both their male counterparts and Austrian women.

Since the 1990s, Austrian women have become increasingly successful at gaining access to the higher income brackets (Biffl, 2002: 262). Although Austrian women work more frequently in part-time jobs than migrant women do, the number of migrant women working in minor employment (with no insurance coverage, except against accidents) is actually higher than that of Austrian women. Roughly half of these migrant women work as domestic workers (as cleaners, nurses or providing care for children or the elderly). Moreover, the large number of migrant women employed for a minimal number of hours in private households suggests that a substantial proportion of their working hours in this sector remains unrecorded (Biffl, 2002: 20).

Biffl states in a comprehensive study on migrant labour in Austria that migrant workers represent a flexible and manoeuvrable workforce within the Austrian labour market (Biffl, 2002: 292). Their level of employment shows a considerable degree of fluctuation. In periods of recession, they are either made redundant or their jobs are taken over by Austrians. In some sectors, however, such forms of substitution do not take place. In the cleaning and housekeeping sector, as well as in health and related services, jobs continue to be occupied by migrant women and not by Austrians, regardless of fluctuations in the general labour market. Austrian women, it would appear, are definitively distancing themselves from (paid) domestic work.

Women's labour migration to Austria

The kind of jobs available to migrant women largely depends on their legal status. Employment possibilities vary depending on whether or not they have status, the nature of their residence permit if they have one, and the length of time that they have resided legally in Austria. Regulations based on the Alien Employment Law stipulate a quota for the employment of third-country citizens and bind employment to specific employers or regions. Frequently, foreign dependants (usually wives) are at least for one year officially excluded from paid labour (for more details, see http://www.ams.or.at; König and Stadler, 2003; Echsel, 2003; Vienna Integration Fund, 2003; Gächter, 1998).

Due to these legal restrictions, migrants are obliged to seek employment within specific professions and/or in the informal sector, in which case they must do without the social insurance benefits linked to formal employment such as unemployment and welfare benefits. Highly qualified migrants often have to accept work below their level of skills, either because of difficulties they experience in getting their diplomas recognised, or because the jobs that fit their qualifications have been given to Austrians, who receive preferential treatment in the labour market.[11] Unemployment hits many migrants from non-EEA countries harder than it does Austrians, since access to welfare payments has been drastically reduced for those not yet in possession of a long-term residence permit.[12] Moreover, applying for and receiving welfare payments can work to the disadvantage of migrants, as it can serve as proof of loss of income, which can furnish a reason to retract residence rights.

Most female migrants who reside legally in Austria do so on the basis of family reunification (Echsel, 2003: 37).[13] Until 2006 in accordance with the annual quotas, wives of third-country citizens admitted for employment in Austria have been allotted a permanent residence permit for all purposes – excluding gainful employment. This means that they had no access to formal employment for at least four years. During their first four years in Austria, therefore, these women remained fully dependent on their husbands, both for their status and for their financial security. A record amendment of the Residence and Settlement Act coming into force on 1 January 2006 brought a significant improvement for family dependants of persons possessing an unlimited entitlement to settlement or an entitlement to asylum. After 12 months of legal stay in Austria they are allotted a 'settlement permit – unlimited' which also includes a permit for gainful employment (Echsel, 2003: 39).[14]

Since the 1990s, more and more women have also been coming to Austria on their own to provide paid care (in both the formal and the informal sectors) or for other jobs, such as sex work.[15] Women have also been coming as students, as refugees and as the wives of Austrian citizens. By 2001, the gender structure of the migrant population was showing a distinct shift towards more women. Although this development has primarily been the result of family migration, the increase in female labour migration has also played a significant role.

During the past 10 to 15 years, the pattern of labour migration to Austria has shown an increase in the number of women coming from Central Europe.[16] Many of them do not come to settle in Austria, but commute on a daily or weekly basis in order to pursue consumer goals or savings plans (Hess, 2001; Huber, 2001; Fassmann et al., 1999). Although the recently introduced measures aimed at creating free movement of services[17] might make it possible for these women to find legal jobs in domestic work via agencies located in their countries of origin, it is more likely that, throughout the transition period,[18] they will continue to take advantage of the regime of free movement to enter Austria as private persons without a work permit, but with the intention of working as a self-employed provider of domestic services.

The significance of women as agents within the migration process should not be measured solely in terms of numbers, but also with regard to the contribution that they make towards the general welfare in the receiving country.

The gendered nature of welfare provision, which prioritises women's role as carers in society, is heightened during migration ... Many of the recent women migrants to Europe have moved to seek jobs in the casualised welfare sector, particularly in domestic work and caring for dependent children, elderly and disabled, as state provision of welfare is not keeping pace with the requirements of ageing populations across Europe.

(Kofman, 2000: 2)

(Migrant) women and the Austrian welfare state

It is of particular interest to examine to what extent the Austrian welfare state encourages women to take on domestic and household tasks or, alternatively, relieves them of these responsibilities. In order to be able to make such an analysis, it is necessary first to consider the basic principles of the Austrian welfare state and the effects prevailing social policies have on women's social and economic position.

Notions of belonging and inclusion in the Austrian welfare state

The conservative corporatist model of the Austrian welfare state is based on a social policy geared towards active intervention in people's lives in order to facilitate their social integration.[19] The purpose of the system is to promote social integration through nationwide redistribution of funds and services, on the one hand, and the local administration of policies, on the other. Social support is provided for those belonging to specifically defined social groups. Rights to social insurance do not accrue to individuals as such, but to members of the nation (Austrian citizens) or to members of an occupational group.

Anyone falling outside of these categories (foreigners, persons lacking employment offering social security benefits, or the casually employed) are excluded from this system or are subject to exceptional regulations. Thus there is differentiated access to emergency assistance (*Notstandshilfe*). Austrian citizens and persons considered equal to Austrians under the law can qualify for this form of social security after they have received unemployment insurance for a period of 20 weeks. However, certain regulations bar non-EEA citizens from receiving these payments, even though they are entitled to unemployment benefits, since these form part of their social insurance (König and Stadler, 2003: 240; Bock-Schappelwein, 2002: 325).

Table 9.3 illustrates the make-up of those registered as unemployed according to gender, eligibility for benefits and citizenship. The table clearly shows that non-Austrian women form the largest group of unemployed who are not eligible for any benefits, a result of the fact that they have formerly held jobs that do not provide for unemployment insurance. The low percentage of

Table 9.3 Percentage of people seeking employment eligible for unemployment benefits and emergency assistance according to gender and citizenship

	Austrians (male)	*Non-Austrians (male)*	*Austrians (female)*	*Non-Austrians (female)*
Unemployment benefits recipients	60%	67%	52%	58%
Emergency assistance recipients	33%	7%	37%	10%
Unemployed persons ineligible for benefits	7%	26%	11%	32%

Source: Bock-Schappelwein, 2002: 336.

non-Austrians receiving emergency assistance is the result of the exclusionary measures discussed above.

Additionally migrants, particularly women who have been admitted on the grounds of family reunification, may be excluded from legal employment and hence also from the social security system. Yet, while many of them are (partly) excluded from the benefits supplied by the welfare state, in fact migrant women contribute a great deal towards maintaining that same welfare state, both via formal employment within the institutions of the social welfare system and through the informal labour that they provide within private households.[20] The unpaid care that they provide for their own families further compounds their contribution in the form of care-work.

Migrant women are actually of double benefit to the Austrian welfare state: to the extent that they are not entitled to social services, they pose no financial risk for the treasury. At the same time they provide social, domestic and care-giving services not only in their own homes but in those of their employers as well, for low pay and under precarious working conditions, which they are forced to accept due to their status of migrant women.

The paradox of the welfare state

The situation of women in the Austrian social welfare system is characterised by a paradox of inclusion and exclusion (Mairhuber, 2000: 223). On the one hand, women profit more from the system than men, either indirectly as the dependants of a male breadwinner or directly as recipients of welfare benefits in their own right. On the other hand, given their allotted roles of unpaid housewife and mother, they are paid relatively low wages and are generally employed part-time, resulting in financial dependency and the risk of ending up in poverty. As a result, they also depend more on social welfare benefits than men do.

Conversely, the welfare state also depends on women's work, both paid and unpaid. The contribution that men make towards maintaining the welfare

175

state is predominantly financial in nature, through the payment of social premiums and taxes. Women's contribution consists largely of the work that they provide as employees of the welfare state or in the form of unpaid and underpaid labour in those sectors of care that fall outside of the state subsidised welfare system. Besides providing care labour themselves, they also act as mediators between families in need of care, social welfare institutions, and others involved in providing care such as grandparents, friends and domestic workers.

In their struggle for emancipation, women are caught in a balancing act between improving their own immediate situation and bringing about substantial change in the long term. The debates surrounding housework and care-work offer a revealing illustration. On the one hand, those domestic and care-giving activities that, given the gendered division of labour, are largely performed by women need to be recognised, revalued and remunerated. On the other hand, remuneration can reinforce the traditional gendered division of labour, since it may dissuade women from looking for alternative forms of employment. Without the simultaneous extension of childcare facilities and other forms of support on the home front, women can never become fully integrated in the paid labour market. But as long as women's jobs continue to be low-paid and their primary responsibility continues to be childcare and housework, policy makers will continue to see this much needed support on the home front as expedient.

The reprivatisation of social services

The most recent trend in the Austrian welfare state has been to balance the national budget at the expense of social welfare benefits and hence at the expense of women (BEIGEWUM, 2002: 112). Budgetary cuts have resulted in social services being transferred from the formal to the informal sector, and in women being forced to serve as unpaid providers of healthcare, education and home care. Those who are either unwilling or unable to fulfil the new tasks ascribed to them must find other persons who can affordably do this work for them, now that the welfare state is withdrawing its support in the form of social services. At the same time, cuts in social services are costing women secure paying jobs. Thus they face pressure on two fronts.

In the hegemonic discourse of tightening budgets, encouraging individual responsibility and stimulating market mechanisms (privatisation and outsourcing), investments throughout Europe have shifted from the public to the private sphere (Sauer, 2003). Part of this process has been the facilitation and promotion of the employment of domestic workers via tax deductions (in France), and through the introduction of service cheques (in Germany) or childcare benefits (in Austria). The discussion surrounding domestic services in Austria presently revolves around the question of meeting the demand for domestic workers. The working conditions of women employed as domestic workers, and particularly their low wages, are hardly matters for discussion.

The terms of the current debate run along the following two closely related lines of argument. On the one hand, the federal government's programme (2000, 2002) as formulated by the Austrian Peoples Party (ÖVP) in collaboration with the Austrian Freedom Party (FPÖ) (resp. Alliance for the Future of Austria (BZÖ)) introduced so-called service cheques, which are supposed to simplify the registration and payment of domestic workers (nannies, maids and nurses for the elderly), thereby making the entire process less bureaucratic.[21] On the other hand, this same programme aims to provide extensive support to women striving to set up their own businesses. The businesses referred to are so-called 'household enterprises'. The government programme suggests the establishment of non-profit home service agencies, which would help reliable and qualified personnel find a job performing family duties. Their view on women's issues is clear, as they define these family duties as services that are normally provided without pay in private households.

The programme does not suggest any alternative options that might, for example, integrate the care normally performed in the home into the social services structure of the welfare state, thus bringing it into the public sphere and out of the isolated private sphere of the family (i.e. that of the wife and mother). Under the guise of progressive initiatives and entrepreneurship, the government's proposal actually threatens to dismantle existing public services in favour of reprivatising care labour. This does little to change the gender-specific division of labour within private households. The proposal is in fact more likely to strengthen women's occupational ties to the private household, placing them in the position of still, or once again, having to provide care labour free of charge. This will, for example, be the case when the housewife-turned-entrepreneur cannot afford reliable and qualified personnel to take over her tasks in the home.

Maria Rauch-Kallat, the Minister of Women's Affairs, defends the government's proposal to promote household enterprises as follows: 'Domestic help is to be made tax-deductible; but this doesn't mean that I support funding servants for the rich. Rather, I aim to contribute to legalizing a real and existing grey area within the labour market . . . that doesn't help the rich, but rather the middle class.' (*Der Standard*, 15 March 2003: 6). But tax deductibility also means tax deficit, evasion of progressive taxation and less revenue for redistribution. This kind of tax policy favours households that can afford a domestic worker and, indirectly, penalises those who cannot. In this way, the more prosperous families can pass on their private expenditures to the public while in poorer families the tensions caused by having to earn a living, on the one hand, while providing the necessary care, on the other are, if anything, further exacerbated.

In various ways, then, the Austrian state is actively engaged in the further privatisation of reproductive work. The financial savings for the treasury are manifold. Formerly subsidised care is now to be privately paid for or performed on an unpaid basis within the home. Migrant women's precarious position in the Austrian labour market, the result of their dependent or undocumented status, works to the advantage of those employing them in their homes and, indirectly, to that of the Austrian state which shares in private employers' interest in keeping the costs of domestic work low. Increasingly, those women who are still being employed by the reduced public services sector are also of foreign origin. Their education, social insurance and future pensions are not being provided for by the Austrian welfare state, but by their own states of origin (Hess, 2001: 208).

Hence, certain reservations must be made when arguing that economic restructuring and the dismantling of the welfare state are occurring at the expense of women. First of all, we must not lose sight of women's status as subjects rather than objects, nor of their scope for action and their decision-making competences. Second, restructuring processes have different effects on different groups of women. The gender dichotomy can be used to highlight women's disadvantages in gaining access to income as well as the unequal distribution of paid and unpaid work. But at the same time, shifts are occurring within gender categories, particularly between women of different classes and nationalities.

Agency and contingency

In this chapter I have tried to reveal structural factors that can help explain the increased employment of migrant women in the domestic services sector. At the same time I have tried to analyse how and to what extent women and men remain actively engaged in organising housework.

The balancing act between strategy and necessity raises dilemmas for both employers and employees. The (usually female) employers of domestic workers, confronted with the competing commitments to family and paid labour, choose or feel compelled to engage someone from outside their home to take over their childcare and housework responsibilities. At the same time, the fact that they can employ a domestic worker gives proof of their privileged position within the fabric of Austrian society, particularly in contrast to that of their domestic worker. The result is that conflicts within the household concerning the division of labour are being resolved through outsourcing, rather than through a radical redistribution of tasks between women and men. The social problem of the gendered division of labour, both within and outside of the home, and of the undervaluation of care-work which is, after all, essential to the maintenance of society, are not being resolved.

Seen from the migrant woman's perspective, work as a domestic worker is by no means the ideal job. But for most of them it does offer one of the few available possibilities for gaining a foothold in Austrian society, given the effects of sexual and ethnic discrimination and the rules excluding many of them from formal employment. Political strategies aiming to improve their position should certainly focus on the precarious and exploitative conditions under which they are obliged to work. On the other hand, care should be taken not to limit the scope of political action, since this can result in migrant women being trapped in the role of domestic workers. It is necessary to carry political analysis further and fundamentally challenge the structural concepts of gender and citizenship that have been instrumental in reducing migrant women's options to those reserved for them as women and migrants; that is, to performing the low-paid job of serving Austrian women as they attempt to maintain their newly won position on their way towards emancipation.

Notes

1 For a detailed description of working conditions in private homes see: Caixeta *et al.*, 2004 for Austria; Anderson, 2000 and Cruz Roja, 2004 for Europe as a whole, and Parreñas, 2000 for the US.
2 According to the former Austrian Minister of Social Affairs, Herbert Haupt, the right to privacy is anchored in the Austrian Constitution. Any form of control carried out by the labour inspection (*Arbeitsinspektorat*) would be an infringement of this right (Ohnemoos, 2000).
3 This applies in particular to the so-called 15th-month bonus salary, specifically introduced for this sector, given the unique working conditions that apply.
4 When employing domestic workers via their own business, employers can deduct salaries as a form of private expenditures. Moreover, they then no longer need pay the 15th-month bonus salary.
5 By contrast, domestic workers are often forced to take unpaid leave when their employers go on vacation.
6 Since these new policies were introduced, the Austrian Labour Market Service (AMS) has reported 9,311 registered au-pairs, of whom approximately 80 per cent originate from Eastern Europe.
7 I prefer the term 'majority population', since it reflects existing power relations, to purely descriptive terms like: 'white, German, Christian, secular, etc.' (cf. Gotlinde Magiriba Lwanga, quoted in FeMigra, 1994: 63).
8 Between 1951 and 2001, the number of women aged 15–64 years employed in paid labour rose from 48.6 per cent to 61.8 per cent respectively – 65.0 per cent if one includes minor employment (Bauer and Eichwalder, 2003: 511).
9 Since 1 May 2004, companies employing more than 20 persons must provide parents returning from paternity leave part-time positions upon request.
10 For more details, see Haidinger, 2004a: 90.
11 Austria's so-called *Inländerprimat* requires that employers, when hiring, give priority to Austrian citizens and that they lay off non-Austrian workers before Austrians. Furthermore, the *Generalvorbehalt* states that migrants can only be employed if their work is both necessary and advantageous for the Austrian economy (see: Bauböck, 2001).
12 Although migrant workers form an integral part of the population, they are not granted any representational rights until they become Austrian citizens, and naturalisation normally takes at least ten years. Until 2005 migrant workers were not even entitled to act as representatives on workers' committees.
13 In Austria, only heterosexual married couples can apply for family reunification.

14 Requirements are: proof of sufficient income, comprehensive health insurance, continuous employment for over one year.
15 In 2001, the Federal Ministry of the Interior issued a decree providing for a specific permit (*Selbständige ohne Niederlassung*) which allows prostitutes or show dancers to work in Austria under restricted conditions (see http://www.servus.at/maiz/gesetz).
16 For example, 71 per cent of the migrants from the Czech Republic and 68 per cent of the Slovakian migrants are women (Vienna Integration Fund, 2003: 10). Most of them are between 20 and 39 years of age.
17 These rules make it possible for persons and companies providing services in one Member State to offer their services on a temporary basis in another Member State.
18 In the transition period, probably until 2011, migrants from the new member countries of the EU, although permitted to reside in Austria, will still be subject to the quota system regarding paid employment.
19 For further details concerning the Austrian welfare state, see Esping-Andersen, 2000: 154; Talos and Obinger, 1998: 7. Regarding the position of women, see Mairhuber, 2000.
20 City council member Karin Landauer (Austrian Freedom Party), who suggested temporarily increasing the employment quota for migrant care workers, stated that: 'nurses from the Philippines are well integrated into Viennese society' (*Der Standard*, 13–14 September 2003, p 9).
21 These 'service cheques', to be filled out by employers, cost €12.50. Employees under the wage limit of €315 per month receive €12 pay and have accidental insurance. Employees earning between €315 and €630 per month only receive €10 of the €12.50, but they have accidental, health, and pension insurance. Employees have to be in possession of a residence permit. The law concerned with the service cheque came into effect on 1 January 2006.

References

Arbeiter Kammer Wien (2000) *Frauenhandel in Österreich*, press release, 11 December
Anderson, Bridget (2000) *Doing the Dirty Work?*, London/New York: Zed Books
Appelt, Erna (2003) 'Frauen in der Migration – Lebensform und soziale Situation', in Fassmann, Heinz and Stacher, Irene (eds), *Österreichischer Migrations- und Integrationsbericht*, Klagenfurt: Drava, pp 144–71
Bauböck, Rainer (2001) *Österreichische Migrationspolitik*; accessed 16 October 2001: http://www.migration.cc/40jahre.html
Bauer, Adelheid and Eichwalder, Reinhard (2003) 'Volkszählung 2001: Lebensunterhalt', *Statistische Nachrichten* 7/2003, Vienna
BEIGEWUM (2002) *Frauen macht Budgets*, Vienna: Mandelbaum
Biffl, Gudrun (2002) *Arbeitsmarktrelevante Effekte der Ausländerintegration in Österreich*, Vienna: WIFO
Biffl, Gudrun (2004) *SOPEMI Report on Labour Migration: Austria 2003–2004*, Vienna: WIFO
Bock-Schappelwein, Julia (2002) 'Die Arbeitslosigkeit ausländischer Arbeitskräfte', in Biffl, Gudrun (ed), *Arbeitsmarktrelevante Effekte der Ausländerintegration in Österreich*, Vienna: WIFO, pp 302–45
Caxieta, Luzenir, Haas, Barbara, Haidinger, Bettina, Rappold, Sonja, Rechling,

Daniela and Ripota, Pamela (2004) 'Hausarbeit und Betreuungsarbeit in Österreich. Eine qualitative Untersuchung unter ArbeitgeberInnen und Arbeitnehmerinnen', unpublished paper

Cruz Roja (2004) *Homes, Caretaking, Frontiers. Immigrant Women's Rights and the Reconciliation of Work and Family*, Madrid: Cruz Roja/EC

Echsel, Katharina (2003) 'Aufenthaltsrechtliche Situation von Migrantinnen in Österreich', in Arbeitsgruppe Migrantinnen und Gewalt (ed), *Migration von Frauen und strukturelle Gewalt*, Vienna Milena Verlag, pp 31–41

Ehrenreich, Barbara (2003) *Arbeit poor. Unterwegs in der Dienstleistungsgsellschaft*, Hamburg: Rowohlt

Esping-Andersen, Gosta (2000) 'Three worlds of welfare capitalism', in Pierson, Christopher (ed), *The Welfare State*, Cambridge: Polity Press, pp 155–69

Fassmann, Heinz, Hintermann, Christiane, Kohlbacher, Josef and Reeger, Ursula (1999) '*Arbeitsmarkt Mitteleuropa. Die Rückkehr historischer Migrationsmuster*', ISF-Forschungsberichte, vol: 18, Vienna: Verlag der österreichischen Akademie der Wissenschaften

Federal Ministry for Social Security, Generations and Consumer Protection/Bundesministerium für Soziale Sicherheit und Generationen (2002) *Geschlechtsspezifische Disparitäten*, Vienna

Federal Ministry for Social Security, Generations and Consumer Protection/Bundesministerium für Soziale Sicherheit, Generationen und Konsumentenschutz/ (2003) *Haushaltsführung und Kinderbetreuung*, Vienna

FeMigra (1994) 'Wir, die Seiltänzerinnen', in Eichhorn, Cornelia and Grimm, Sabine (eds), *Gender Killer*, Berlin: ID-Archiv, pp 49–65

Gächter, August (1998) 'Rechtliche Rahmenbedingungen und ihre Konsequenzen', in AMS (ed), *AusländerInnen in Österreich*, Vienna: Wissenschaftsverlag, pp 10–27

Gather, Claudia and Meissner, Hanna (2002) 'Informelle Erwerbsarbeit in privaten Haushalten', in Gather, Claudia, Geissler, Birgit and Rerrich, Maria S (eds), *Weltmarkt Privathaushalt*, Münster: Westfälisches Dampfboot, pp 120–40

Haidinger, Bettina (2004a) 'She sweeps for money! Beschäftigungsverhältnisse und strukturelle Bedingungen bezahlter Haushaltsarbeit von Migrantinnen in Österreich', unpublished thesis, Wirtschaftsuniversität, Vienna

Haidinger, Bettina (2004b) 'Ich putze Dreck, aber ich bin nicht Dreck! – Migrantinnen in der bezahlten Haushaltsarbeit. Eine qualitative Untersuchung unter Arbeitgerber/innen und Arbeitnehmerinnen', in Hartl, Katja and Kreimer, Margareta (eds), *Am Rande des Arbeitsmarktes: Haushaltsnahe Dienstleistungen*, Materialien zu Wirtschaft und Gesellschaft 90, Vienna: AK Wien, pp 63–81

Hess, Sabine (2001) 'Transnationale Überlebensstrategien von Frauen', in Hobuss, Steffi (ed), *Die andere Hälfte der Globalisierung*, Frankfurt/Main: Campus, pp 197–225

Hess, Sabine (2002) 'Au Pairs als informalisierte Haushaltsarbeiterinnen', in Gather, Claudia, Geissler, Birgit and Rerrich, Maria S (eds), *Weltmarkt Privathaushalt*, Münster: Westfälisches Dampfboot, pp 103–19

Höglinger, Andrea and Berka, Gerhard (1994) *Arbeit in Privathaushalten*, Vienna: AK Wien.

Huber, Peter (2001) 'Teilprojekt 10: Migration und Pendeln in Folge der EU-Erweiterung', in Mayerhofer, Peter and Palme, Gerhard (eds), *Strukturpolitik und*

Raumplanung in den Regionen an der mitteleuropäischen EU- Aussengrenze zur Vorbereitung auf die EU-Osterweiterung (Preparity), Vienna: WIFO

Kassberger, Ferdinand and Schwarzl, Reinhold (2000) 'Zur Vollständigkeit der BIP/ BSP-Berechnunges', in *Statistische Nachrichten 2/2000*, Vienna, pp 142–8

Kofman, Eleonore (2000) *Gender and International Migration in Europe. Employment, Welfare and Politics*, London/New York: Routledge

König, Karin and Stadler, Bettina (2003) 'Entwicklungstendenzen im öffentlich-rechtlichen und demokratiepolitischen Bereich', in Fassmann, Heinz and Stacher, Irene (eds), *Österreichischer Migrations- und Integrationsbericht*, Klagenfurt: Drava, pp 225–61

Mairhuber, Ingrid (2000) *Die Regulierung des Geschlechterverhältnisses im Sozialstaat Österreich*, Frankfurt: Peter Lang Verlag

Ohnemoos, Elisabeth (2000) 'Hausgehilfinnen im 3. Jahrtausend', *Journal Panorama*, Ö1, 18 December

Parreñas, Rhacel S (2000) *Servants of Globalization*, Stanford: Stanford University Press.

Sauer, Birgit (2003) *Gender Makes the World Go Around. Geschlecht und Globalisierung*; accessed 8 November 2003 at: http://www.copyriot.com

Statistik Austria (2003) *Familienarbeit bleibt Frauensache*, press release 7.899–148/03, Vienna: Verlag Österreich

Statistik Austria (2004) *Volkswirtschaftliche Gesamtrechungen*, Vienna: Verlag Österreich

Statistik Austria (2005) *Statistisches Jahrbuch Österreich 2004*, Vienna: Verlag Österreich.

Talos, Emmerich and Obinger, Herbert (1998) 'Sozialstaaten nach dem goldenen Zeitalter', in Talós, Emmerich (ed), *Soziale Sicherung im Wandel*, Vienna: Böhlau, pp 7–30

Vienna Integration Fund/Wiener Integrationsfonds (2003) *MigrantInnen in Wien*, Vienna.: Wiener Integrationsfonds

Young, Brigitte (2000) *Die Herrin und die Magd*; accessed at: http://www.trend. partisan.net/trd0900/t190900.htm, edition September 2000

10

RESPONSE AND RESPONSIBILITY

Domestic violence and marriage migration in the UK

Aisha Gill and Kaveri Sharma

Immigrants to the UK constitute a diverse population of ethnic, cultural and national groups. Increasing attention is being given to the 'problem' of immigration and asylum seeking in the UK at the point of entry, yet there is little attention from researchers and policy makers to subsequent experiences of immigrants. Women who are the victims and survivors of domestic abuse face issues common to all abused women, whether they are citizens or recent immigrants; but there are also issues specific to new immigrant women, including significant cultural and legal barriers to seeking safety, which need to be considered. Specifically, immigrant women who are abused by their partners or sponsors face very particular difficulties in accessing personal safety and protection. If these women do not have indefinite leave to remain (ILR) in the UK, or are at risk of removal or deportation for other reasons, the consequences of leaving an abusive partner can complicate their immigration status. While immigration legislation and policies lack a gender dimension, forms of persecution can clearly be very gender specific. Due to their role and status in society generally, and more specifically within family and kinship systems, women may be exposed to human rights abuses different from those of their male counterparts.

The term domestic violence[1] is used to describe various forms of assault, including psychological, verbal and mental abuse, physical beating, kidnapping, rape, threat of bodily harm, murder, dowry-related abuse,[2] attempted or actual forced marriage and honour-related violence. While domestic violence in the United Kingdom is perpetrated on men, women and children, most victims are women.[3] Such abuse of women is not an isolated phenomenon, but present in every socio-economic, cultural and ethnic group. Domestic violence against women occurs with alarming frequency and severity in the UK: it claims 150 lives each year, accounts for 25 per cent of all violent crime, and has more repeat victims than any other crime. This chapter focuses on the fact that each year approximately 500–600 immigrant women to the UK suffer domestic violence; and most of these women are married to or have relationships with UK citizens or men with indefinite leave to remain in the UK.

Growing public awareness of the prevalence and frequently lethal nature of domestic violence has led to legislation designed to protect women and punish their abusers. This chapter evaluates various relevant UK legislative measures (from the 1980s onwards) and uses case studies of immigrant women from South Asia to highlight issues that have wider relevance for all immigrant women. This chapter examines some of the obstacles faced by immigrant women and how these have increased over the last decade, and also explores legal strategies for protecting this vulnerable population from domestic violence. We conclude with policy recommendations emphasising the necessity for and obligation of a welfare state to guarantee women and dependent children a basic human right: freedom from violence and a safe place of residence. The strong premise of this chapter is that the need to protect vulnerable immigrant women experiencing domestic violence is a prime duty of the legal and welfare system, and one that should weigh more heavily than the often conflicting need to prevent illegal immigration.

Legislative responses to domestic violence

Immigration and marital status: policy and procedure

International migration is an important phenomenon in Britain, and during the last 60 years immigration to the UK has become a key policy issue. It is a theme of immediate political relevance and is being discussed by all mainstream political parties. In the immediate historical past immigration policy has been determined largely by relations with Commonwealth countries. Following the 1948 British Nationality Act, immigration to the UK was restricted to citizens of the Commonwealth, those with the legal right to enter the UK. In the next two decades, this open immigration was curtailed to reduce immigrants from the New Commonwealth (NCW) and Pakistan. With continued immigration for family reunification permitted, the inflow of migrants from the New Commonwealth and Pakistan continued (Schuster, 2003). Since the 1980s, successive UK governments have tightened immigration restrictions.[4] This has occurred in conjunction with greater freedom of travel from the enlarged EU to the UK. Among non-EU immigrants, acceptances for settlement by the Home Office declined from about 70,000 per annum in the early 1970s to 50,000 per annum in the early 1990s. The proportion from NCW countries declined from about 60 per cent in the 1970s to less than 50 per cent in the 1980s. By the late 1980s, more than two-thirds were entering as husbands, wives or dependants (mainly children). Among immigrants from the Indian subcontinent, there was a sharp decline in the number of children admitted, though some increase in the number of fiancées and spouses (Coleman and Salt, 1992: 453). These flows reflect path-dependent effects of earlier labour migration. The shift from children to spouses reflects the decline in young first-generation immigrants and the maturing of the second generation. A relatively small proportion of those accepted for settlement have been refugees. Those granted asylum[5] or 'exceptional leave to remain' were the fastest-growing category between 1980 and 2002 (Dobson *et al.*, 2001: 257).

From the early 1990s, the 'threat' vocalised in contemporary political discourse increasingly echoed by governments concerned the number of asylum seekers. Asylum seekers have increasingly been stereotyped as poor and unskilled 'economic migrants' rather than genuine asylum seekers. There was also growing concern about the immigrants entering Britain on tourist visas who subsequently claimed asylum. The Asylum and Immigration Act of 1993 removed a visitor's right of appeal if refused entry. The Act halved the number of people granted asylum between 1993 and 1994, increased dramatically the number held in detention pending decisions, and raised the number repatriated. The Asylum and Immigration Act of 1996 removed the right to all state and local authority benefits (including housing) for those claiming asylum after arrival and for those whose applications had been rejected but who still remained in the UK. The Immigration and Asylum Act of 1999 further modified the asylum and appeals system, strengthened enforcement powers, and increased sanctions against carriers of illegal entrants. A key part of this Act was an attempt to minimise alleged 'economic incentives' for people to claim asylum either on entry or on the expiration of other types of visa (such as student visas). In summary, the focus of legal reforms during the 1990s was on efforts to combat illegal immigration (Schuster, 2003).

The specific problems of immigrant women are long-standing and pre-date even the contemporary political crackdown. The UK government had by the early 1980s introduced a set of rules to prevent potential immigrants entering the UK on the basis of marriage to a resident. Of particular relevance to our discussion were the *primary purpose rule*, the *one-year immigration rule* and the *no recourse to public funds rule*. The primary purpose rule required applicants to prove that the primary aim of the marriage was not settlement in the UK. Hence, unless proven otherwise, all marriages of non-UK citizens with UK residents were seen as bogus and intended only as a means of securing residence. The one-year rule introduced the requirement that people coming to the UK to join their spouse must remain in the marriage for at least one year before applying to remain indefinitely. A further requirement was that the immigrant spouse's application had to be supported by the resident spouse. A consequence of this rule was that the immigrant spouse not applying for indefinite leave to remain in the UK before the expiry of the one year spousal visa automatically became an 'overstayer',[6] committed a criminal offence and became liable to deportation. The immigrant spouse whose marriage breaks down in the first year faced possible deportation.

The no-recourse to public funds[7] rule required that immigrants coming to the UK must be financially self-sufficient or supported by their spouses. They are not entitled to any welfare benefits, council housing, public funds or facilities funded by public funds, including refuges (Joshi, 2003) until getting indefinite leave to remain. When an immigrant spouse comes to the UK on the basis of marriage, they come on a two-year spousal visa and during those two years or 'probationary period' (increased from one to two years as of 1 April 2003), they have no access to public funds. After the two years of marriage, the sponsoring British spouse has to make an application to the Home Office on behalf of the immigrant spouse requesting a grant of indefinite leave to remain. Access to public funds is then permitted. The probationary requirement is problematic and reinforces power imbalances within marriages – the threat of deportation can be used as a powerful tool to force immigrant women to remain in relationships against their will. The existence and extension of the probationary period are a clear demonstration that that the legal system assumes migrants are seeking illegitimate access to the UK. The burden of proof is placed squarely on the shoulders of the immigrant.

This inherent bias in the structure of the legal system has not gone unchallenged. Against a backdrop of increasing black and Asian radical activism, key campaigns led by women in the 1980s and 1990s highlighted the extent and seriousness of male violence against women. During this period, groups like Southall Black Sisters (SBS) and Newham Asian Women's Project (NAWP) highlighted the failure of the state to intervene appropriately in cases of domestic violence in minority ethnic communities. These groups recognised the need to foster better understandings of women's actual experiences of violence within the family, the frequency and nature of violence, and how structures of authority are constituted within the family (Gill and Rehman, 2004: 75–83).

Over the last 30 years domestic violence against women and children has appeared as a prominent feminist theme in debate. This has led to a heightened awareness of inequalities embedded in the interlocking systems of race and class and underpinned by religion, gender and location. It has also led to an increase in demand for a woman's right to control her own life and body. Successful alliances between women activists of all ethnicities and academics led to the emergence of mass protests in campaigns against rape, immigration laws, rights of women who had been imprisoned for killing their abusers, and forced marriages and more generally institutionalised racism and religious fundamentalism (Bhabha and Shutter, 1994; Gill and Rehman, 2004: 75–83).

After vigorous and sustained campaigning from women's groups, in 1997 the primary purpose rule was abolished and in June 1999 a concession won and incorporated with some changes in evidence requirements, into the Immigration Rules[8] of December 2002. This concession clawed back some space in the legal system for victims of domestic violence. Henceforth immigrant spouses or unmarried partners who wanted to leave their partner as a result of domestic violence within the probationary period were allowed to remain in the UK, even though no longer living with their spouse. This concession has come with a price. In order to prove that domestic violence had occurred, individuals have to provide *one* of the following:

(a) an injunction, non-molestation order or other protection order made against the sponsor;
(b) a relevant court conviction against the sponsor; or
(c) details of a relevant police caution issued against the sponsor.

The obvious problem with this standard of evidence is that it sets the bar very high. For many women suffering abuse the concession was irrelevant, since they could not approach the police or the courts to report domestic violence; further this concession did not apply to women who had already become overstayers (Lewis, 2004). This problem is of particular relevance to newly arrived immigrant women who are more likely to lack the cultural capital permitting them to go beyond the confines of their newly acquired family structure to access the resources of the legal system. Again this was challenged.

In April 2003, the Immigration Rules were amended to state that if one of the above pieces of evidence was not available, *more than one* of the following should then be provided:

- a medical report from a hospital doctor confirming that the applicant has injuries consistent with domestic violence;
- a letter from an examining GP who was satisfied injuries were consistent with domestic violence;
- an undertaking given to a court that the perpetrator of violence will not approach the applicant who is the victim of violence;
- a police report confirming attendance at the home of the applicant as a result of domestic violence;
- a letter from social services confirming its involvement in connection with domestic violence; or
- a letter of support from a women's refuge.

Again the concession has less substance than might first appear. There remain formidable obstacles for abused immigrant women seeking protection from the legal system. Under the two-year rule, women are dependent on their partners to sign their application form to remain in the UK after two years. If partners fail or refuse to do this (likely in the case where a woman has left an abusive spouse), the Home Office treats the woman as an 'over-stayer' who then faces automatic deportation. The position of overstayers who do not meet these requirements is far more difficult, leaving them vul-nerable. In practice, this applies even to women who have faced domestic violence – a woman whose application[9] is three days late is treated as a 'long-term overstayer'.

Overstayers need to satisfy the Home Office that their removal from the UK would violate the UK's obligations under the European Convention of Human Rights (ECHR) and therefore amount to a breach of human rights,[10] i.e., by arguing an Article 8 (or any other qualified right)[11] breach or a real risk;[12] Article 3[13] (or any other absolute right); that the woman should be con-sidered a refugee under the terms of the Refugee Convention[14]; or that there are other compassionate circumstances prevailing and that the Secretary of State should exercise discretion and grant leave to stay in the UK (Lewis, 2004). In practice such applications are extremely difficult. According to Home Office figures for the situation covered by the Immigration Rules for the years 2000 to 2002, of the 119 women who applied for indefinite leave to remain under the domestic violence concession, only 60 per cent were granted settlement; it is unclear how many women were deported because they were unable to report domestic abuse (Southall Black Sisters, 2004).

New initiatives on domestic violence

A review of the literature on violence against women reveals the prevalence of such violence is difficult to establish. Still, there are now official reports citing the incidence, prevalence and consequences of male-partner violence against women worldwide (World Health Organisation, 2002). It is accepted that domestic violence, and most other forms of violence against women and children, are likely to be under-reported and that current data are therefore likely to be under-estimates. Progress so far has been because of work on the part of the women's movement through global, national and local activities. In the UK violence against women only really started being addressed by legislation in the early 1970s (Hanmer and Maynard, 1987). The Domestic Violence, Crime and Victims Act 2004 is the latest example.

In June 2003, the UK Home Office issued a consultation paper entitled *Safety and Justice*, which made various suggestions for amendments to law and policy on domestic violence. The paper acknowledged that immi-grant women experiencing domestic violence face a great many problems – especially those resulting from the lack of access to public funds rendering them trapped in abusive relationships. The paper did not then suggest any measures to redress the situation. In December 2003, the consultation paper was transformed into the Domestic Violence, Crime and Victims Bill and on 15 November 2004, received Royal Assent. Provisions in the Act strengthen the rights of victims and witnesses, and seek to ensure they receive necessary help, support and protection. If successful, the Act could transform the way women are treated. It has the potential to reduce violence against women and point to effective strategies to control other forms of violence. However, as it stands the Act does not contain any targeted provisions for specific problems faced by immigrant women. In particular, the government has resisted making public funds available to these women (Home Office, 2003: 45). At most, abused immigrant women may benefit from the spill-over effects of legislation targeting the more general problem of domestic violence.

The *Home Office Development and Practice Report 35* (2005), is the latest report produced by the Home Office on the issue of domestic violence as experienced by members of black and minority ethnic (BME) communities. While the report mentions immigration as an aggravating factor to accessing help, it does not mention the severe problems faced by immigrant women in domestic violence situations.

Intended benefits and unintended consequences of domestic violence legislation

Social context

Legislative responses to domestic violence take this phenomenon out of the private, family context and move it into a public, legal realm where abusive behaviour is recognised as criminal conduct. The implementation of domestic violence legislation can be evaluated most effectively by examining the interaction between the social and private contexts of domestic abuse, particularly in the case of immigrant women.

The first step in this analysis is to explore the social context in which the domestic abuse of immigrant women takes place. For two reasons, the danger and severity of domestic violence are particularly acute for immigrant women of uncertain immigration status. First, living outside of the dominant culture, immigrant women are often unaware of their legal rights as individuals. Second, some immigrant women come from cultures where domestic abuse is tolerated or condoned; women are often unaware that the treatment they are suffering is illegal. Immigrant victims in general and South Asian women who are abused in particular (DasGupta, 2000) are reluctant to report crime and co-operate with state authorities. Language barriers further bar many immigrant women from access to social programmes and police support (Raj and Silverman, 2002). There may also be strong cultural values on keeping 'family problems' private, preventing women from reporting abuse (Wachholz and Miedema, 2000). These women fall victim to the 'quadruple whammy' of marginalisation resulting from their immigration status, gender, ethnicity and abuse.

Case histories of abuse victims and survivors provide critical insights into the particular situations of abused women. These insights illustrate a variety of social and personal consequences of laws designed to protect women. Building on these case histories, we then evaluate the effectiveness of legislation designed to help vulnerable immigrant women. The legislation described in the previous section illustrates the UK government's partial commitment to providing assistance for victims of domestic violence. As we have discussed, this occurs in the context of another and potentially contradictory aim – that of controlling immigration. The discussion that follows highlights the unforeseen pitfalls of these laws.

Intersectionality theory[15]

Many immigrant women facing abuse by their partners balance triple identities: being new immigrants, victims of domestic violence and women of colour. These multiple identities converge and heighten the massive social barriers that they must overcome to end the violence in their lives.

A particular problem for immigrant women leaving an abusive marriage is the threat of poverty. Leaving a marital home often implies cutting oneself off from family and any wider social support structures. Immigrant women are particularly vulnerable to the denial of benefits because they face significant obstacles to independence. They often lack the language or other skills and may also, as a result of the violence, be ill equipped emotionally or physically to maintain steady employment. The loss of benefits may force women to remain in or return to threatening situations because they cannot afford the alternatives (Erez, 2000). Welfare funding is therefore essential for helping abused women make a transition into a productive and safe livelihood.

After years of campaigning by Asian women's groups, the Home Office ruled that an immigrant woman would have the right to apply to stay in the country if she could provide evidence of domestic violence. Again we see the benevolence of government legislation undermined by its other aim – controlling potential illegal migration. Women in this situation have 'no recourse' to public funds such as income support, housing benefits or council housing. This forces immigrant women and their children into destitution, making it almost impossible for them to survive the long process of obtaining a decision from the Home Office. Most women's refuges cannot afford to provide refuge services to immigrant women, as the refuges themselves rely on the rental and housing benefit for their income. Even where a refuge may be able to provide support to a woman without recourse to public funds, it is normally limited to one space a year, which is clearly far less than the numbers required.

Instead of viewing the barriers associated with being female, being a member of a minority group and being an immigrant as separate and unrelated entities, it is more productive to understand how these factors overlap to create the unique dynamic that immigrant women experience, 'the location of women of colour at the intersection of race and gender makes [their] actual experience of domestic violence . . . qualitatively different than that of white women' (Williams-Crenshaw, 1991: 358). This highlights a specific focus of our discussion, that the experience of abused immigrant women is different from that of both the male immigrant and of native-born women of colour. This cannot be tackled or understood by reference to legislation concerned with 'immigration' and 'domestic violence' as entirely separate and distinct matters of public policy. For the abused women highlighted in our case studies, abuse and immigration interact in a vicious circle, and any proposed solution needs to recognise this. Each facet of an abused immigrant woman's identity hinders her ability to obtain legal protection and acquire the necessary public benefits to escape domestic violence.

In the next section we examine two case studies reported to Newham Asian Women's Project[16] (NAWP) in 2004. We recognise potential reservations about the general applicability of lessons from case studies. These case studies are drawn from a very culturally specific group, and as we have noted, the experience of domestic violence is a highly cultural-specific phenomenon. Nevertheless we are focusing here on the precise problem of abused immigrant women. We believe strongly that there are very definite issues common to this group, irrespective of nationality, class or religion.

Domestic violence and Asian immigrant women: case studies

In this section we present two case studies of clients at Newham Asian Women's Project.

Case study 1: Parvinder

Parvinder[17] came to the UK seven years ago on a one-year spousal visa after marrying her British husband. She had been facing abuse from almost the beginning of her marriage. This resulted in hospitalisation on one occasion, severe bruises several times, and emotional scarring from constant verbal abuse. After enduring more than a year of abuse, she found the courage to call the police. After she did so, her husband told the officers on call that she was living in the UK illegally. Parvinder had by this time become an overstayer, her visa had expired. She was arrested, taken to the police station and later released. The same occurred on two other occasions, Parvinder then stopped approaching the police.

After more than six years of abuse, she approached NAWP. With the help and support of NAWP she obtained a non-molestation order against her husband. When her immigration application was reviewed under the domestic violence concession, the Home Office rejected the application stating that her marriage had not broken down within the probationary period during which she should have regularised her stay in the UK. Being an overstayer, she has not been given the right to appeal this decision and is liable to be deported to her country of origin where she will likely face persecution for leaving her husband.

Parvinder has no entitlement to public funds and her status as an over-stayer renders her ineligible to work in the UK. Parvinder now wants to leave her violent marriage but faces few options. Without access to public funds there is a very remote possibility of finding a refuge space. NAWP have been unable to locate her a refuge space in England. Parvinder has recently been served with an eviction notice by her mother-in-law (the home owner) from the marital home. The experience of Parvinder illustrates the tension in the legal system. Despite securing a public and legal acknowledgement of her husband's abuse, she was still subjected to the legal provisions in place to control illegal migration.

Case study 2: Nina

Presenting a different set of problems, another of NAWP's clients, whom we shall call 'Nina', was arrested on allegation of being an illegal immigrant. Nina's husband, who had been extremely abusive to her, made the com-plaint. She had fled domestic violence and has been living with strangers for over six months. After returning to the marital home to collect personal belongings, her husband called the police. Her spousal visa at this point was not due to expire until a few months later. Nina was not carrying her pass-port at the time, so she was arrested and kept in custody for eight hours. Only after her NAWP case worker took her passport to the police station was she released. Nina does not have proof of domestic violence, as she was never allowed out of the marital home, not even to register with a GP.

The issues raised by Nina's experiences highlight our basic theme, namely the bias in the legal system. Nina was viewed first as a potentially illegal migrant and only second as a victim of domestic abuse. Why was she not allowed to show her passport to the police at the time of her arrest? Why did the police not take into account her statement detailing abuse towards her? Where would she get the 'proof' of domestic violence for her ILR application to the Home Office? How is she supposed to sustain herself in the UK while her application is being considered?

The data in Table 10.1 have been collated from the case files of 14 clients of the NAWP with immigration-related problems between September 2004 and February 2005. All these clients are of South Asian origin: six are from India, five from Bangladesh and three from Pakistan. They had all come on spousal visas, except one who had come on a financée visa; all women reported fleeing some form of domestic violence, from the husband and/or the extended family. None of the women feels able to go back to their home country due to fear of being persecuted by their natal family and community.

Nine women had valid spousal visas at the time of making the application for ILR, while four had become overstayers. Four of the women had 'enough' proof of domestic violence, as required under the Immigration Rules. In seven of the cases, women had made complaints that were not pursued or had a letter from a refuge worker supporting the woman's statement; three of the women did not have any proof of domestic violence. On an average, it took women 5.5 months to make an application for ILR after being separated from the perpetrator of violence. In seven cases, after an average of 13 months, the application was still pending before the Home Office.

Ten of the 14 women relied on friends or distant relatives for some kind of subsistence support, of whom seven lived with personal or family friends while waiting for the Home Office decision. The rest have been supported at some stage or continue to receive money, food or clothes from friends while they live in a refuge. Four of the women received some kind of support from the state, most under the community care law; two of the women with children receive child benefit.

These data clearly illustrate the vulnerable position in which immigrant women fleeing domestic violence can find themselves. In the next section, we explore these and other issues within the context of the current legislative framework and then move on to make suggestions for change.

Different standards at different stages of the proceedings

There is a tension between the government's humanitarian interest in protecting abused women and the contemporary political need to demonstrate being tough on immigration. This has been demonstrated in our outline of formal legislative changes, challenges to them and subsequent amendments and also in our case studies. This section looks at another aspect of this tension – the disparities in the standards set by the Immigration Rules at different stages of immigration proceedings.

The experience of domestic abuse can be grievously complicated for the victim when she is not a citizen and her legal status depends on co-operation from the abuser. An abused spouse may be deterred from taking action to protect herself and her children – including the filing for a civil protection order, filing criminal charges or calling the police – because of the fear of deportation. An abuser's control over a woman's residence status and threats of deportation are powerful tools that lock women into abusive relationships, isolate them from help, and ultimately exacerbate the lethality of the violence they experience.

One group of women who are not included in the new Immigration Rules are those who become overstayers in the UK and whose visas expire. It is important to understand the circumstances in which immigrant women who face domestic violence become overstayers. As presented in the case of

Table 10.1 Demographic information about clients at Newham Asian Women's Project

Name	Ethnicity	Age	Dependants	Date of entry in UK	Immigration status at the time of HO application	Evidence of domestic violence	Date of separation from perpetrator of violence	Date of application for ILR to HO	Date of HO decision	Interim support provided by	Current status in UK
Khalida	Bangladeshi	28	None	Sep 2003	Valid spousal visa	Police complaint, GP report	March 2004	Aug 2004	Dec 2004	Local Council u/s 21 of NAA	Has ILR
Nasima	Indian	26	None	July 2003	Valid spousal visa	Police complaint of marital rape	Dec 2003	March 2004	Dec 2004	Accommodation by a refuge and depends on friends for sustenance	Has appealed against the HO decision
Poppy	Bangladeshi	29	1 son (6 years)	1997	Overstayer	Letter from refuge worker	June 2003	Dec 2003	Awaited	Accommodation by a refuge and gets child benefit (£16.50 pw)	Overstayer but awaiting decision by HO
Harjeet	Indian	30	1 son (6 years)	1998	Overstayer	Police complaints, injunction orders, medical report	Dec 2004	Many applications made since 2000	All applications rejected, last decision Sep 2004	Continued to live with the perpetrator until Dec 2004, now dependent on friends for support	Overstayer
Yasmin	Pakistani	31	None	Jan 2003	Valid spousal visa	Police complaint, injunction order	Dec 2004	Jan 2005	Feb 2005	Family friends	Has ILR
Noreen	Bangladeshi	24	Pregnant	June 2002	Valid spousal visa	Police complaint	March 2004	June 2004	Awaited	Family friends	Awaiting decision from HO
Parmjeet	Indian	28	Pregnant	Jan 2006	Valid spousal visa	Police complaint, GP report	Jan 2005	Yet to be made	–	Friends	Spousal visa
Deepa	Indian	27	None	Aug 2003	Valid spousal visa	None, was not allowed out of the house	June 2004	Yet to be made	–	Friends	Spousal visa

Name	Ethnicity	Age	Dependants	Date of entry in UK	Immigration status at the time of HO application	Evidence of domestic violence	Date of separation from perpetrator of violence	Date of application for ILR to HO	Date of HO decision	Interim support provided by	Current status in UK
Zahida	Pakistani	26	1 son (3 years)	Mar 2001	Overstayer	Letter from refuge worker	June 2003	Sep 2003	Awaited	Accommodation by a refuge and assistance u/s 17 of CA	Overstayer, awaiting decision from HO
Rehana	Bangladeshi	22	None	Oct 2002	Valid spousal visa	999 call record	July 2004	Oct 2004	Awaited	Friends	Awaiting decision from HO
Nisha	Indian	27	None	Jan 2002	Valid spousal visa	None	Aug 2003	Oct 2004	Awaited	Earlier by friends and then by local authority u/s 21 NAA	Awaiting decision from HO
Manpreet	Indian	28	None	June 2001	Overstayer	None	Aug 2001	Nov 2003	Awaited	Friends	Overstayer, awaiting decision from HO
Nilofer	Bangladeshi	22	None	Dec 2003	Valid spousal visa	Police complaint	Oct 2004	Yet to be made	–	Friends	Spousal visa
Nargis	Pakistani	29	1 son (4 years)	Mar 2004	Not known	None	July 2004	Jan 2005	Awaited	Friends	Awaiting decision from HO

Key:
HO: Home Office
ILR: Indefinite leave to remain in the UK
NAA: National Assistance Act, 1948
CA: Children's Act, 1986

Parvinder, many immigrant women do not have access to information and services provided in the UK because they are not able to report domestic violence, and second, they are not able to make applications to the Home Office to regularise their residency. It is important to note that for many immigrant women, the perpetrator of domestic abuse will be their point of contact with the outside world, through power and control exercised by him but also because of the language barrier. This leaves women in such situations almost completely oblivious to the options and services that may be available and to delays in women making appropriate applications before the expiry of their initial spousal visa, resulting in them becoming overstayers. As the law stands, if such women make applications for indefinite leave to remain after becoming overstayers, they are not given any right to appeal against the Home Office decision. An asylum seeker who is the dependant on her husband's claim and who suffers domestic violence would be in a very similar situation to an overstayer. She would either need to satisfy the Home Office that she has her own claim for asylum or that there are human rights reasons for her to be granted leave to stay in the UK.

Conclusion

There has been much effort by the UK government to provide assistance to immigrant women experiencing domestic violence. The most progressive changes have been prompted by women's groups campaigning for greater legal protection and economic assistance, a notable case being the June 1999 abolition of the primary purpose rule. We recognise that changes in legislation have been well meaning, yet there remain serious problems in implementation, as well as serious unintended consequences, of legislation that limit its effectiveness. The most important fault lies in the conflict between the humanitarian aim of the government to protect those suffering from domestic violence, and the political need to be seen to be tough on illegal immigration. The system at present hinders an abused immigrant woman's fight for independence and security. As Lewis argues, '[t]he Government appears to be trying to tackle the issue of domestic violence but the legislation is discriminatory when considered holistically' (Lewis, 2004: 14). A sharp turn towards more conservative immigration and asylum laws has put vulnerable immigrant women at an extreme disadvantage as compared to women citizens, specifically with regard to social support and criminal justice response.

To better respond to the demonstrated needs of immigrant women, a number of measures should be implemented. To name only two, bolstering funding for emergency shelters and providing women access to public support systems would go a long way to supporting the needs of immigrant women. Abused women, whether they are citizens or not, deserve to feel safe; and this means ensuring easy access to affordable housing, healthcare and decent employment opportunities, so women can establish a better quality of life for themselves and their children. Furthermore, immigrant women require culturally sensitive services to accommodate their language, culture and religious diversity, and should have access to legal aid within a more gender-sensitive justice system (Joshi, 2003). What abused immigrant women need is not that much different from the needs and wants of the other disenfranchised groups, such as the homeless. The government, in its role as representative of a democratic population and protector of public trust, has an obligation to fulfil the basic human rights and ensure dignified living conditions for all their citizens, especially those who are the most vulnerable.

The UK has made a commitment to victims of domestic violence through the new Domestic Violence, Crime and Victims Act 2004. The purpose of the Act is to amend existing civil and criminal protection for victims of domestic violence and to address the rights of victims of crime through new legislation. Despite suggested amendments to the Act made by Women's Aid and Southall Black Sisters, the House of Lords rejected suggestions that victims of domestic violence be allowed access to public funds during their probationary period. We echo those suggestions put forward by many women's groups and argue for the need to change the Domestic Violence, Crime and Victims Act 2004 to better support immigrant women who face domestic violence. Specifically:

(a) all victims of domestic violence who are subject to immigration control should receive benefits and housing under the Housing Act 1996;
(b) the government should retrieve these funds from spouses, provided that there is no further risk of harm to the victim or her family;
(c) the Domestic Violence Immigration Rule should be extended to all victims of domestic violence subject to immigration control;
(d) the types of evidence required to prove domestic violence under the Domestic Violence Immigration Rule should be extended, and include: adjudicator decisions, victim and witness testimonies and reports, and letters from voluntary and statutory sector agencies.

One of the most dangerous times for an abused woman is the moment following her decision to leave her abuser (Women's Aid, 2004). For such women who find the courage to flee, access to public benefits is the safety net that enables them to create safe and secure lives for themselves and their children. The UK government must ensure that *all* women, including vulnerable immigrant women, have access to public funds and assistance when they attempt to separate from their abusers. If not, instead of providing women with a way out, the government will be condemning these women to a life of danger, violence or even death. Like most immigrants, women who are undocumented as result of domestic violence seek a future that includes families, homes and careers. They feel, however, unable to do so because of their tenuous legal status in the UK.

In 2004 the government provided a small amount of funding (£40,000) for a 'Last Resort Fund' to pay for safe refuge spaces for women with no other recourse for a maximum of two months each.[18] This fund was primarily administered by Women's Aid, who also raised a further £40,000 to add to the fund. Southall Black Sisters in 2004 calculated that the sum of £80,000 will only support 46 women for two months each, which is a fraction of the estimated 500 to 600 women with no recourse who are affected by domestic violence (Southall Black Sisters, n.d.). While this fund intended to help with paying rent and meeting daily living costs, its restriction to two months' support is unlikely to cover the period required for a woman to be granted indefinite leave to remain under the *Immigration Rules*.

In 2004/5 the government paid £120,000 into Women's Aid Last Resort Fund, with the aim of improving access to, and expanding the Fund, and to monitor its take-up. Government funding meant that the Fund could be extended to help women with money to pay refuge rents and meet living expenses for themselves and any children for up to eight weeks. Women's Aid secured additional funds to support this work and between April 2004 and March 2005, around 124 women were helped to access a place of safety, at a cost of £165,000 to the Fund. This is still a fraction of the estimated 500 to 600 women with no recourse who are affected by domestic violence annually (Southall Black Sisters, n.d.). In May 2005, the government advised Women's Aid there would be no further money made available for the Last Resort Fund, and it is currently suspended due to lack of funds. Although government's national action plan on domestic violence acknowledges the Last Resort Fund is only a temporary solution and that 'in the coming months ... Government Departments will be looking for long-term solutions for those victims with no recourse to public funds', no further announcements have been made about how this problem will be addressed.

Southall Black Sisters has calculated the total average cost of supporting women in a refuge for a period of one week at approximately £217 (Southall Black Sisters, n.d.). The application of a woman whose leave to remain has not expired is estimated to take approximately six weeks to process. Thus, the total cost of supporting all abused immigrant women in refuges while their applications are processed would cost (using the estimate from Southall Black Sisters) over £700,000. The problem for women's refuges is not simply then a question of identification and 'rescue' of the victims of domestic violence. There exists a massive shortfall of recourses relative to potential need. If a woman's leave to remain in the UK has expired and the woman subsequently becomes an 'overstayer', her application can take between one and two years to process. Supporting women in refuges for two years rather than six weeks is clearly an impossibility. This illustrates the vital long-term need for the legal system and welfare system to enable women to become self-supporting in employment rather than ostracise them and create a demand on the very limited resources of crisis organisations.

As the issue of domestic violence has begun to receive more attention in the UK, the special problems faced by immigrant women have started to receive attention and recognition. However, a piecemeal approach to the difficulties faced by abused immigrant women will not alleviate the problem of domestic violence. A comprehensive framework that addresses the plight of immigrant women through regulation, legislation and community-based efforts is urgently needed.

The statutory framework that has emerged in the UK makes some advances towards addressing domestic violence. For some immigrant women who are fleeing domestic violence, the framework goes a long way to help them escape their lives of abuse. While many uncertainties and ambiguities remain, this framework is still a significant improvement. However, protection for immigrant women fleeing domestic violence needs to be extended further to provide more than simply a glimmer of hope. Effective protection would allow women to make applications to remain legally in the UK on grounds of domestic violence, but this conflicts with the motivations framing the wider legal system that continue to undermine women's ability to achieve financial independence and remain separate from their abusers. There needs to be recognition within the legal system of the need to address the economic realities and consequences that immigrant women are confronted with when they leave abusive marriages. The different racial, cultural, economic and linguistic realities of immigrant women cannot be ignored. Any solutions must take such concerns into account, acknowledging that these are factors that shape an abused immigrant woman's assessment of her options.

Though we recognise that there can very well be a trade-off between the need to help abused immigrant women and the desire to control immigration, we take the strong view that the protection of vulnerable immigrant women experiencing domestic violence is a prime social duty of the legal system, one that should weigh more heavily than the need to prevent potential illegal immigration. The balance at present, we believe, is wrong. Whilst much is made by central government of its commitment to a fair and just immigration policy, it is clear that fairness and justice do not extend to ensuring the needs of some of the most vulnerable people are addressed or even recognised. The UK has committed itself to combating domestic violence, but this commitment will be undermined if not all women residing in the UK are effectively protected. Women's groups have recognised this fact, as has been made evident by the alliances involved in campaigns around all aspects of domestic violence, including the immigration law issues. If the government truly wishes to implement effective policies, it will have to acknowledge this fact as well. We end here with the powerful words of frustration issued by one of our clients with no recourse to public funds:

What is my fault in all this? I left my home, country, family and everything that I had ever known and came to the UK to live with my husband. In the last seven years that I have been here, not only have I been abused by my husband but by the state as well. I have been discriminated against only because I belong to a culture where women as upholders of family honour are expected not to complain against their husband and so I did not leave him even though my visa had expired. Now that I have left him, I have no support from the state because I did not leave him soon enough.

Acknowledgements

The authors would like to thank and acknowledge the clients of Newham Asian Women's Project for allowing us to refer to their experiences in this chapter. We would also like to thank Bryn Williams-Jones, Sarah van Walsum and Thomas Spijkerboer for their invaluable comments on an earlier version of this chapter.

Notes

1 We are aware that attempts to define violence remain a contested problem (Kelly and Lovett, 2004). Numerous factors exist which complicate simplistic definitions of domestic violence. The term itself is a symbolic, hence rhetorical construction, subject to contested meanings. Feminist advocates and researchers working in the field of domestic violence have been active in attempting to challenge the definition of the problem, to re-examine the scope and social construction of 'public' problems and to present and represent the face of the victim.

2 Though the dowry system was abolished in India in 1961 and in Bangladesh in 1980, more than 5,000 dowry deaths occur each year and many go unreported. Dowry is the money or gifts given at the time of marriage by parents of the bride to the groom and/or his family members (Oldenburg, 2002).

3 The UK government report *Safety and Justice* (Home Office, 2003), while repeating the one in four women statistic, adds that one in six men will be a victim of domestic violence in their lifetime. While the former statistic is now well established in policy statements (e.g., 'one in four: the London domestic violence strategy'), no corollary 'one in six' strategy has yet been devised for male victims of violence, possibly because of the recognition that the effects of domestic violence on men and women are incommensurable.

4 Although immigration from the countries of the New Commonwealth has been the focus of debate and policy, it accounts for only one-quarter of total immigration (Solomos, 2000).

5 In 2003, the UK received 49,405 applications for asylum (excluding dependants). The UK ranked ninth amongst European countries in 2003 in terms of asylum seekers per head of population. This was one lower than 2002, when the UK ranked eighth. France received more asylum applications than any other European country in 2003 (18 per cent of applications in Europe). Applications in Ireland, Germany and the Netherlands fell by 32 per cent, 29 per cent and

28 per cent respectively, while applications in France, Greece and Italy rose by 7 per cent, 44 per cent and 85 per cent respectively.

6 An overstayer is someone who has stayed in the UK after their visa expired and is considered an illegal resident, in breach of the immigration law and not permitted to remain in the UK (Lewis, 2004).

7 Anyone coming to live or stay in the UK must be able to support and accommodate themselves during this period without claiming certain benefits. These are: income support and jobseeker's allowance; housing and homelessness assistance; housing benefit and council tax benefit; working families' tax credit; a social fund payment; child benefit; or any disability allowance.

8 Paras 289 and 289A of HC395 as amended.

9 An application for indefinite leave to remain under the Domestic Violence Rules takes, on average, 47 days to process and a minimum of three months for the representative to prepare the application (including obtaining the relevant evidence). If the application is refused, the appeal procedure is timely. The woman will probably therefore be left in a precarious financial position while awaiting a decision.

10 As laid down in *R v Special Adjudicator (Respondent) ex p Ullah (FC) (Appellant); Do (FC) (Appellant v Secretary of State for the Home Department (Respondent)* [2004] UKHL 26.

11 Right to private and family life.

12 *Chahal v UK*, (1997) 23 EHRR 413.

13 Right to freedom from torture, inhuman or degrading treatment.

14 Most EU states base their definition of a refugee on Article 1 of the 1951 Geneva Convention:

> for the purposes of the present Convention, the term 'refugee' shall apply to any person who: . . . (2) As a result if events occurring before 1 January 1951 and owing to a well-founded fear of being persecuted for reasons of race, religion, nationality, membership of a particular social group or political opinion, is outside of the country of his nationality, and is unable or owing to such fear is unwilling to avail himself of the protection of that country . . .

Different states interpret this article differently. A refugee enjoys the rights specified in the Geneva Convention while an asylum seeker has far fewer rights.

15 Intersectionality as a framework, developed within critical race theory, constitutes a critique to traditional ethnic and feminist research which assumes that all women experience oppression in the same form.

16 Newham Asian Women's Project is a charity based in the London Borough of Newham. It provides advice, information, support, training, counselling and safe accommodation to women and children fleeing domestic violence.

17 All the names in this chapter have been changed to protect the identity of the clients.

18 Since this chapter was submitted in 2004 the situation for this group of women has significantly deteriorated in terms of their access to support from the government.

References

Bhabha, Jacqueline and Shutter, Sue (1994) *Women's Movement: Women under Nationality, Immigration and Refugee Law*, Stoke-on-Trent: Trentham Books

Coleman, David and Salt, John (1992) *The British Population: Patterns, Trends and Processes*, Oxford: Oxford University Press

DasGupta, Shamita (1998) 'Women's realities: Defining violence against women by immigration, race, and class', in Bergen, Raquel Kennedy (ed), *Issues in Intimate Violence*, Thousand Oaks, CA: Sage

DasGupta, Shamita (2000) 'Charting the course: An overview of domestic violence in the South Asian community in the United States', *Journal of Social Distress and the Homeless* 9, pp 173–85

Dobson, Janet, Koser, Khalid, McLaughlan, Gail and Salt, John (2001) 'International migration and the United Kingdom: Recent patterns and trends', *Research, Development and Statistics Directorate Occasional Paper 75*, London: Research Development and Statistics Directorate, Home Office

Erez, Edna (2000) 'Immigration, culture conflict and domestic violence/woman battering', *Crime Prevention and Community Safety: An International Journal* 2(1), pp 27–36

Gill, Aisha and Rehman, Gulshan (2004) 'Empowerment through activism: Responding to domestic violence in the South Asian community', *Gender and Development* 12(1), pp 75–83

Gupta, Rahila (2003) *From Homebreakers to Jailbreakers: Southall Black Sisters*, London: Zed Books

Hanmer, Jane and Maynard, Mary (eds) (1987) *Women, Violence and Social Control*, Basingstoke Macmillan.

Home Office (2003) *Safety and Justice: The Government's Proposal on Domestic Violence*, London: Home Office, the Research, Practice and Statistics Directorate

Home Office (2005) 'Tackling domestic violence: Providing advocacy and support to survivors from Black and other minority ethnic communities', *Home Office Development and Practice Report* 35, London: Home Office, The Research, Practice and Statistics Directorate.

Joshi, Poonam (2003) 'Jumping through hoops: Immigration and domestic violence', in Gupta, Rahila (ed), *From Homebreakers to Jailbreakers: Southall Black Sisters*, London: Zed Books

Kelly, Liz and Lovett, Jo (2004) *What a Waste: An Argument for an Integrated Approach to Violence against Women*, London: Women's National Commission

Lewis, Kate (2004) *Victims of Domestic Violence: Disparities Accessing Legal and Social Welfare Assistance under EU and Domestic Legislation*, London: JCWI

Oldenburg, Veena (2002) *Dowry Murder: The Imperial Origins of a Cultural Crime*, Oxford and New York: Oxford University Press

Raj, Anita and Silverman, Jay (2002) 'Violence against immigrant women: The roles of culture, context and legal immigrant status on intimate partner violence', *Violence against Women* 43, pp 1311–26

Schuster, Liza (2003) 'Common sense or racism? The treatment of asylum-seekers in Europe', *Patterns of Prejudice* 37(3) pp 233–56

Sen, Purna, Humphreys, Catherine and Kelly, Liz with WOMANKIND Worldwide (2003) *CEDAW Thematic Shadow Report: Violence against Women in the UK*, London: Womankind

Solomos, John (2000) *Race and Racism in Britain*, Basingstoke: Macmillan

Southall Black Sisters (n.d.) The Two Year Rule (formerly The One Year Rule) Campaign, accessed at: http://www.southallblacksisters.org.uk/campaign_oneyearrule.html

Wachholz, Sandra and Miedema, Baukje (2000) 'Risk, fear, harm: Immigrant women's perceptions of the "policing" solution to woman abuse', *Crime, Law, and Social Change* 34, pp 301–17

Williams-Crenshaw, Kimberly (1991) 'Mapping the margins: Intersectionality, identity politics and violence against women of colour', *Stanford Law Review* 43, pp 1241

Women's Aid (2004) *Annual Report*, available at: http://www.womensaid.org.uk

World Health Organisation (2002) *World Report on Violence and Health*, Geneva: WHO

11

FRENCH IMMIGRATION LAWS

The *sans-papières'* perspectives

Catherine Raissiguier

This chapter contrasts the ways in which undocumented immigrant women are constructed by and through French media and legal discourses to the ways in which some immigrant women narrate themselves in the context of the *sans-papiers* movement. The chapter opens with a discussion of discursive processes that place these women under erasure. It then moves on to show how legal narratives as well as legal/social practices in France are locating and locking some immigrant women into 'domestic' and 'traditional' roles within French society. The chapter ends with a discussion of four women's narratives, which offer provocative critiques of current French administrative and legal practices.

In the chapter, I argue that undocumented women are kept out of the sphere of rights in part through discursive and material practices that tie them to the family, matrimony and motherhood. It has been argued that undocumented immigrants in France are relegated to a zone of infra rights (Lochack, 1985). Here I suggest that for women, these infra rights are in part produced by gendered relations that affect all women in France, but that affect immigrant women in particular and contradictory ways. On the one hand, being a mother (especially of a child born on French soil) has been one of the most successful bases for legalisation for undocumented immigrant women seeking to obtain a change of status. On the other hand, derivative rights acquired through family reunification have robbed many immigrant women of their legal autonomy and placed them in vulnerable situations vis à vis their families and the French state.

Moreover, once located in the realm of domesticity and 'tradition', immigrant women become the privileged signifier and constant reminder of certain immigrant communities' failure to integrate into French society. Here, old notions of African women drawn from France's colonial imaginary are rearticulated into the current context of post-colonial population movements. In particular, the image of an overly fecund African mother haunts current discussions of the 'immigration problem' in France. These rearticulations

204

place immigrant women at the centre of anti-immigrant and racist developments in contemporary France and render them particularly vulnerable to
such developments.

The *sans-papiers* movement: women under erasure

In the spring of 1996 a group of post-colonial immigrants launched a resistance movement that transformed common understandings of grassroots
immigrant politics in France. This group, now referred to as the *sans-papiers*
(literally 'without papers'), are undocumented immigrants and refugees
sometimes under threat of deportation. The term *sans-papières* refers specifically to immigrant *women* who are without papers. The *sans-papiers* organised early as collectives and demanded that the French state legalise their
status. The movement gained national and international attention when,
in August 1996, the police forcibly removed 300 *sans-papiers* from the
Saint-Bernard church in Paris, which they had occupied for two months.[1] By
directly confronting the legal impasses that the French law has created for
them, undocumented immigrants have been forcing France to look at the
contradictions embedded within the laws of the republic.

Women have always constituted a significant presence within the movement, especially in the early stages of the struggle. However, there has been
little to no serious attention given to that presence. And while women tend to
be graphically evoked whenever the French media report on the movement
(they are everywhere in the background of the coverage of the *sans-papiers'*
demonstrations, sit-ins and hunger strikes) – in fact one might argue that
they have become a visual staple of the *sans-papiers* story backdrop – there is
an obvious erasure of them and their specific issues. For instance, in spite of
such graphic visibility, I was initially unable to determine the number of
women involved and their particular stake in the movement. When I clipped
the written press, I found that the St Bernard *sans-papiers* were mostly
from Mali but also from Senegal, Cameroon, Guinea, Mauritania and the
Maghreb. I also discovered that among them were some 100 children and
around 12 polygamous families – but rarely was mention made of the women
themselves. When a leader was interviewed in the paper or on TV, it was
likely to be a male figure with the notable exception of Madjiguène Cissé,
who emerged as one of the strongest leaders and spokespersons for the
movement.

Despite the numerical importance of women in the Saint-Bernard collective (more than 30 per cent of the adults were women) and despite their
continued substantive presence in the movement, the dominant representation of the *sans-papiers* struggle is one that does not seriously take women
into account. One only need look at the French daily newspaper *Le Monde*
between 14 August and 30 August 1996, to witness the literal erasure of
women (and children) from the struggle. This is the two-week period when

negotiations were at a standstill, and the movement received continuous coverage from the French press. At that moment, ten *sans-papiers* engaged in a hunger strike for more than 40 days were physically at risk. Negotiations between the government and the *sans-papiers* were interrupted, and the French government planned the evacuation of the church but was reluctant to implement such a forced removal in the context of an (inter)national movement of solidarity mounting in support for the Saint-Bernard 300.

By looking at the *Le Monde*'s illustration of the crisis, we can see, among other things, that the movement is conceptualised and presented as a story whose main protagonists are men – especially French men. In the cartoons published by the newspaper, the conflict is represented as *une affaire d'hommes (blancs)*, white men's business. The stories themselves, however, present a more nuanced take on the struggle. The *sans-papiers*, in fact, have become so central to the culture that they are also used to illustrate other stories for the paper. In the 14 August 1996 issue of *Le Monde*, the front-page story is about the decline of vacation-time road accidents in France. Next to it, one can also read a story about the *sans-papiers,* and the help they are increasingly receiving from left and humanitarian organisations. The cartoon, which

Le nombre de morts sur les routes est le plus bas depuis 1956

La Sécurité routière constate une plus grande sagesse des Français

Les soutiens sans papiers

Associations et opposition

LA SEMAINE du 15 août s'annonce très chargée sur les routes de France. Au traditionnel chassé-croisé des vacanciers s'ajoutera un grand nombre de départs en week-end prolongé, le 15 août permettant cette année de « faire le pont » quatre jours durant. *En 1991, année présentant la même configuration calendaire, on avait enregistré un week-end record pour les retours, avec un grand nombre de bouchons »*, rappelle la direction de la Sécurité routière, qui a classé « rouge » la journée du 17 août en province et « orange » les retours vers l'Ile-de-France le lendemain.

Le dernier bilan publié par la Sécurité routière témoigne d'une plus grande sagesse des automobilistes français : durant le premier semestre 1996, la route a tué 7,7 % de personnes en moins qu'au premier semestre 1995 et le mois de juin 1996 fut le onzième mois consécutif de baisse importante du nombre des victimes.

Entre juillet 1995 et juin 1996, 8 105 personnes sont décédées sur les routes. Ce chiffre est le plus faible depuis que les statis-

tiques de la Sécurité routière ont été créées en 1956. La continuité, depuis le début des années 90, des politiques publiques visant à renforcer la réglementation, et, surtout, le nouveau comportement des Français face aux risques de la route semblent être

à l'origine de cette évolution. Celle-ci doit néanmoins se confirmer, la France figurant seulement au huitième rang des pays européens les plus prudents.

Lire page 20

LES DIX GRÉVISTES de la faim sans-papiers de l'église Saint-Bernard, hospitalisés quelques heures de force par la préfecture de police de Paris lundi 12 août au matin, poursuivaient tous leur mouvement de grève, mardi 13 août.

Figure 11.1 Cartoon by Plantu.

Source: Le Monde, 14 August 1996.

represents a French policeman driving a whole African family back to the border, is cleverly used to illustrate both stories. One of the black back-seat passengers says: 'The French, they are driving better and better!' The white policeman, as the driver, is at the centre of the image. In the back seat, one adult male is surrounded by a 'slew' of children and one woman – presumably his wife and the mother of all the children. This representation of an African woman in relation to the *sans-papiers'* struggle is both exceptional and typical. It is exceptional in that usually women are not present in these cartoons and typical in the sense that she is the quintessential African woman who gets conjured up when the African presence in France is in need of a trope. Tellingly, she is silent in the cartoon and half-hidden by the car's window frame. This visual narrative, however, belies the more complicated story unfolding in the Saint-Bernard church. Indeed, the reader need only turn to page six of the paper to discover the story of Marianne Camara. The 27-year-old Malian mother of two is angry and determined. She has just joined the four other women involved in the hunger strike in protest of the forced hospitalisation of the strikers: 'Babies were crying, perhaps the riot police were trying to scare us so that we'd abandon the struggle. But we will not give up. We are not afraid of a church evacuation' (*Le Monde* 14 August 1996).

Camara, then, is a mother who, unlike the woman in the cartoon, is speaking and acting. Burying Camara's story in the back pages of the paper is another way of erasing the active presence of women within the struggle. Camara's story is the kind of counter-narrative that I want to foreground in this chapter. This is a narrative that resituates immigrant women at the centre of the story and looks at the ways in which they participate in and transform the discursive and social practices that shape French politics of immigration at the beginning of the new millennium. By engaging this counter-narrative, my aim is to complicate and disrupt hegemonic representations of post-colonial immigrant women in France. This chapter then, at the very least, brings visibility to the heterogeneous presence, work and transformative agency of women involved in the *sans-papiers* movement. A larger aim is to suggest that some immigrant women are being constructed in ways that emphasise and reinforce their domestic roles in the family and locate them primarily in the sphere of the private and the 'traditional'. In a contradictory logic, immigrant women emerge as symbols of 'tradition' and backwardness, and at the same time are locked in material realities that reproduce them as radically foreign. Old colonial/patriarchal beliefs about African women are rearticulated here to racialise certain immigrant communities and to politicise the very question of immigration in France. Legal discourse is an arena where we can see this paradoxical logic at play.

Changes in French laws: from derivative rights to legal autonomy?

While French law is gender-neutral (it refers to spouses rather than wives or husbands), institutions, cultural norms and social interactions are not (Lesselier, 2003: 45). It has been amply demonstrated, for instance, that the so-called end of legal work immigration in 1974 hastened and deepened an already existing momentum toward the feminisation of immigration in France. After 1974, family reunification became one of the few ways to enter the country legally and migratory profiles began to change dramatically in the 1970s and the 1980s. Indeed, in the second half of the 1970s we begin to see men migrating to France after having married a legal immigrant or a young French woman of immigrant descent. While these changes might be read as interesting reversals of existing gender patterns, it has been noted that these new migratory profiles might anchor (and strengthen) otherwise on-the-wane matrimonial practices. Young women, as a result, find themselves in difficult situations that sometimes result in profound unhappiness and domestic violence.[2]

For the past three decades legal scholars, grassroots immigrant women's organisations and international agencies have underscored and deplored the specific legal vulnerability of immigrant women in France. Many of their rights, at least until 1984, have been defined as derivative rights (Scales-Trent, 1999; Rude Antoine, 1996; Gaspard, 1995; Rahal-Sidhoum, 1987). Because most immigrant women entered the French territory through the process of family reunification, their immigration, citizenship, income-generating power and social benefits are connected to the status of a male family member. In other words, it is the legal status of a spouse (or father) that determines the legal status given to a woman. The severing of familial and marital relationships can put immigrant women and their daughters in a legal bind vis à vis the French state and, in the worst-case scenarios, usher them into the realm of illegality.

Before 1984, spouses and children introduced through the procedure of family reunification were granted a residency card that mentioned their status as 'family members' and did not include the right to seek employment. Residency and work permits were separate documents. Those family members who wished to work for a wage needed to request a work permit once they could document they had secured a job.

A law introduced on 17 July 1984 established two types of sojourn/work cards: a temporary sojourn card (whose length can vary but cannot exceed one year) and the residency card which is valid for ten years. Both cards entitle the recipient to legal work. Since 1984, family members who enter the country through the procedure of family reunification obtain the same card as the resident member; renewal is automatic for those who obtain a ten-year residency card. For those who receive a temporary card, renewal is tied to their ability to provide for themselves should the familial link be severed. This particular change in the law of 1984 marks the end of strict 'derivative' rights for immigrant women in French immigration law.[3]

However, women are still rendered legally vulnerable by the common administrative practice of the non-immediate issuance of residency and temporary cards and the handing out of application receipts (*récipicés*), which are valid for three months only and must be renewed repeatedly to ensure the person legal protection. The most recent of the immigration laws (2003) codified the practice by stipulating that rejoining spouses would only be granted a temporary card for the first two years; a clear setback from the gains of 1984.[4]

In March 1993, a conservative government, with Charles Pasqua in the position of Prime Minister, developed and implemented a stringent politics of immigration control. Among other things, the 1993 immigration law increased immigrant women's legal vulnerability. It made legal family reunification much harder to achieve and stipulated that in the case of divorce or estrangement within a year after the issuance of legal residency papers, these could be taken away from or not renewed for the foreign spouse.[5] When in rupture of legal status, women could be deported to their countries of origin. Mothers of French children are protected from such deportations under French law, but could become undocumented and therefore unable to work legally or to claim and receive social and health benefits. The Pasqua laws of 1993 also prohibited the entry of polygamous families into France through the process of family reunification (only one wife and her children can be brought into the country through the procedure). It also prohibited the renewal of residency permits of foreigners in polygamous situations. Such restrictive measures created the very conditions that were to produce many undocumented immigrants in France – among them family members who entered the country outside the bounds of legal family reunification – and who swelled the ranks of the *sans-papiers* movement in the mid-1990s.

In spite of some improvements, the 1998 Chevènement Law did little to diminish the dependency of women on their spouse's legal status. The law did codify the notion of 'familial and private life' as one of the criteria that would be taken into account for legalising undocumented immigrants. Theoretically the law opened up the notion of 'family' to include bonds outside those of matrimony such as common law marriage (*concubinage*) and civil unions of straight and gay couples. However, the notion of 'family and private life' is often very narrowly interpreted by the administration.[6] Polygamous family members who entered the country prior to 1993 can have their residency papers renewed as long as they can document that they are no longer bound by a polygamous union and are no longer co-habiting. This specific measure has put some women in extremely vulnerable positions, especially given the limited availability of affordable housing.

A brief review of family reunification in France since the mid-1970s underscores that the contradictory circumstances created by French immigration legislation often put immigrant women and the children who depend on them in vulnerable and precarious situations and work against their long-term integration within French society, which has been a stated goal of French governments for the past 20 years. I shall suggest here that legal narratives (as well as popular and scholarly ones) draw some of the discursive and material boundaries within which immigrant women begin to understand and narrate their own selves.

Four women/four trajectories

For the purpose of this chapter, I have decided to focus on four women who are currently active in *sans-papiers* collectives. It should be clear, however, that this is a different phase of the movement; we are now six years into the struggle, all the St Bernard *sans-papiers* with a few exceptions have obtained a change of status, and the demographics of the collectives have changed drastically (North Africans, Eastern Europeans and Asians are now present in large numbers and increasingly active in the movement).[7] The key issues, perspectives and strategies of the movement are also different from those that emerged in the first stages of the struggle. For instance, while activists still claim that they are fighting for a collective change of status, asking for *des papiers pour tous!* (papers for everyone), it is clear that at this particular juncture all negotiations happen and are resolved at the individual level. While these four women do not represent the full range of immigrant/activist experiences revealed by my interviews, they do give us a sense of the great variety of experiences and some of the recurring themes emerging from all the interviews.[8]

Louisa: struggling for women's legal autonomy [9]

I met Louisa in Marseilles in the spring of 2002. She was 25 at the time of my interview. Like Camara, quoted above, Louisa is a young immigrant woman struggling to define for herself the contours and the meanings of her presence in France. Louisa is a young Muslim woman from the Comoro Islands who arrived in 1993, aged 17, to be with her older sister and to study in France. She entered the country with a three-month visa hoping that she would obtain a change of status by having her sister become her legal guardian. Her applications took over a year to be processed and when she finally obtained an answer it was negative: by then she was too old – at 18 – to be under the guardianship of her sister. Instead of going back to aging parents, a dislocated economy and a bankrupt educational system, Louisa decided to stay and join the ranks of the thousands of undocumented immigrants who now live in France in the most precarious conditions. She enrolled in a

French private school in 1995, learned French and obtained excellent results. However, she was unable to take the national end of high school exam (*le baccalauréat*) because she did not have appropriate short-stay residency papers. In 1997 she applied for a change of status but her application was rejected. She became involved in the *sans-papiers* movement in 1998. Between her first application and the time she actually obtained a change of status in 2001, she appealed four times and was rejected four times.

Louisa's critique of the French authorities and how they handle undocumented immigrant women's applications for changes of status is quite telling. Louisa recounts that Marseilles immigration officials recommended that she get married in order to obtain a change of status:

> Literally at the *Préfecture*, they would tell us: If you have a hard time getting your papers, just get married and then you will obtain a change of status – that's easy and there won't be any problem . . . with a French national of course [laughter], but I did not want that! If you want papers, just have kids . . . this is not a written policy but that is what the civil servant working the counter would tell us. Perhaps they think they are helping us that way . . . but it is not my choice, it is not my choice! I wanted to build my life before . . . that is the battle to win.[10]

Louisa goes on to discuss the dire effects of these administrative practices on women who follow the advice of various administrative agents. Her interview refers, in part, to the perverse effects of the issuance of *récipicés* to women who are actually entitled to residency papers and to the fact that women have to stay married for a minimum of two years before they can keep their papers:

> I have seen women who listened to that, got married with guys they did not love, and then found themselves under constant threat because even if you are married and you have your residency papers, you have to wait three years to be fully autonomous . . . you cannot divorce, you cannot argue with your husband because you are afraid that he will ask for a divorce. So these women found themselves in worse situations than mine – without papers. Some got kids with men who did not declare the children and therefore they were not able to get their papers in the end . . . that's why [I am organising] to show to all these women that you can obtain what you want through struggle!

Louisa's testimony underscores the fact that immigrant women in France are literally being tied to the family through a variety of quasi-legal, political and social practices. Later on in the interview, she explains how single

211

women are always suspect characters in the eyes of the French administration: 'How can a single woman live in France for ten years without papers?' Because women are always thought of as depending on a man, it becomes impossible to imagine them independently migrating, getting an education, obtaining paid work, and supporting themselves in spite of the fact that hundreds of them do just that. According to Louisa, the French administration treats immigrant women as perpetual minors. She sees this basic fight for immigrant women's legal autonomy at the core of the *sans-papiers* movement.

Clairette: gendering 'security'

> If today I ask to stay in France, it is because I have nothing left. I have nothing left at home! If I retire, I do not have a house any longer. My house has been broken, destroyed. I have nothing left . . . I know I can have a position there, but I would have to start again as if I were at the beginning of my career.

Clairette, a highly religious (Christian) and unassuming woman in her early fifties, is from the Republic of the Congo (RC). I met her at the *sans-papiers* collective in one of the working-class suburbs of Paris – where she attended meetings on a semi-regular basis. Unlike Louisa, Clairette did not flee her homeland because of dire poverty and the destructuring of basic public services in her country. What set her on a trajectory of displacement and immigration were the brutal civil wars that have erupted in the RC since the early 1990s, and recurring health problems connected to the traumas she experienced during these civil wars. Like most of the other *sans-papiers*, her relationship to France preceded the troubles that made her leave the Congo.[11] Connected with a Franco-African network of bio-medical researchers (especially around the treatment and prevention of AIDS/HIV), she had already travelled to France many times.[12] Her only daughter and former husband lived in France with regular papers. In fact, Clairette makes it quite clear in the interview that she could have invoked 'family reunification' in the 1980s and early 1990s (when her daughter was still under 18) if her primary interest had been to stay in France for familial or economic reasons.

Clairette needs to say here, she claims, to protect her safety, to take care of her health, and to be able to maintain a relationship with her daughter and her grandchildren. In fact, what Clairette sees as the ideal situation for her is a legal status that would allow her to come and go between the two countries as she pleases:

> Yes, for me the ideal would be to be able to come and go. That would be perfect. That way, I could continue [to live] in my country because I am entitled to my retirement [benefits] back home. But when I need

to come and visit my daughter and my grandchildren, to be able to do it without problems so that I can be the grandmother to my French grandchildren. Yes, to be able to come without difficulties so that I can get treatment [when I need it]. So for me the ideal situation is not necessarily to hold a position here – if they [the French authorities] are afraid of that – but to be able to work a little bit here, to draw a salary, to save some money, and then leave for my country.

The tightening of immigration laws, throughout Europe, in the 1980s and the 1990s has made such legal standing and flexible arrangement next to impossible. Once in France, immigrants who have overstayed their legal sojourn (often after one month for a tourist visa) are likely to stay without papers because they know that if they return, their chances of coming back are very slim.

Clairette, who clearly sees herself as highly educated and part of an elite middle class, resents that she cannot leverage her educational and class status to parlay her change of status or at least a job that would enable her to support herself while waiting for a legal decision on her case to be made:

I personally think that if a person has difficulties getting a change of status, then they [the French authorities] should at least take into account the competency level of the person ... to let that person support herself while she is waiting for her papers. Yes, at least, check the skills of the person as far as work is concerned. It is not because you are an immigrant that you have nothing to offer. I personally think that it is the immigrants who build the country so you should be more considerate [toward them]. Not only you don't give them papers, but you don't want them to work either. And then, later, people are surprised by the fact that [in France] we have an insecurity problem ... people become aggressive when they do not have ... and the woman, if she is not grounded, it can even lead to prostitution! That's it! It does push [some] women who are alone, who have no help to turn to prostitution. Then, we are surprised that AIDS/HIV rates [of infection] are on the rise ... and those who have to beg because they are destitute. It is not a good thing for a country to have people begging on the street. Wouldn't it be better to give these people a job instead to have them begging or turning to prostitution?

Clairette connects the fact that the *sans-papiers* are de facto incapable of supporting themselves legally to larger social and epidemiological problems that are plaguing France and are fuelling the 'immigration panic' in the country. She sees women as particularly vulnerable and, like Louisa, she is highly critical of the social and political practices that push women to consider motherhood and marriage as means to attain a change of status and leave behind their *sans-papiers* status:

> I want territorial asylum ... because I am not safe [at home].[13] People are pushed ... I have seen other people who are forced to give birth in order to get their papers or to marry; that is something I disagree with. Often folks find themselves with a child that they do not want because that child for sure [was begotten] to have papers ... that is a terrible thing ... or you get married ... that is not, that is not, I think that it is belittling, I mean degrading because I have seen some people who were married at home and here they are forced to remarry in order to obtain their papers ... or to abandon their family back home.

Karina: post-colonial crossings, gender inequalities

Karina, a young Algerian mother of two, has a long history of familial connections with France and especially with the city of Marseilles. Although she was born in Algeria, like many of her closest relatives, Karina has spent most of her life in France. However, at the end of a common tale of several moves back and forth between the two countries, Karina re-entered France in 2000 with a short-term visa and found herself *sans-papiers* after her visa expired. Her story illustrates the complex post-colonial backdrop of the trajectory and the lived experience of many *sans-papiers*. It also underscores the fact that gender hierarchies at play on both sides of the Mediterranean have shaped Karina's own trajectory and need to be analysed to fully understand how she, unlike her brothers, finds herself without papers in a country where she grew up, went to school, and where a large part of her family has long-standing roots.

In 1962 (when Algeria won its independence) Karina's father left Algeria to seek work in France. In fact, Karina's grandfather had done the same thing in 1915 and had spent his life split between the two countries. Karina's grandfather lived and worked in Marseilles for eleven months of each year and would spend one month in Algeria with his wife and young children. While in Marseilles he managed several restaurants, employed his sons in his business, and over the years had several French companions who bore him eleven children. Throughout the years, he brought several of his (Algerian) sons to work in his restaurants. After a few years of one-month visits to Algeria, Karina's father sent for his family. Karina's mother, Karina and her brothers arrived in France in the late 1960s through the legal procedure of family reunification. Her mother would have three more children in France: two daughters and a son. When Karina was 4 she was sent back to Algeria to keep her grandmother company. However, when she turned 6, she came back to Marseilles and started school in the French public educational system.

Karina would stay, grow up, and be educated in France until 1987, when her parents decided they wanted to return home, retire and live in the villa they had had built for them. Karina made the conscious (but with hindsight problematic) decision to follow them:

> My father wanted to get closer to his mother. I followed along with the younger children. I thought that I would go to Algeria . . . France is not so welcoming to foreigners. I thought I would go back to Algeria and teach. I [thought I] was not losing much by going back to Algeria. We used to go every year. We did not realise it was a developing country when we were there on vacations . . . I studied education for two years and I became a teacher of French. That's where I met my husband – he too was a former immigrant [and he too is now *sans-papiers* in Marseilles].

In 1989, Karina's mother decided to bring the whole family back to Marseilles to flee a dangerous civil war. Karina and a brother decided to stay in Algeria. Karina explains that she was bound by a contract to the Algerian state whereby she had agreed to teach for a number of years after her state-sponsored teacher's training. Karina also explains how her parents failed to protect her by making sure she would maintain a legal connection to France in case she decided to return – something they had done for her brothers:

> As a woman – my rights were not foregrounded. If you fail to come back to France after a six-month absence, you lose your [residency] papers. The boys kept going back and forth so they would not lose their legal standing. I didn't.

In the rest of the interview Karina explains how she and her husband felt in danger in a country where fundamentalists targeted teachers and civil servants. As a woman, the threats were particularly frightening:

> I was not wearing the veil. I was teaching [in a school] where the girls were wearing the veil. We [her husband and herself] were like extra-terrestrials – in the city things are a bit more open, but [in the rural area where we taught] we were pariahs . . . One day the fundamentalists called for a general strike. On that day, I was the only teacher at work, the only one!

After several years of struggle and careful planning, in 2000, Karina, her husband and their two children arrived in France on a short-term visa and with FF 200,000 (slightly over $30,000) in savings. When I met Karina in 2002, most of the money was gone, both she and her husband worked 'illegal' jobs, and both were activists with the Marseilles *sans-papiers* collective.

She sees her participation in this struggle as a way to transform the gender relations that contributed to turning her into a *sans-papière*. At the end of the interview she concludes:

> Now that I feel like my head is above water, I want to continue [the struggle] for other women. When I tell women 'there is a march on Saturday,' they reply: 'Wait, I have to talk it over with my husband.' That has got to stop!

Malika: a small room of one's own

I met Malika at a public demonstration in Paris. In front of a mixed crowd of *sans-papiers*, Malika drummed, chanted and led the other demonstrators in spirited songs about the plight of the *sans-papiers*. A *sans-papiers* delegate in her collective, Malika was one of the most active organisers and certainly the most active woman for that particular collective. In her mid-thirties, Malika was one of the many single *sans-papiers* for whom a legal change of status would prove difficult to obtain.

Malika was born in Morocco and lived in extreme poverty until she turned 18 and was forced to marry a man much older than herself. While her economic status slightly improved after her marriage (her husband was a migrant worker in Iraq), her life turned into a nightmare of abuse, domestic violence and marital rape. She still bears the marks of four years of abuse she endured on her body and her soul. Malika fled Morocco not to escape poverty, not to escape civil war, but simply to save herself and to leave behind a life of abuse, fear and gender-based violence. She is the only one among the four women featured in this essay to have entered France illegally. With a sister living and established in France, Malika – like many others – tried to obtain a short-term tourist visa:

> My sister did send me the [proof] that she could put me up. But I was denied a visa because I had no salary and I had no bank account – neither I, nor my father. I just wanted a short-term visa – even for two weeks. I wanted to get out – I had no choice. It was like death for me. Everything was black. When I saw a man, any man, on the street it was torture. On top of that I was dirt poor. I was alone – my whole family is here in France [except for her father] and when I saw them, when they visited for a vacation, they would tell me how France is a beautiful country and how it is the country of man's [sic] rights and that women can have all kinds of things, that in France you can prosecute [an abusive husband], you can do this, you can do that . . . I could only think of France. But I was not granted the visa. I came in, like that, without a visa, illegally. . . . I passed with the papers of another woman who looked like me.

216

Malika found work almost immediately after she entered the country illegally. Working as a live-in maid for three years, Malika managed to save money, learn French, and little by little reconstruct herself as a whole person. She recounts with delight her first months at her employer's home:

> It was the first time in my life that I had a small room of my own. I knew, I totally knew my place – I was a maid, but it was something that I will never forget: for the first time in my life a small room of my own: a bed, a small TV. I had never had a TV in my whole life, I mean until I was 25. I was 25 when I arrived in France. See, that was amazing. They were good people . . . I like to read, because I did not go to school for very long – five years: you can hardly accomplish anything. But I always loved to read. So I bought a little book. It is written in Arabic and translated in French. [I used it] to understand what the parents were saying to their children. I asked what are you saying? What does this mean? Then I used the book to locate the words and memorise them – it is thanks to them that I learned how to speak little by little – they helped me improve my French.

Malika learned much more than language skills through her work experience. What the 'small room of her own' provides her with is a personal space to look at her life, heal some of the wounds of gender oppression, and make crucial connections between different forms of oppressive and exploitative relations:

> See, I did not want to stay at my sister's. I wanted to work. I wanted to be independent. Because when you live like this, like an object, after you revolt. I wanted to know what the freedom of a woman to decide all alone, to have a pay-check, not depend on someone else, was [like]. So for me it was great that I was able to work immediately. . . . But why was it great for me? Because at that time I did not know what it meant to work [for a wage] – I did not know about working hours. I did not know. All I could see was that I was in a castle. It was only a villa, but for me it was a castle that I could not dream of. It was my little room that I never had until then, it was people who respected me. I did not care about the work, for me it was normal. I did not negotiate my salary, I did not . . . I did not know! Even if they had told me you have to work Saturdays and Sundays, I would have probably said yes, because I did not know.

Malika's 'little room' and the privilege it represents can also be seen as screens that initially mystify the exploitation that she is experiencing and prevent her from 'knowing'. As time goes by, however, Malika began to revolt against the exploitative working conditions that often come with the territory of live-in domestic work. Little by little, she recounts, her employers asked her to perform tasks that Malika saw as outside the boundary of her live-in maid contract: working in the garden, washing her employer's car, and baking 'speciality' cakes for the whole family. Malika also clearly resents that neither her family nor the family who employed her – in the three years she worked for them – ever took the time to take her to Paris (both lived in the suburbs):

> I never went to Paris, never! Each time I asked my sister, she'd reply: 'Cops are everywhere.' So I thought the cops were circling the subway, I did not know!

When she asked her employers to give her a formal work contract so that she could seek a change of status, her employers demanded that she sign a ten-year work contract. Malika refused the terms of their offer and walked out:

> I said no. NO, I said ten years that's a whole life! I don't know what is going to happen. I do not want to sign a contract. If you want to [employ me legally] then you do it. If you don't you don't, what can I tell you?

Malika finds illegal work again fast and easily. She is working as a maid in a third-class hotel run by a Kabyle. She asks him to get paid at the end of each day of work (FF 150 – under $30 at the beginning; FF 300 – around $50 at the end) in order to avoid being robbed of a salary should the hotel close or her boss suddenly decide to disappear. Malika probably gleaned this piece of knowledge through conversations with other *sans-papiers*. During my research I heard several stories of *sans-papiers* being robbed of their salary by unsavoury employers taking advantage of their illegal status. So after almost nine years of life and full-time employment in France, Malika cannot 'prove' that she has been here for that long (she has no lease to show, no stamp dating her entry on her passport, and no other records that are asked of her by the French authorities). Neither can she 'prove' that she has been gainfully employed for all these years (she has no working contract, pay stubs, or even proof of a bank account in France).

So Malika in November 2001 joined a *sans-papiers* collective to come out once again and fight for her dignity, her rights and her independent status as an immigrant woman. Her interview echoes a recurring theme in these four women's interviews. For them, immigrant rights and the *sans-papiers* struggle are deeply connected to gender rights and the legal autonomy of women. For them, women's and gender issues are at the core of this important social movement. For them immigrant rights and women's rights are all basic human rights and engage the very dignity of the person:

Yes I am a human being. If I am on earth it is for a purpose; it is not for nothing. I have a role to play as a woman and my papers I want to obtain my papers as a single woman! I have had several marriage proposals; I have had . . . even some French guys. I said NO! Why do I need to be married to obtain these rights? NO! I exist as a woman. If I work it is my strength, it is not the strength of someone else. If I am well it is for me. And if I want papers it is for personal reasons. It is for *me*! Because I have been so degraded, so crushed that now I want to exist and I want to be able to look in the mirror and say: after all I am somebody who accomplished something . . . I succeeded without anyone's help!

Conclusion

Requests for legal autonomy have been at the centre of immigrant women's organising efforts in France. In a 1984 article in *Hommes et Libertés* – the publication of the leading French human rights organisation (*Ligue des droits de l'homme*) – the authors clearly indicate that legal autonomy was at the forefront of immigrant women's organising in the early 1980s:

> A dossier constituted by the Collective of Immigrant Women (*Collectif des femmes immigrées*) analyzes – and denounces – the politics of family reunification. Composed of 25 organizations and various individuals, the Collective, created in 1982, has given itself the goal of defending 'the right of immigrant women to exist as persons with the same rights as French women,' and of 'denouncing any legal or judiciary practices that maintain de facto immigrant women in dependency'.
>
> (De Oliviera *et al.*, 1984: 40)

Other immigrant women's groups pointed out the dangers of derivative rights for women and the increased dependency and vulnerability connected to lack of legal autonomy. In 1985 the organisers of '*Permanence femmes immigrées/femmes sans papiers*' (an immigrant women/undocumented women advocacy group), with foresight, alerted the French community to the fact that restrictions in family reunification were bound to create 'new categories of undocumented immigrants' especially among women and children (Lesselier, 2003: 55).

At the European level, non-governmental organisations have lobbied to put this issue on the agenda. They have asked the European Community 'to ensure migrant women an independent legal status and to recognise – on personal grounds – their right to obtain a work and residency permit, which should reduce their vulnerability in case of divorce, domestic violence, sexual abuse, and rape' (Vetter, 1997: 12). As a result of these pressures, the European parliament has begun to turn its attention to the particular situation of immigrant women.

Interestingly, and in spite of what many *sans-papières* think and advocate, the need for women's legal autonomy and the individuation of immigration rights are claims that never became central within the *sans-papiers* movement at large. It is not enough to accept the obvious feminist reading of this situation that it is men and male leaders who determine the common agenda. In addition, it is important to suggest other reasons for the continued non-prioritisation of such claims. As stated above, undocumented women have often used their status as mothers to seek a change of status. This focus on the family within the movement is complicated and worth examining in terms of some of its unexpected and contradictory effects.

Nine years after the genesis of the movement, many undocumented women have been legalised as members of families (as spouses and mothers). Most of the individuals still left out of the process of regularisation are single men not likely to obtain a change of status in the near future. The early focus on the humanitarian need to keep families together is now used by the state to deny legalisation to many individuals who cannot claim familial linkages in France including, needless to say, gays and lesbians without papers.

Non-governmental organisations and allies, in France and elsewhere, have also been quite successful at presenting immigrant and undocumented women as victims in need of protection (of sex traffickers, abusive husbands, exploitative bosses, etc.).[14] One of the pernicious, and often unintended, effects of this strategy is to reinscribe problematic notions about women and the 'third world' (Mohanty, 2003: 1991). However, immigrant women are hardly simple victims and their active participation in struggles like that of the *sans-papiers* – even when orchestrated around family (mother/wife) issues – produced a double displacement of the French leader and the male head of the family as the privileged speaking subjects of the struggle.

While immigrant organisations and the *sans-papiers* movement continue to challenge French immigration laws and to create breaches for autonomous actions and development for immigrant women, French legislation still pronounces (and French popular and scholarly discourses still construct) these women as dependent on their husbands. This essay begins to address the problems generated by such legal and discursive contradictions and to invite feminist scholars and activists to understand the limits and the dangers (for all women) of representational practices that uncritically rely on tropes of women as dependants and victims.

As long as some immigrant women are imagined and constructed as wives and mothers in a meaning system that continues to ignore that wives and mothers are engaged in all kinds of productive and resistive activities inside and outside the wage-labour force and both inside and outside of the polity, we will fail to see them and engage them as the complex social actors they truly are. We will also fail to provide them with the full range of social and civil rights to which they are entitled.

Notes

1 The *sans-papiers* started their movement on 18 March 1996, by occupying the church of Saint-Ambroise in Paris. For a detailed chronology of the first three years of the movement, see Madjiguène Cissé 1999: 245–9.
2 See Tribalat, 1999 cited in Chaïb, 2001 and personal interview with Claudie Lesselier from the RAJFIRE (unpublished interview on file with author, 9 April 2002).
3 Since January 1985 family reunification can only be initiated by the immigrant already legally residing in France and while family members are still in the home country.
4 After this chapter was written, a new immigration law was promulgated, further restricting family reunification rights (24 July 2006).
5 For a detailed critique of the Pasqua laws, see Naïr, 1997: 22–24.
6 The 1998 Law reduced the legal residency requirement to one year before an immigrant can apply for family reunification. Under the Chevènement Law, the person requesting the procedure must demonstrate housing considered 'normal for a family living in France', a stable income (equivalent to the minimum wage) and a full-time job. Authorisation to enter the territory can only be granted after the Office des Migrations Internationales (OMI) has determined that housing and resource requirements have been met.
7 It is interesting to note here that Madjiguène Cissé, the most vocal and visible woman of the St Bernard collective, never obtained a change of status and has now returned to Senegal.
8 I conducted all interviews in Paris, Lille and Marseilles in 2002, with the bulk of them conducted in Paris and Marseilles.
9 All names have been changed to protect the anonymity of the women interviewed.
10 The *préfecture* is the governing body of the Interior Ministry at the level of the *département*. As such, it is in charge of delivering identity papers and immigration documents.
11 Civil wars erupted in the Republic of Congo in 1993, 1997 and 1998. The fighting in Brazzaville caused material damage, large-scale population displacements and thousands of casualties. Clairette herself recounts how she fled Brazzaville in 1997 and walked 600 kms (400 miles) in order to reach Pointe Noire and Dolizi, which were protected because of the oil industry located in the area. During the journey, she vividly recounts the atrocities she witnessed which still haunt her today.
12 In 1990, she did a three-month internship at the Pitié Salpêtrière Hospital in Paris.
13 Territorial asylum was created in 1998, through the Chevènement legislation, to offer some form of asylum to individuals who did not fall under the strict guidelines of the Geneva Convention. In particular, this was introduced to address the situation of Algerians. However, the vast majority of territorial asylum claims are being denied by the French authorities.
14 See Lessellier, 2003; and Bhabha in this volume.

References

Chaïb, Sabah (2001) *Facteurs d'insertion et d'exclusion des femmes immigrantes dans le marché du travail en France: Quel état des connaissances?* Document de travail élaboré pour la Confédération Française Démocratique du Travail, January.

Cissé, Madjiguène (1999) *Parole de sans-papiers*. Paris: La Dispute

De Oliviera, A, Silva, E and El Mahalawi-Nouet, Martine (1984) 'L'Aspiration à l'autonomie des femmes immigrées', *Hommes et Libertés* 33, pp 39–41

Gaspard, Françoise (1995) 'Statut personnel et intégration sociale, culturelle et nationale', *Hommes et Libertés* 84, pp 3–15

Hersent, Madeleine and Zaidman, Claude (eds) (2003) *Genre, Travail et Migrations en Europe*, Paris: Presses Universitaires de France

Le Monde, 14 August 1996

Lesselier, Claudie (2000) 'Pour une critique féministe des lois sur l'entrée et le séjour des personnes étrangères en France', *Brochure du RAJFIRE*, 2 March

Lesselier, Claudie (2003) 'Femmes migrantes en France: Le genre et la loi', in Hersent, Madeleine and Zaidman, Claude (eds), *Genre, Travail et Migrations en Europe*, Paris: CEDREF, pp 45–59

Lochack, Danièle (1985) *Étrangers: De Quel Droit?* Paris: Presses Universitaires de France

Mohanty, Chandra (2003) *Feminism without Borders: Decolonizing Theory, Practicing Solidarity*, Durham, NC: Duke University Press

Mohanty, Chandra, Russo, Anne and Torres, Lourdes (eds) (1991) *Third World Women and the Politics of Feminism*, Bloomington: Indiana University Press

Naïr, Samir (1997) *Contre les Lois Pasqua*, Paris: Arléa

Rahal-Sidhoum, Saïda (1987) *Eléments d'analyse de statut socio-juridique des femmes immigrées en vue d'un statut pour l'autonomie des femmes immigrées en France*, Paris: Convention CFI/FNDVA

Rude-Antoine, Edwige (1996) 'Des épouses soumises à des régimes particuliers', *Migrants-Formation* 105, pp 45–61

Scales-Trent, Judy (1999) 'African women in France: Citizenship, family, and work', *Brooklyn Journal of International Law* XXIV (3), pp 705–37

Tribalat, Michèle (1999) *De l'Immigration à l'assimilation. Enquête sur les populations etrangères en France*, Paris: La Découverte/Ined

Vetter, Mady (1997) *Situation juridique et sociale des femmes agées etrangères (en région P.A.C.A.)*, Marseille: Bureau Régional de Ressources Juridiques Internationales

12

CROSSING BORDERS

Gender, citizenship and reproductive autonomy in Ireland

Siobhán Mullally

This chapter examines the challenge posed by the migrant female subject to Ireland's gendered borders and focuses, in particular, on recent constitutional debates on citizenship and family life. In June 2004, a referendum on citizenship was held in Ireland. The referendum and subsequent constitutional amendment led to restrictions being imposed on the constitutionally protected right to citizenship by birth. The citizenship referendum followed a period of heated debate on the meaning of citizenship and the terms on which migrant families would be allowed to remain in Ireland. The 1990s had witnessed significant changes in Irish society with Ireland becoming, for the first time, a country of net inward migration. Asylum and immigration, rather than emigration and depopulation, became pressing political issues. Against the background of this changing migration context, Ireland quickly forgot its own history of seeking refuge on distant shores. As the number of migrant workers and asylum applications grew, official discourse in Ireland fell quickly into the fold of 'fortress Europe' developing its own 'fortress Ireland mentality'.[1]

Increasing immigration coincided with constitutional change, change that was due to peace negotiations in Northern Ireland and a desire for compromise in the ongoing dispute between Ireland and the United Kingdom concerning the status of Northern Ireland. As a result of these peace negotiations and the subsequent Belfast Agreement,[2] the territorial claim to Northern Ireland, enshrined in the Irish Constitution since 1937, was removed, and replaced by a new article 2 affirming the right to self-determination of the people of Northern Ireland and the entitlement of anyone born within the 'island of Ireland' to Irish citizenship.[3] The *jus soli* principle recognised in common law and in Irish legislation[4] was given constitutional recognition for the first time. The coincidence of constitutional change with increasing immigration was described by the Irish Supreme Court as an 'accident of history'.[5] It is an 'accident' that led to significant changes in the concept of citizenship and in the legal protections afforded to migrant families within the state.

The debate on birthright citizenship placed migrant women's roles in reproduction at the centre of legal and political debate in Ireland. Migrant women's bodies, their sexuality and childbearing roles became the subject of heightened scrutiny, with newspapers reporting daily on the numbers of migrant women availing themselves of maternity services in Irish hospitals. Introducing the proposal for a referendum on citizenship, the Minister for Justice, Equality and Law Reform highlighted the perceived threat posed to the nation-state by migrant women coming to Ireland. 'How', he asked, 'do we respond?' To require non-national women of childbearing age to make declarations of pregnancy when arriving in the state was, he said, 'clearly unworkable – especially in a common travel area'.[6] That requiring a migrant woman to make a declaration of pregnancy might amount to degrading treatment, a violation of a woman's right to privacy or her right to bodily integrity, did not appear to be a concern.

Of course, the intersection of gender, national identity and reproduction is not new to Ireland. Women's reproductive rights in Ireland have long been a contested terrain. Defining Ireland in exclusively 'pro-life' terms served as a distinguishing mark of Irish identity. The family, sexuality and reproductive rights fell within the boundaries of the private, the sphere of domestic jurisdiction and served to underpin the nation-state's claim to a distinct cultural identity. The Catholic right in Ireland, concerned with preserving the conservative ethos that permeates the Irish Constitution, has portrayed feminism and human rights discourse as a threat to Ireland's 'pro-life' and 'pro-family' traditions, and as a threat to Ireland's sovereignty. In debates on citizenship and migration, however, the concern to protect the sovereignty of the state and to control immigration trumped 'pro-life' and 'pro-family' traditions, provoking little response from the Catholic right. Where migrant women have invoked the constitutional protections afforded to the family or the state's duty to 'defend and vindicate' the right to life of the 'unborn', the state has been quick to appeal to requirements of comity with other nations and its inherent and universal right to control immigration. Migrant women coming to Ireland and bearing children posed a threat to the racial homogeneity of the nation and to the ever fragile process of nation-building. While post-colonial Irish nationalism celebrated women's roles as mothers, migrant women's reproductive roles were not to be celebrated. Mother Ireland was to remain 'white' Mother Ireland.

In the citizenship debates in Ireland, women were defined yet again by their reproductive roles and, yet again, the assertion of reproductive autonomy was rejected as a threat to the nation's ethno-cultural identity – an identity that has been revealed both as deeply gendered and deeply racialised. The exclusivity of the family unit that is provided with constitutional protection was also revealed. Migrant families, denied the protection of the state, were not considered to be 'indispensable to the welfare of the Nation or the state' (see Article 41, Constitution of Ireland). Migrant women, choosing Ireland as their children's birthplace destabilised Ireland's claim to racial homogeneity and Irish understandings of 'the nation', 'the family' and 'the citizenry' (Lentin, 2003).

The *jus soli* principle and citizenship debates in Ireland

The 1937 Constitution of Ireland, *Bunreacht na hÉireann*, left open the question of how citizenship was to be allocated, providing only that citizenship status would be determined in accordance with law.[7] It was presumed that the *jus soli* principle of citizenship by birth would continue to apply as part of the inherited body of common law. In 1956, the Irish Nationality and Citizenship Act was passed, providing for citizenship by birth or descent. The primary concern within the legislature was to ensure that all those born in the island of Ireland would be entitled to citizenship. Citizenship laws could transcend the partition of the island into North and South. The still nascent project of nation-building required an open and inclusive concept of citizenship. Emigration and depopulation were threats to the project of nation-building and so the *jus sanguinis* principle, allowing for citizenship by descent, was also provided for. This inclusive concept of citizenship was not all-embracing, however. From the beginning, debates on the meaning and significance of citizenship in Ireland were deeply racialised. Speaking on the passage of the Irish Nationality and Citizenship Act in 1956, Deputy Esmonde noted that while the entitlement to citizenship by birth was desirable, 'in one sense', such an entitlement also carried with it a 'certain amount of danger'. There were, he noted, 'a great number of people [in the world] who would be undesirable to us in Ireland'. Esmonde's comments reflect an assumed commonality within the Irish nation and a denial of the humanity of the stranger. This assumption and denial was to continue to surface in debates on immigration and citizenship in Ireland.

Ireland's jurisprudence on fundamental rights is steeped in the traditions of natural law. Steeped as they were in the jurisprudence of natural law, one would not have expected that the legal notion of citizenship would greatly influence the Irish courts' determinations on the rights of non-nationals within the state. In many cases, however, a concern to protect the state's 'inherent right' to control immigration trumped the claims to fundamental rights made by non-nationals. This concern has been particularly evident in debates surrounding the rights of residence claimed by undocumented migrants with Irish citizen children. While the children acquired citizenship by birth, the precise nature of their birthright and the terms on which they belonged to the Irish nation were much disputed. The case of *Osheku v Ireland*[8] was one of the earliest cases to deal with the right to family life in the context of immigration decisions. Gannon J, speaking for the High Court, concluded that the fundamental rights protected by the Constitution were not absolute. In an oft-quoted statement, he defended a quintessentially state-centred view on the limits and scope of fundamental rights. There were, he said, 'fundamental rights of the state itself as well as fundamental rights of the individual citizens, and the protection of the former may involve restrictions in circumstances of necessity on the latter'.[9] In a statement that reflects the exclusionary impulse behind the nation-state, he noted that the 1935 Aliens Act reflected the philosophy of the nation-state: 'Its unspoken major premise is that aliens have, in general, no right to be on the national territory'.[10] As we shall see, it is this exclusionary impulse that has guided, or misguided, legislative and judicial responses to the claims made by migrant families in Ireland.

The position of children born in Ireland with non-national parents became the subject of debate in the 1990 decision of the Supreme Court, *Fajujonu v Minister for Justice*.[11] The *Fajujonu* case involved a husband and wife, of Nigerian and Moroccan nationality respectively. The couple were living in Ireland without documentation. When the matter finally came before the Supreme Court, Mr and Mrs Fajujonu had been resident in the state for more than eight years. The third named plaintiff, their eldest daughter, Miriam Fajujonu, had been born in Ireland and was a citizen by birth. The Fajujonus had two further Irish citizen children. Finlay CJ, speaking for the majority of the Supreme Court, concluded that a citizen child had a constitutional right to the 'company, care and parentage of their parents within a family unit'. Subject to the 'exigencies of the common good', this was a right, he held, which could be exercised within the state. Particular emphasis was placed on the Fajujonus' residence for 'an appreciable time' within the state. Walsh J, concurring with the majority judgment, placed greater emphasis on the rights of the family as a constitutionally protected unit and the need to protect the integrity of the family. The children, he said, were of tender age, requiring the society of their parents. In the particular circumstances of this case, to move to expel the parents would be inconsistent with the constitutionally protected rights of the family.[12]

The findings of the Supreme Court and, in particular, the judgment of Walsh J, reflect the cardinal value of citizenship for a child: 'the ability to enjoy the company, care and parentage of their parents within a family unit within the state' (Bhabha, 2003). Following on from this judgment, applications for residence from undocumented migrant parents were routinely granted. However, over the next decade, the migration context in Ireland was to change dramatically. The number of non-national parents claiming residency on the basis of Irish citizen children increased from approximately 1,500 in 1999 to over 6,000 in 2001.[13] At the beginning of 2003, more than 11,500 applications for residence from undocumented migrant parents were pending with the Ministry. As the numbers of families claiming residence rights increased, political pressure to deny these claims grew. Bowing to this pressure, the Minister for Justice, Equality and Law Reform began to refuse or stay applications in late 2002, leading finally to the Supreme Court judgment in the *L* and *O* cases in January 2003.[14] By this time, the right to citizenship by birth had been enshrined as a constitutional right, following the Belfast Agreement and the Nineteenth Amendment to the Constitution Act, 1998.[15]

The *L* and *O* cases involved two families of Czech Roma and Nigerian origin, each with Irish citizen children. Deportation proceedings were commenced against *L* and *O* following the failure of their asylum applications. Seeking a judicial review of the deportation orders, *L* and *O* both asserted a right to exercise a choice of residence on behalf of their citizen children, and on behalf of their children claimed the right to the company, care and parentage of their parents within the state. The majority of the Supreme Court distinguished the *Fajujonu* case on the basis of the length of time the parents had lived within the state and the changing context of immigration in Ireland since then. Using the terms of Finlay CJ's judgment in *Fajujonu,* the majority of the Supreme Court concluded that neither family had been within the state for 'an appreciable time', such as to give rise to a right to residence. Keane CJ distinguished the nature of citizenship claims enjoyed by children and adults. While an adult citizen had an automatic right to reside in the state, he said, the position of minors was 'significantly different'.[16] The right to reside within the state could not vest in a minor until she or he was capable of exercising such a right. And, while the parents could assert a choice of residence on behalf of their citizen children, any claims made by the parents were subject to the exigencies of the common good. The requirements of the common good were defined by the Court solely with reference to the state's interest in controlling immigration and in maintaining the 'integrity of the asylum system'.

The *L* and *O* cases also raised questions concerning the constitutional commitment to protecting the 'inalienable and imprescriptible' rights of the family. Article 41 of the Constitution assigns the family an exceptionally important status and role in the 'welfare of the Nation and the state'. The rights of the family are described in the constitutional text as being 'antecedent and superior' to all positive law, including, this would suggest, to immigration and asylum law. Ireland's commitment to the protection of the family unit has frequently been invoked as a marker of Ireland's distinct national identity.[17] In *McGee v Attorney General*, Walsh J noted that the family, as the 'natural primary and fundamental unit group of society', had rights that the state could not control.[18] In the *L* and *O* cases, however, the Court concluded that the state's right to control immigration and to safeguard the integrity of the asylum and immigration systems took priority over any claims asserted by undocumented migrant family units. Only certain kinds of families, it would seem, are deserving of the constitutional protection afforded by the very entrenched provisions on family life. The findings of the Supreme Court in the *L* and *O* cases stand in marked contrast to the Court's deference to the family unit in previous cases. Just one year earlier, in the *NWHB* case, Keane CJ held that the family, because it derives from the 'natural order', was endowed with an authority that the Constitution itself recognised as being superior even to the authority of the state. He went on to argue that the Constitution outlawed any attempt by the state to usurp 'the exclusive and privileged role of the family in the social order'.[19] In the same case, Murphy J noted that the express terms of the Constitution relegated the state to a subordinate and subsidiary role.[20] The circumstances that could justify intervention by the state in the family unit, he said, must be exceptional indeed. Such exceptions have been found to arise where the best interests of the child required intervention. In the *L* and *O* cases, however, this line of reasoning was turned on its head, with the state's interest in immigration control invoked to challenge the exercise of parental authority and to undermine the child's best interests.

Removing the right to citizenship by birth: migrant women challenging borders

Despite the Supreme Court judgment in the *L* and *O* cases and change in practice, migrant women continued to travel to Ireland and to give birth to their children within the state. Predictions that the judgment would stem the flow of inward migration to the state failed to materialise. The government decided, therefore, to take further action and in April 2004, announced its intention to hold a referendum on a proposed constitutional amendment, to impose restrictions on the right to citizenship by birth where a child was born within the state to non-Irish nationals.[21] In the months preceding the citizenship referendum, the government repeatedly emphasised the crisis posed to the state's maternity services by migrant women arriving in Ireland:[22]

> Our maternity services come under pressure because they have to deal at short notice with women who may have communication difficulties, about whom no previous history of the pregnancy or of the mother's health is known . . . Hospitals cannot predict the demand on resources from month to month . . .

The migrant woman, because of her possible childbearing role, posed a threat to the state's overriding concern with immigration control. Predictability in immigration numbers could not be guaranteed. In presenting the proposed amendment, the government was anxious to portray its move as a compassionate one, designed to minimise the risks faced by migrant women taking 'hazardous journeys' to come to Ireland at late stages of their pregnancy.[23] To reduce such risks, it was necessary, they said, to remove the incentive that induced women to take such journeys in the first place. This meant removing the right to citizenship by birth.[24]

Discussion of migrant women's childbearing and reproductive roles allowed for a circulation of racist imagery, in a way that was unsanctioned. Media headlines included: 'Racial time bomb set to explode as crisis deepens';[25] 'State alert as pregnant asylum seekers Aim for Ireland'[26] and 'Non-nationals fuel pregnancy crisis'.[27] In 2002, an elected councillor (member of local government) publicly commented that 'refugees and asylum seekers are breeding like rabbits here'.[28] This reiteration of racialised imagery, through reproduction and sexuality, contributed to a climate of inequality and fear. The National Consultative Committee on Racism and Interculturalism reported that pregnant black women and black women with children were becoming targets of verbal and physical abuse.[29] The National Women's Council of Ireland, representing more than 300,000 women, responded to the government's proposal by calling for a no vote in the referendum. The government, they said, was blaming migrant women and children for the state's repeated failure to properly resource the Irish maternity and health services. What was needed, they argued, was 'a fair and comprehensive immigration policy that is compassionate, anti-racist and recognises the rights and needs of women'.[30] The Irish Human Rights Commission, in presenting its observations on the proposed referendum, pointed out that much of the evidence offered in support of the proposed amendment was anecdotal in nature and inconclusive.[31] Specifically, the Commission concluded that the data offered were insufficient to allow anyone to draw inferences as to the motives of non-national parents giving birth in Ireland to the extent argued by the government.[32] Such particularities were erased as all migrant women were presented as a threat to the state's interest in immigration control or as victims of unscrupulous traffickers. The Commission also pointed out that the proposed changes were discriminatory, as they imposed restrictions on one category of citizens with 'no substantial historical or familial connection to Ireland', while not addressing the citizenship entitlements of other equivalent groups, including those who obtained citizenship by descent without having to establish any substantial connection with the state.[33]

Despite these concerns, however, the electorate voted, by a majority of almost four to one, in favour of the proposal. The Nationality and Citizenship (Amdt) Act, 2004, subsequently enacted, provides that children may acquire citizenship by birth only if their parents have been lawfully resident in the state for three years or more. No provision is made to regularise the status of children born to undocumented migrant parents who remain in the state for a substantial period of time. The position of migrant families with citizen children born prior to the commencement of the 2004 Act was finally addressed in January 2005, when the government announced the introduction of a new set of procedures to assess residency applications.[34] Although the move to end the uncertainty surrounding the legal status of many immigrant families has been welcomed, the process has attracted criticism. Again a reluctance to protect the right to family life of migrant families is evident. Applicants for residence are required to sign a declaration on family reunification, accepting that permission to remain in the state does not give rise to any 'legitimate expectation' that family members living abroad would be given permission to reside in Ireland.[35] The declaration raises, yet again, the question of whether and how the right to family life of migrant families is valued. Announcing the introduction of the new proposals, the Minister for Justice, Equality and Law Reform, Mr Michael McDowell, stated that residence would only be granted to those parents who could show that they have 'not been involved in criminal activity' and are 'willing to commit themselves to becoming economically viable'.[36] As yet it is unclear how a criminal record that arose in an applicant's country of origin will be considered or whether this reference will be limited to non-political crimes. The requirement of 'economic viability' raises questions as to whether a parent that is unable to be economically self-sufficient will be denied residence.

This latter requirement echoes the distinctions made by the ECJ in the *Chen* case, a case that arose prior to the citizenship referendum in Ireland, and added a further legal twist to the domestic debates.[37] Man Lavette Chen, a Chinese national and mother of a Chinese national child, went to Northern Ireland to give birth to her second child, Catherine. Catherine acquired Irish citizenship by virtue of being born on the island of Ireland. Chen and her daughter, Catherine, subsequently moved to Cardiff in Wales, UK, and applied for a long-term residence permit. Their application was refused. On appeal, the immigration appellate authority referred the case to the ECJ for a ruling as to whether Community law conferred a right of residence in the UK to Catherine and her mother. The Advocate General Tizzano, issuing his opinion on 18 May 2004, concluded that a young child who is a national of a Member state has a right to reside in another Member state so long as he or she has sickness insurance and sufficient resources so as not to become 'an unreasonable burden' on the public finances of the host Member state.[38] In addition, he concluded that to deny Chen's right to residence in the UK would render her daughter's right of residence totally ineffective. The Advocate General's opinion was upheld by the ECJ in its ruling on 19 October 2004. The Court dismissed the UK's contention that Chen should be denied residence because she had improperly exploited Community law in deciding to give birth in Northern Ireland so as to secure Irish and consequently EU citizenship for her daughter. The UK, the Court concluded, was attempting to impose additional conditions on the acquisition of rights arising from the grant of nationality by another Member state.[39] Chen had acted within the boundaries of the law and should not be subject to further limiting requirements.

The Court's judgment reflects one of the fundamental inequalities in

Community law. Catherine and her mother, if not independently wealthy, could not have availed of the freedoms of Community law under either Article 18 EC or Directive 90/364. Catherine's status as a citizen of the Union could not ensure the cardinal value of citizenship, the right to reside in the country of which one is a national (Bhabha, 2003). That right was subject to having sufficient independent resources so as not to become 'an unreasonable burden' on the host state. Despite these limits, however, the *Chen* judgment does go some way towards recognising the networks of relationships into which a child is born and his or her dependency on those relationships for the effective vindication of Community rights. The role of the mother as carer is recognised as being essential to the effective vindication of the child's right to nationality and residence. This relational understanding of the EU citizen recognises, albeit with many limitations, a citizen child's right to family life and a relational understanding of the subject of rights. In contrast, the Irish Supreme Court, in the *L* and *O* cases, was willing to effectively deny the children's right to residence within the state by deporting their carers and subjecting the children to de facto deportation. The child's right to residence, as an Irish citizen, was qualitatively different and would not be vindicated by the state until the child was capable of exercising such a right on his or her own behalf.[40] This limited understanding of the child as a bearer of rights allowed the state to justify its failure to vindicate the citizen child's right to residence. Despite the well-entrenched family life and fundamental rights provisions in the Irish Constitution, Community law, with its relatively underdeveloped rights jurisprudence, ultimately granted the citizen child greater protection than did Irish constitutional law.

Family values and reproductive rights in Ireland: gendered borders and gendered identities

Women's assertion of reproductive autonomy in Ireland has required the crossing of many borders, both the territorial borders of the state and the jurisdictional borders between international and domestic law. In May 1971, almost one hundred women boarded a train in Dublin. They travelled to Belfast, where they purchased large quantities of contraceptives. They returned to Dublin by train, marching illegally through the customs barriers at Connolly Station waving banners, posters and condom balloons. The 'Condom train', as it subsequently became known, transgressed many boundaries. In crossing Ireland's disputed border with Northern Ireland and openly flouting the legislative ban on importing contraceptives, the women's movement challenged the borders set by the conservative Catholic consensus in the Republic of Ireland. They exposed the inequalities between women, North and South, and the closure of Irish society to difference in matters of sexual and reproductive health. They also exposed the hypocrisy of a state that lay territorial claims to Northern Ireland but refused to accommodate religious diversity in matters concerning sexuality and reproduction (Jackson, 1993; Connolly, 2002).

Women seeking to terminate their pregnancies have been forced to leave the state and have travelled, usually to the UK, to access safe abortion services. Women have also sought to transgress the borders of domestic law, appealing to international and European human rights standards, pointing to the gender-differentiated nature of Irish citizenship and seeking support for their claim to reproductive autonomy in treaties such as the 1979 UN Convention on the Elimination of All Forms of Discrimination Against Women,[41] the 1966 International Covenant on Civil and Political Rights and the European Convention on Human Rights. In the past, women have left the state to access contraceptives. Today, more than 7,000 women travel to the UK each year to access safe abortion services.

Prior to the Eighth Amendment to the Constitution, there was no explicit constitutional prohibition on abortion, though it was widely believed that the right to life of the foetus was protected as an unenumerated personal right under Article 40.3.[42] The move to introduce a constitutional amendment prohibiting abortion arose from a concern that the Supreme Court's recognition of a right to marital privacy could be invoked to strike down legislation criminalising abortion. The *Roe v Wade*[43] decision in the US was preceded by a Supreme Court decision, recognising the right to have access to contraceptives as an aspect of the right to privacy.[44] Anti-abortion campaigners were concerned that the same line of reasoning might be invoked by Irish courts. Already, fundamental rights jurisprudence had extended far beyond the limits of the constitutional text, transforming the relationship between citizen and state.

The Pro-Life Amendment Campaign (PLAC) was launched in 1981, composed primarily of groups drawn from the Catholic right. The amendment campaign and the bitter debates that ensued have been described as a 'second partitioning' of the state (Hesketh, 1990). Although PLAC was careful to employ secular language in its campaign, it clearly drew on a conservative Catholic ethos to support its claim to the absolute inviolability of foetal life (Kingston *et al.*, 1997). Recognising this, each of the Protestant Churches in Ireland issued statements opposing the proposal for a 'pro-life' amendment (Fletcher, 2001). Their concerns were echoed by the anti-amendment campaign who argued that an absolute constitutional prohibition on abortion would deny equal rights to citizenship to non-Catholics and perpetuate a politics of exclusion in the Irish Republic. PLAC, however, continued to represent abortion as a violent colonial tool threatening the integrity of the Irish nation (O'Reilly, 1992). Ultimately, the pro-life campaign won the day. The 1983 referendum led to the Eighth Amendment to the Constitution, acknowledging the right to life of the unborn.[45] Significantly, however, the amendment recognised also the need for 'due regard to the equal right to life of the mother'. Almost a decade later, the requirement of 'due regard' was to give rise to one of Ireland's most controversial constitutional debates.

In February 1992, the Attorney General secured an injunction restraining a pregnant 14-year-old girl from leaving the country for a period of nine months.[46] Effectively, she was imprisoned within the state. The girl at the centre of the X case was pregnant as a result of a rape, her case coming to the attention of the Attorney General, because of an ongoing criminal investigation into the rape. The X case provoked a huge outcry at national and international levels. Weeks of media attention followed. International media reported Ireland to be 'backward', 'barbarous', punitive', 'priest-ridden' – a portrayal that did not sit well with the modernising image of an expanding economy (Smyth, 1990). Newspapers, drawing on the Irish government's opposition to policies of internment in Northern Ireland, reported X as being interned within the state, without charge (Fletcher, 2001). The Supreme Court finally lifted the injunction, concluding that the equal right to life of the mother allowed for the termination of a pregnancy where it was established that there was a real and substantial risk to the life, as distinct from the health, of the mother. The risk to life could include a threatened suicide.[47]

While the Court's judgment on the substantive issue of abortion was welcomed by 'pro-choice' activists, the ruling on the right to travel for the purposes of terminating a pregnancy raised some concern. The High Court had ruled that the state's duty to protect the life of the unborn amounted to a 'public policy' derogation and was, as such, permitted by Community law. The Supreme Court upheld the High Court's finding, concluding that the right to travel, *simpliciter*, could not take precedence over the right to life of the unborn, unless the mother's life was in danger.[48] Public policy, interpreted so as to reflect an ethno-cultural identity at national level, defined the limits of the European integration project (Phelan, 1992). The potential restriction on women's freedom of movement and with it, the spectre of 'pro-life' groups seeking injunctions to restrain pregnant women from travelling to the UK, provoked widespread criticism. Further constitutional referenda and amendments were necessary to ensure protection of women's right to travel. Despite repeated constitutional referenda on abortion, however, the legal framework regulating abortion, including the right to travel to avail of abortion services elsewhere, remains unclear.

In 1997, the centre-right Fianna Fáil and Progressive Democrats coalition government was formed.[49] A minority government, they were dependent for support on the votes of four independent members of parliament. This support was secured by the promise of yet another abortion referendum. In March 2002, the Irish people were asked to vote again on the issue of abortion law reform. The Twenty-Fifth Amendment of the Constitution (Protection of Human Life in Pregnancy Bill)[50] proposed a prohibition on abortion except in circumstances where there was a risk to the life of the mother. In an attempt to limit the effect of *Attorney General v X*, drafters of the bill excluded the risk arising from a threatened suicide as a ground for permitting abortion.

The referendum on the Protection of Human Life in Pregnancy Bill was held on 6 March 2002. It was defeated by the narrowest of margins, with 49.58 per cent voting 'Yes' and 50.42 per cent voting 'No'.[51] The decisive factor in the 'No' vote was the split in the anti-choice movement. Although the Catholic Church mobilised behind the government's referendum proposal, extremists in the anti-choice movement called for a 'No' vote because of the Bill's failure to protect human life prior to implantation in the womb.[52]

While the abortion referendum was dominating the political arena, the rights of the 'unborn' were being tested again in Ireland's Supreme Court.[53] *Baby O & Another v Minister for Justice Equality and Law Reform* involved a Nigerian woman who was seven months pregnant and subject to a deportation order from the state, following a failed application for asylum. The woman challenged the validity of the deportation order, arguing that the state's duty to defend and vindicate Baby O's right to life prevented the state from deporting her to Nigeria, where infant mortality rates were substantially higher and the standard of living substantially lower. The Attorney General, acting on behalf of the Minister for Justice, Equality and Law Reform, appealed to the common good, to the need to defend and vindicate the territorial integrity of the state, and to the Minister's right to deport failed asylum seekers.[54] The Supreme Court agreed with the submissions of the Attorney General. The threat posed by higher infant mortality rates could not invoke the protection of Article 40.3.3°.[55] The state's duty to defend and vindicate the right to life of the unborn did not extend to ensuring the health and well-being of Baby O, or even to ensuring a safe delivery. Article 40.3.3° could not be relied on to invoke unenumerated social and economic rights, which the Court held, were not implicit within the constitutionally protected right to life.[56] The Court upheld the deportation order and also refused a final application to stay the order pending a petition to the European Court of Human Rights. The 'common good' required a speedy deportation of the mother and foetus. Again, the narrative of nation was to prove exclusionary. The self-styled 'pro-life' movement, preoccupied with another referendum on abortion, had little to say in support of Baby O or her mother.

The Treaty on a Constitution for Europe, concluded under the Irish Presidency of the EU, is supplemented by a Protocol, providing that the constitutional prohibition on abortion in Ireland would not be affected by the adoption of a Constitution for Europe.[57] Again we see the limits of the European integration project and the willingness of states to accommodation difference through limits imposed on women's reproductive health (Mullally, 2006). Against the background of this political wrangling, more than 7,000 women will continue to travel to the UK each year to terminate their pregnancies. For unemployed women or women earning low wages, this freedom to travel remains illusory.[58] For asylum-seeking women, the freedom to travel does not exist. Travel documents, however, have been provided on an ad hoc basis for asylum-seeking women wishing to travel to the UK to avail themselves of abortion services, which raises questions as to the legality of the legislative restriction imposed on travel for such women and conversely, of the legality of the state's ad hoc response.[59] The Irish Human Rights Commission in its submission to the CEDAW Committee on Ireland's *Combined Fourth and Fifth Reports* under the UN Convention on the Elimination of All Forms of Discrimination Against Women, notes that the number of women from immigrant communities seeking the services of crisis pregnancy agencies has risen significantly and that an increasing number of reports of back-street abortions amongst immigrant communities are under investigation by the police force.[60] The failure to safeguard the reproductive rights of specific groups of women, such as asylum-seeking women, was highlighted by the CEDAW Committee in its Concluding Observations on Ireland's second and third periodic reports.[61] The UN Human Rights Committee highlighted Ireland's obligation, under Article 7 of the ICCPR and General Comment 28, to ensure access to safe abortions for women who become pregnant as a result of rape.[62] For asylum-seeking women, such access is not ensured, given the travel restrictions imposed while waiting for determination of asylum claims. This raises questions as to whether women are being compelled to continue with pregnancies, whether 'forced pregnancies' are occurring, contrary to the state's human rights treaty obligations.

Concluding remarks

Migrant women coming to Ireland have turned debates on reproductive rights on their head, exposing the hypocrisy of a state that purports to defend and vindicate the right to life of the unborn and to protect the family. Migrant women's assertion of reproductive autonomy, in choosing to give birth within the state and secure citizenship status for their children, has been met with a rapid unfolding of legal restrictions, designed to remove incentives for women who may wish to come to Ireland. In the citizenship debates in Ireland, the familiar gender tropes – of women as wives, mothers, victims or demonised 'others' – were evident yet again. Migrant women were victims of unscrupulous smugglers, forced into taking 'hazardous journeys' or were 'demonised others', responsible for the crisis in the state's maternity services, the dilution of cultural identity, and violation of the state's borders. In the *Chen* case, Chen stood accused of abusing immigration law and policy, despite the fact that she had acted clearly within the boundaries of the law. The complexity of the migrant female subject, the push and pull factors that might have induced her to migrate, were ignored.

The voices of migrant women were rarely heard in the citizenship debates as legal interventions were designed and pursued solely from the perspective

of the state's interest in immigration control. Women's agency or reproductive autonomy was not foregrounded in these debates as it is not foregrounded in debates on abortion or reproductive health in Ireland. The legal
and political responses to immigration in Ireland, at times disciplinary and at
times punitive, have not sought to empower women's human rights but
rather to restrict women's mobility and agency. Such responses are not, of
course, unique to Ireland. They reflect broader trends in migration law and
policy, trends that are underpinned by a politics of risk and security and
demonisation of alien 'others', both women and men.

In responding to a changing migration context, Ireland has failed to 'turn
the gaze back', to reflect upon its own history of seeking refuge and economic prosperity on distant shores. For Irish women, 'turning the gaze back'
reveals the many reasons why women migrate and cross borders. For Irish
women in the nineteenth and twentieth centuries, migration represented economic opportunity, but also a route through which reproductive autonomy
and sexual desire could be pursued. As a result, migrant Irish women were
frequently identified as a threat to communally oriented Irish modernity
(Gray, 2004a). Though migration concealed differences in sexual practices
and identities, anxiety about reproductive and sexual autonomy amongst the
diaspora remained. Assertions of individualism and autonomy in matters of
reproduction and sexuality, whether at home or amongst the diaspora,
threatened the unity of a nascent nation-state and the process of nation-
building. 'Turning the gaze back' also reveals the ways in which migrant Irish
women in Britain were racialised through their roles in reproduction. Irish
women played key roles in low-wage occupations in the nineteenth and twentieth centuries. They were not noticed for such roles, however, but rather for
their roles in reproduction, frequently being represented as bodies out of
control, with too many children, making unreasonable demands on welfare
systems and threatening English ways of life (Walter, 2001).

Appeals to the sanctity of family life and to 'pro-life' traditions, have
served to limit women's human rights claims in Ireland since the foundation
of the state. The priority accorded to such appeals have led to repeated
attempts to restrict women's freedom to travel and to a notion of citizenship
that is deeply gendered. While such attempts have often focused on restricting women's freedom to exit the state, legal responses to migrant women's
assertion of reproductive autonomy have sought to restrict entry to the
state. Common to both sets of legal responses is the curtailing of women's
reproductive autonomy. In the context of migrant women, appeals to the
constitutional provisions on family life and to the state's duty to defend and
vindicate the right to life of the unborn have met with little success. The
state's interest in immigration control, an interest that, in the words of the
High Court, is recognised 'universally and from earliest times',[63] has been
granted priority. In the citizenship debates in Ireland, we see clearly the
power of citizenship laws to exclude. Women, migrant families and their

children are all excluded from a polity that prides itself as being cosmopolitan. Through the vilification and increasing control of migrant women's bodies, we see a re-assertion of a limited form of national sovereignty and a racism that functions through reference to reproduction, 'understood as gendered, classed, racialised labour that can be carried out for the state – or against the state' (Luibhéid, 2003: 85). Migrant women's assertion of reproductive autonomy threatened to destabilise the racial homogeneity of the nation-state. In response to this 'threat', Ireland has introduced citizenship laws that seek, yet again, to restrict women's autonomy, mobility and agency.

Notes

1 In 1995 Ireland received 420 asylum applications. In 1999, this number had increased to just under 8,000 and at the end of October 2000 to 9,080. In 2004, this number had fallen to approximately 4,500. Source: Office of the Refugee Applications Commissioner, Dublin.
2 See: Agreement Reached in Multi-Party Negotiations (the Belfast Agreement), concluded 10 April 1998 and the Agreement between the government of the United Kingdom of Great Britain and Northern Ireland and the government of Ireland (British-Irish Agreement) reproduced in: (1998) 37 ILM 751. See generally Harvey and Livingstone, 1999; Harvey, 2000; Harvey, 2001.
3 See: Nineteenth Amendment to the Constitution Act, 1998. The full text of Article 2 of the Constitution of Ireland (as amended) reads:

Article 2

It is the entitlement and birthright of every person born in the island of Ireland, which includes its islands and seas, to be part of the Irish Nation. That is also the entitlement of all persons otherwise qualified in accordance with law to be citizens of Ireland. Furthermore, the Irish nation cherishes its special affinity with people of Irish ancestry living abroad who share its cultural identity and heritage.

4 1956 Irish Nationality and Citizenship Act.
5 See *Lobe and Osayande v Minister for Justice, Equality and Law Reform*, [2003] IESC 1 (23 January 2003) *per* Fennelly J, para 451.
6 McDowell M, Minister for Justice, Equality and Law Reform, 'Proposed citizenship referendum', *Sunday Independent*, 14 March 2004.
7 Article 9 of the Constitution.
8 [1986] IR 733.
9 Ibid., p 746.
10 Ibid., p 745.
11 *Fajujonu v Minister for Justice* [1990] 2 IR 151; [1990] ILRM 234.
12 In a statement that is likely to have relevance to many families facing deportation proceedings in the future, Walsh J went on to point out that deportation proceedings could not be taken against a family that included citizen children, simply because of poverty, particularly where that situation of poverty was induced by the absence of a work permit.
13 *Irish Times* 'What's to befall these Irish children?' 9 April 2002.
14 See n 5 above.
15 See n 2 above.
16 Ibid. *per* Keane CJ para 34.

17 See *Norris v Ireland* judgment of 26 October 1988. 13 EHRR 186.
18 [1974] IR 284, at p 310.
19 *North Western Health Board v HW and CW* [2001] 3 IR 622.
20 Ibid., p 732.
21 The Twenty-seventh Amendment of the Constitution Bill 2004 proposed that a new section be added to Article 9 of the Constitution to read as follows:

> 9.2.1 Notwithstanding any other provision of this Constitution, a person born in the island of Ireland, which includes its islands and its seas, who does not have, at the time of his or her birth, at least one parent who is an Irish citizen or entitled to be an Irish citizen is not entitled to Irish citizenship or nationality, unless otherwise provided for by law.

22 McDowell M, Minister for Justice, Equality and Law Reform, 'Proposed Citizenship Referendum', *Sunday Independent*, 14 March 2004.
23 Ibid.
24 Ibid.
25 *Irish Independent*, 27 January 2002, by Ralph Riegel and Geraldine Niland.
26 *Irish Examiner*, 4 December 2001, by Donal Hickey.
27 *Irish Examiner*, 21 February 2001, by Fionnuala Quinlan.
28 *Irish Times*, 16 April 2002, by Sean Keane 'Councillor says asylum seekers are "breeding like rabbits" '.
29 See: 'Pregnant blacks facing citizenship jibes – report', *Irish Times*, 14 March 2002, by Nuala Haughey.
30 National Women's Council of Ireland, Press Release, Tuesday 8 June 2004.
31 Irish Human Rights Commission. Observations on the Proposed Referendum on Citizenship, 2004. Available at: http://www.ihrc.ie/documents/documents.-asp?NCID=6&L=1.
32 Ibid., para 5.9.
33 Ibid.
34 Department of Justice, Equality and Law Reform 'Minister announces details of revised arrangements for residency', 14 January 2005, available at: http://www.justice.ie.
35 Department of Justice, Equality and Law Reform, Appl IBC/05.
36 Department of Justice, Equality and Law Reform, 'Minister announces revised arrangements for processing claims for permission to remain from parents of Irish born children', 14 December 2004.
37 Case C-200/02 *Chen v Secretary of State for the Home Department*, 19 October 2004.
38 See Article 1(1) of Directive 90/364.
39 See above, n 37, para 39.
40 See above, n 16 *per* Keane CJ.
41 See Women's Human Rights Alliance *Shadow Report: Irel004* (WHRA, 2004).
42 See *McGee v Attorney General* 1987 IR 284 *per* Walsh J (*obiter*), p 312.
43 410 US 113 (1973).
44 *Griswold v Conneticut*, 381 US 479 (1965).
45 Article 40.3.3', inserted following the enactment of the Eighth Amendment to the Constitution Act, 1983, reads: 'The state acknowledges the right to life of the unborn and, with due regard to the equal right to life of the mother, guarantees in its laws to respect, and, as far as practicable, by its laws to defend and vindicate that right.'
46 [1992] 1 IR 1, *per* Costello J, p 7.
47 Ibid., pp 57–58 *per* Finlay CJ.

48 O'Flaherty J, dissenting on this point, held that restricting a woman's right to travel would interfere to an unwarranted degree with the individual's freedom of movement, the authority of the family, and the protection of the dignity and freedom of the individual.

49 Fianna Fáil is one of the oldest and largest political parties within the Irish state. Further information available at: http://www.fiannafail.ie. The Progressive Democrats were a minority party in the coalition government. They were formed as a political party in 1985 and at the time of writing hold eight seats in the Irish Parliament. Further information available at: http://www.progressivedemocrats.ie/.

50 Twenty-Fifth Amendment of the Constitution (Protection of Human Life in Pregnancy) Bill, No 48 (2001) [hereinafter Proposed Twenty-Fifth Amendment]. The Bill draws on similar legislation introduced in Poland in 1993, the Family Planning, Protection of the Human Foetus, and Conditions Permitting Pregnancy Termination Act. Prior to 1993, abortion on social grounds was permitted in Poland.

51 Mark Brennock, 'Taoiseach rules out abortion legislation following defeat', *Irish Times*, 8 March 2002, p 1.

52 For example, Press Release, SPUC, 'International pro-life leaders call for a no vote in Irish abortion referendum', 28 February 2002, available at: http://www.spuc.org.uk/releases/20020228.htm.

53 *Baby O v Minister for Justice, Equality and Law Reform.* Unreported Supreme Court Judgment, [2002] 2 IR 169.

54 Ibid., p 173

55 Ibid. *per* Keane CJ, p 182.

56 Ibid., p 182

57 See Protocol on Article 40.3.3 of the Constitution of Ireland.

58 See Irish Council for Civil Liberties (Women's Committee), *The Need for Abortion Law Reform in Ireland: The Case against the Twenty-Fifth Amendment of the Constitution Bill, 2001* (2002), available at http://www.iccl.ie/women/abortion/abortion_paper2002.html.

59 See 'Asylum seekers allowed to travel for abortions', *Irish Independent*, 15 October 2001.

60 Irish Human Rights Commission, *Submission to the UN Committee on the Elimination of All Forms of Discrimination Against Women* 2005, available at: http://www.ihrc.ie/documents/documents.asp?NCID=6&L=1.

61 *Concluding Observations of the Committee on the Elimination of Discrimination Against Women: Ireland*, 1 July 1999. UN Doc A/54/38, paras 161–201, para 185.

62 Human Rights Committee, Sixty-ninth session. *Concluding Observations of the Human Rights Committee: Ireland*, 20 July 2000. UN Doc CCPR/CO/69/IRL, para 18. See also CCPR/C/21/Rev.1/Add.10, CCPR General Comment 28, 29 March 2000, para 11.

63 [1986] IR 733, p 746 *per* Gannon J.

References

Bhabha, Jacqueline (2003) 'The citizenship deficit: On being a citizen child', *Development* 46, pp 53–9

Connolly, Linda (2002) *The Irish Women's Movement: From Revolution to Devolution*, London: Palgrave

Constitution Review Group (1995) *Report of the Constitution Review Group*, Dublin: Government of Ireland Publications, pp 247–51

Fletcher, Ruth (2001) 'Post-colonial fragments: Representations of abortion in Irish law and politics', *Journal of Law and Society* 28(4), pp 568–89

Gray, Brenda (2004a) *Women and the Irish Diaspora*, London/New York: Routledge

Gray, Brenda (2004b) 'Remembering a "multicultural" future through a history of emigration: Towards a feminist politics of solidarity across difference', *Women's Studies International Forum* 27(4), pp 413–29

Harvey, Colin J (ed) (2000) 'Governing after the rights revolution', *Journal of Law and Society* 27, pp 61–97

Harvey, Colin J (ed) (2001) *Human Rights, Equality and Democratic Renewal in Northern Ireland*, Oxford: Hart Publishing

Harvey, Colin J and Livingstone, Stephen (1999) 'Human rights and the Northern Ireland peace process', *European Human Rights Law Review*, pp 162–77

Hesketh, Tom (1990) *The Second Partitioning of Ireland: the Abortion Referendum of 1983*, Dun Laoighre: Brandsma Books

Jackson, Nuala (1993) 'Family law: Fertility and parenthood', in Connolly, Alpha (ed), *Gender and the Law in Ireland*, Dublin: Oak Tree Press, pp 109–29

Kingston, James and Whelan, Anthony with Bacik, Ivana (1997) *Abortion and the Law*, Dublin: Roundhall Sweet & Maxwell

Lentin, Ronit (2003) '(En)gendering Ireland's migratory space', paper presented at Migrant Women: Transforming Ireland Conference, Dublin

Luibhéid, Eithne (2003) 'Globalisation and sexuality: Redrawing racial and national boundaries through discourses of childbearing', paper presented at Migrant Women: Transforming Ireland Conference, Dublin

Mullally, Siobhán (2005a) 'Debating reproductive rights in Ireland', *Human Rights Quarterly* 27(1), pp 78–104

Mullally, Siobhán (2005b) 'Citizenship and family life in Ireland: Asking the question "Who Belongs?" ', *Legal Studies* 25(4)

Mullally, Siobhán (2006) *Reclaiming Universalism: Gender, Culture and Human Rights*, Oxford: Hart Publishing

O'Reilly, Emily (1992) *Masterminds of the Right*, Dublin: Attic Press

Phelan, Rossa (1992) 'Right to life of the unborn v promotion of trade in services: the European Court of Justice and the normative shaping of the European Union', *MLR* 55, p 670

Smyth, Aibhe (ed) (1990) *The Abortion Papers: Ireland*, Dublin: Attic Press

Walter, Bronwen (2001) *Outsiders Inside: Whiteness, Place and Irish Women*, London: Routledge

13

SOCIO-POLITICAL AND LEGAL REPRESENTATIONS OF MIGRANT WOMEN SEX LABOURERS IN ITALY[1]

Between discourse and praxis

Isabel Crowhurst

Since the late 1980s an increasing number of migrant women originating primarily from economically developing countries started to operate in the Italian sex industry.[2] Their presence brought about a profound epistemological disruption in the conventional formulation of knowledge about migrant women in Italy who were previously either ignored or identified as non-threatening and submissive.

This chapter presents an analysis of the genealogies of representations of migrant women sex labourers in Italy in order to explore the extent to which significance attached to their multiple constructions affects the formulation and implementation of policies and legal provisions specifically addressed to them. A number of features in the destination country, including socio-political factors (Italian collective identity construction, political opportunism, etc.), normative values and cultural practices (historical stigmatisation of prostitutes, racialisation of the 'ethnic other', etc.) are explored here as they play a significant role in determining the reception and response to these new migrants; at the same time they are observed as part of a dynamic process whereby social and political systems, hierarchies and the discourses informing them evolve under the process-oriented force of migration.

I argue that since their arrival, migrant women operating in the sex industry have been criminalised and racialised as dangerous and unsettling 'others', following a pattern that had more commonly been applied to male migrants. However, after the discovery that some female migrants in the sex industry are forced into the business and live in slavery-like conditions, the so-called 'foreign prostitutes'[3] often came to be represented as passive victims of sexual trafficking. The reconstruction of a new ontology of migrant women sex labourers according to this image has never been definitive, resulting in a schizophrenia in their representation as either victims or criminals, in the response of the population oscillating between pity and contempt, and in the strategies enacted by the state varying from granting residence and protection to brutal policing and deportation.

The chapter is structured as follows: the next two sections explore how dominant discursive frameworks of migration and prostitution in Italy evolved in the last decades to incorporate the presence of migrant women sex labourers. The subsequent reconstruction of the circumstances of the first 'encounters' between female migrant sex labourers and the Italian population lays the ground for more specific considerations on how their socio-political representations map out in legal and social practices.

Recent developments in the representation and reception of migrants to Italy: a background picture

For more than a century after unification in 1861, Italy's mass migrations 'have been among the most important of the modern world' (Gabaccia, 2000: 3), with over 26 million Italians emigrating between 1876 and 1965 (Wrench and Solomos, 1993). In the 1970s, the international migration turn-around from net emigration to net immigration in Southern Europe (King and Black, 1997) ended Italy's long history as one of the most prolific exporters of people and labour (Gabaccia, 2000) and marked its passage from a traditional sending country to a new[4] country of destination. The International Organization for Migration (IOM) reports that in three decades the number of migrants to Italy has risen 'from 300,000 to an estimated 1.6 million at the end of 2001, representing 2.8 per cent of the population' (IOM, 2001), reaching approximately 2.6 million, i.e. 4.5 per cent of the population, three years later[5] (Caritas/Migrantes, 2004).

The socio-political impact of and response to migration in Italy has been the object of analysis of a florid scholarly production which has concordantly observed that Italy, as a destination country, has progressively developed exclusionary policies and practices towards newcomers. The literature suggests that since the late 1960s – at the onset of migration flows – and until the early 1980s, the steady arrival of migrants had been internalised by the local population as a social fact, with little normative debate about its causes and possible consequences (see, for example, Andall, 2000; Dal Lago, 1999; Statham, 1998; Campani, 1993). As Statham points out, structural factors such as the migrants' 'relatively low numbers ... their uneven regional dispersal across the country and their insecure type of labor' contributed to obscure their presence (Statham, 1998: 25), hence the migrants were not initially conceived of as a public issue because they were not yet identified as part of the public.

By the end of the 1980s, this situation was being replaced by an increasing fear of the cultural and economic threat represented by the immigrants (Andall, 2000). Accordingly, the old conceptualisation of migration as the movement of people in search of better opportunities was substituted with that of an illegal activity that needs to be stopped. This approach is reflected in the various pieces of legislation on migration that since 1986 (see Table 13.1) have progressively introduced tighter restrictions for entry of the so-called *extra-comunitari* (extra-communitarians), an Italian term used to refer specifically to people who are not citizens of the European Union.

This shift in attitude is believed to have been accelerated by the so-called 'Albanian crisis' of 1990 and 1991, when the large number of Albanians fleeing to Italy from the deepening political crisis of their country became the object of a sensationalised representation by the media which reported their arrival as a national emergency that rendered the country 'under siege' (Dal Lago, 1999; Wrench and Solomos, 1993). After this episode the discourse on immigration – whether generated in the political arena or reproduced through media channels – has been constantly filled with visual and verbal images of invasion and attack from 'outsiders'.

The development of politics and policies of exclusion has to be explained also in the context of the drastic end of the first Italian republic[6] in 1991,

Table 13.1 Italian laws on immigration: 1986–2002

Law 943 of 1986 was the first Italian law on immigration. It included an amnesty for undocumented aliens residing on Italian territory, being primarily aimed at prohibiting clandestine migration. It did not include a provision for asylum, a realistic appreciation of the social conditions of immigrants and ultimately, it failed to provide a rational and coherent migration regime (Statham, 1998).
Law 39 of 1990 (also known as the Martelli Law) granted a second amnesty for regularisation, it included specific norms on the working conditions of migrants and established the right to asylum. It reflected the government's policy to regularise migrants already in Italy, whilst at the same time prohibiting further entry of non-European nationals, in compliance with the further closure of European borders resulting from the Schengen agreements.
Law 40 of 1998 (also known as the Turco-Napolitano Law and Consolidated Act (CA) of the provisions concerning the regulation of immigration and rules on the conditions of the foreigners), aimed at bringing some order into the coacervation of Italian immigration laws and codes. It moved along three main guidelines: entry programming within annual quotas; fight against illegal immigration and criminal exploitation of illegal migration; and social integration policy for legal migrants. It introduced new provisions for a special residence permit for migrant victims of violent acts and serious forms of exploitation. After the fall of the leftist government coalition in 2001 and the victory of Berlusconi's right-wing Cabinet, which includes members of the far-right Northern League and the neo-fascist National Alliance, more initiatives were enacted to curtail immigration into Italy with:
The (so-called) 2002 Bossi-Fini law, which amended the 1998 CA by further restricting the conditions of residence, and introducing stricter illegal immigration deportation practices.

when the explosion of a major corruption scandal threw the political system in turmoil. As a crisis of legitimacy crystallised within the dominant culture, the migrants became a perfect new ideological alterity to contrast with the rebuilding of a new political identity. The openly xenophobic and racist Northern League has been the most prominent and successful political party to exploit the constructed image of the migrant as 'inimical other' in order to claim its own legitimacy and authority.[7] In general, however, a much broader spectrum of political parties has focused on the migrants as common enemies, sharing the ideology that '*our* identity consists of being *their* antagonists' (Saunders, 2003: 33).

Gendering otherness

In the Italian collective discourse, the migrant is often represented with the following features: male, undocumented and usually engaged in criminal activities related to drugs, money laundering and/or trafficking in women. Indeed, the deconstruction and 're-assembling' of the 'other' have involved a process of masculinisation combined with one of criminalisation that charges it with a more threatening 'appeal'. This is why the terms *immigrato* (male immigrant) and *extra-comunitario* (male extra-communitarian) are impregnated with so many negative underlying connotations that now, when adopted, they invariably echo the stigma they have absorbed in common usage, and may even be used as insults in colloquial language.

The placard of the Northern League shown in Figure 13.1 is a good example of the hyperbolic stereotyping of the attributes ascribed to migrants. All four men depicted – a street vendor, a drug dealer, a man cleaning cars at the traffic-lights, and the fourth unzipping his pants ready to rape – are represented in an attitude of threatening imposition of their 'requests'. This selective representation is symbolic of the mechanism of curtailing the wholeness of the 'other' who, deprived of its multiple diversities, loses 'its power to signify, to negate, to initiate its historic desire, to establish its own institutional and oppositional discourse' (Bhabha, 1994:13, quoted in Saunders, 2003: 16), and is forced to exist only in the ontological role of enemy.

Women from the Philippines, Eritrea, Cape Verde and Somalia who had been migrating to Italy for as long as men, were not included in the category of 'deviant and criminal' because they did not fully conform to the image of threat to the country's social cohesion and social order: their prevalent occupation as domestic workers, confined to the invisibility of their employer's home, was perceived as benign and socially useful (Campani, 1993; Wrench and Solomos, 1993; Bonifazi, 1992). The same treatment was not reserved for those women who started to migrate to occupy positions in the Italian sex industry at the end of the 1980s. The contrast between the 'new' migrant woman, so visible as street prostitute, and the old one, invisible and domesticated, caused a major epistemological rupture in the typical representation

Figure 13.1 Placard of the Northern League, August 1998: 'Stop them! They are arriving in their millions'.[8]

of migrants as 'deviant males and submissive females', which resulted in the creation of yet another compartmentalisation in the public discourse: migrant women started to be dichotomised through an ethnic divide. The 'older' and trusted female migrants, the Filipinas, Peruvians, Cape Verdians, etc., maintained their synonymity as domestic workers, whereas the 'new' migrants such as Nigerians, Albanians and Romanians, were immediately labelled as 'whores' and incorporated in the category of 'criminals' in the company of male migrants. This is clearly visible in the Northern League's placard (see Figure 13.1) which reproduces the historical racialised hyper-sexualisation of black women by showing a woman, the only one, of African origin in an aggressive and lascivious posture, asking 'do you want to fuck?', presumably to an Italian male.

These considerations suggest that one of the critical factors that results in the social rejection of women sex labourers is their involvement in prostitution. The next section delineates an overview of the representation of prostitution in Italy, so as to fully grasp the social meanings of the space that 'new' female migrants came to occupy.

Approaches to prostitution in Italy

The first law on prostitution in Italy was passed in 1860 when, in the very midst of the wars of unification, the Italian nation was still in the making (Gibson, 1999). The ruling class and the new bourgeoisie maintained that they had to consolidate their hegemony in a climate of morality, where the so-called dangerous classes – of which prostitutes were singled out among the most prominent representatives – had to be kept under severe surveillance. Nevertheless, prostitutes were not considered full criminals as their function was thought to be essential for the preservation of social equilibrium: despite being 'morally and hygienically dangerous', they served the function of a 'safety valve' for the male sex drive which would otherwise be directed towards 'honest' women. For this reason, the state opted for a strict regulation of prostitution in circumscribed spaces, the so called *case chiuse*, closed houses, i.e. brothels, which allowed for social décor to be preserved (Gibson, 1999).

The end of the regulamentarist regime came in 1958 with the establishment of a new abolitionist[9] piece of legislation that has been in force ever since. It forbade the establishment of new brothels and ordered the closure of existing ones. Thus, while prostitution can be performed in the streets, and by one woman only in her own apartment, the criminalisation of activities such as loitering, kerb crawling, soliciting, etc., have created an aura of unlawfulness around prostitution itself that contributes to its further stigmatisation and its association with deviant social behaviour (Danna, 2004), despite the fact that such regulations were instituted to defend specifically the person-prostitute.[10]

In 1983 two sex workers founded the Committee for the Civil Rights of Prostitutes (Comitato per i diritti civili delle prostitute: 'The Committee' thereafter) after street prostitutes operating around the area of Pordenone (north-east Italy) had organised a protest against the physical and verbal violence they had suffered at the hands of soldiers stationed at the United States Army base. Since its foundation the Committee has been actively

REPRESENTATIONS OF MIGRANT WOMEN SEX LABOURERS

fighting against the social exclusion and marginalisation of prostitutes and promoting the decriminalisation of prostitution – rather than its recognition as work – as a legitimate activity among consenting adults.

Carla Corso, the Committee's president, suggests that prior to 1958, regulation by the state conferred upon prostitution institutional validity and public acceptability as prostitutes were recognised as important social actors; the subsequent closure of state-regulated brothels resulted in prostitutes resurfacing to the visibility of the streets, thereby becoming much more vulnerable to social rejection. As Corso emphasises:

> When they closed the brothels and prostitutes ceased to be con-
> trolled by the state, they became perceived as a dangerous people, as
> they are still today. Before [the law of 1958], going with a prostitute
> was for men a goliardic experience, to the point that they talked
> about it openly, it was a reason to show off, now they are ashamed of
> it, they come hiding themselves, as if they were thieves. And not
> because they realise that they are cheating on their wife who is at
> home, but simply because they think they are doing something
> transgressive; they copulate with women who do not have a social
> function, while before the whole thing was regulated.
>
> (Corso and Landi, 1991: 169, author's translation)

The drastic and repressive methods used by the police against street prostitution forced Italian sex workers to either abandon their activities altogether or transfer from the streets into private apartments; hence by the mid-1980s, very few Italian women, in many cases drug addicts, were present on the streets (Corso, 2003). The renewed lack of visibility of prostitution contributed to a subsiding of general public hostility towards it, and its consequent removal from the public agenda as a major issue of concern. Pia Covre of the Committee went as far as to believe that throughout the years the population was even starting to accept prostitution:

> Looking back to the 1980s, I really thought that for prostitutes the
> social stigma could be defeated. I thought that we would have a great
> 'opening up' and that we could even talk about 'work'. Even in some
> sectors of public opinion there was this evolution and there was the
> idea that one could think of prostitution as an acceptable phenom-
> enon, limited as it was at that time, as something that had the right to
> exist, and that maybe could have been acceptable as a job. This is
> obviously based on the kind of prostitution we had at that time.
>
> (Personal interview, 2002)

In an international conference of prostitutes in Germany in 1984, the members of the Committee were informed that both in Germany and in the

Netherlands migrant women were progressively starting to occupy positions in the sex industry, and the same phenomenon was expected to expand to southern Europe as well. In fact, the systematic migrations of women sex labourers that reached Italy in the late 1980s brought again a significant shift in the societal response to prostitution, as further explained in the following section.

Encountering migrant women sex labourers[11]

Women sex labourers became socially visible in Italy in the early 1990s when local prostitutes were the first to gain an awareness of the conditions in which they operated; in some instances they received the new 'colleagues' with hostility, due to the much lower price of the services they offered which inevitably attracted more clients, and which increased competition amongst sex labourers. Nevertheless, as will be shown, they were also the first to take action to create structures of support for this new group of migrants. In her autobiography published in 1991, Carla Corso mentions women migrants operating in prostitution in Italy and gives an insider's sense of the very first impressions of this phenomenon;

> Exploitation is experienced by prostitutes of colour, there are many women who live this drama, and in my opinion it is a really explosive situation. These are awful things . . . they are imported, just as at the times of the white slave trade, now however they are black, South Americans, from South East Asia, it's a real trade. . . . They definitely have to be very powerful organisations, because these women keep staying here, otherwise one cannot understand how they can stay for months and months on our streets without a visa, with no paper, at times even without a passport. The police just look and keep going, the majority of the times they say nothing . . . The drama of these women is that they have not chosen to be prostitutes, the majority of the times they come here because someone promised them another job.
>
> (Corso and Landi, 1991: 186–7; author's translation)

Although this narrative is still based on vague notions of the phenomenon, surrounded by an aura of mystery – the unclear origins of the women, the criminal mafia, etc. – Corso had been prophetic at that time, in understanding that the situation would assume much bigger dimensions. Furthermore, while initially the police ignored them, the population reacted to the renewed visibility of street prostitutes with immediate hostility. The phenomenon came to be seen as a *disagio*: the Italian word that is used to indicate a state of hardship, of disturbance of the public peace. As a result, a number of local communities started to organise street demonstrations to intimidate the women, to chase them out of the area and in some cases they even made punitive expeditions 'legitimated as the defence of public decency, nocturnal quiet and the innocence of the neighbourhood's children, as well as the protection of local women from harassment by clients' (Danna, 2004: 166). The first neighbourhoods to feel affected by the phenomenon in the early 1990s were generally those of bigger cities such as Milan, Turin, Rome, Naples and Palermo, and a few years later, similar reactions took place in smaller localities when women migrant sex labourers expanded their territory.

A social worker from a non-governmental organisation that provides support to women trafficked for sexual purposes said that it was 1995 when in the city of the north-east where she operates, the population started to feel affected by the presence of street prostitution. Immediately after that:

> a public debate at the city level opened up on the problem of clan-
> destine immigration, drug and the safety problems that the citizens
> were experiencing. So, on top of micro-crime, such as drug dealing,
> the population expressed their *disagio* towards the presence of these
> women on the streets, even if at the beginning they were very few. But
> in any case they were a disturbing factor ... The debates were very
> intense and there was a lot of talk about prostitution and about the
> fact that nobody wanted it ... at that time the phenomenon was new
> for everybody, for the citizens, and for the public administration. The
> social services knew nothing about it, it was new for the police, and
> this was the same all over Italy.
> (Personal interview, summer 2002, author's translation)

The first to be identified as 'foreigners' *and* prostitutes were black women who were commonly referred to as 'the Africans'. Only at a later stage, after being approached, were they renamed: a process that resulted in the creation of very inaccurate pseudo categories based primarily on stereotypical and undistinguished notions of the 'other'. All the 'Africans' become Nigerians; the 'whites' became Albanians, Romanians or Eastern Europeans. Indeed, the knowledge of these women's origin, lives, migration patterns, moti-vations, etc. remained for the first years of the 1990s very imprecise and ambiguous. Therefore when the public outcry over the phenomenon of sex trafficking assumed overwhelming proportions also in Italy, the new image of migrant women unknowingly lured into prostitution and forced to live in slavery-like conditions easily penetrated the mainstream discourse on migrant women sex labourers, together with the equally popular and threatening image of deviancy ascribed to them.

Social and political mobilisation: a plurality of responses

The Committee was the first to mobilise in order to get to know better who these 'other' women were, so as to establish a dialogue and be able to provide, when needed, better targeted support. This is how Tampep,[12] what Pia Covre defines the 'mother of all support projects', was born:

> We have been working with Tampep since 1993 . . . We were working already as an association, as Committee . . . on the streets to give information, to help with the prevention [of STDs] with groups of our associates. It was something very self-organised and self-managed. That's how we started to conduct a more systematic intervention towards the foreigners, because before we even had difficulties with the materials [leaflets, instructions, etc]. With Tampep we created a real methodology of intervention, we started to understand better who these prostitutes were, so that we gave a more solid basis and validity to our interventions.
>
> (Personal interview August 2002, author's translation)

Since then the Committee has coupled practical interventions on the ground with a variety of other advocacy-oriented activities, in which it progressively stressed the recognition of subjectivity and personal agency of migrant women sex labourers, and criticised the false pity for victims displayed by state authorities who, ironically, harass and deport them at the same time. Through its vocal interventions in these topical issues, the Committee gained special public recognition for a brief period under the centre-left governing coalition (1996–2001), when it became an important interlocutor of the Government's Equal Opportunity Unit on issues pertaining to prostitution and trafficking in women, and with a much stronger influence than the multiple voices of other women's movements (Danna, 2004). For instance, while the very opposite feminist ideological stand that views prostitution as sexual slavery enhancing male supremacy à la Barry (1984, 1995), Dworkin (1981) and Jeffreys (1997) has had relatively widespread support among Italian feminists, their keen concern with issues of abortion and divorce somehow sidelined their interest in prostitution. This topic therefore assumed relevance only sporadically, when new proposals were made to change the existing law. Only recently has prostitution come back onto the agenda of some Italian women's movements, including the Federation of Housewives (Federcasalinghe). This large and 'very conservative group', which very clearly states its non-affiliation with feminist movements, in 1998 'launched a campaign to gather signatures for compulsory medical examinations of prostitutes, for the purpose of defending the family' (Danna, 2004: 166).

The manifestation of strong opposition to 'foreign prostitution' and mobilisation to eliminate or strictly regulate it has also characterised the activities of religious and political groups, although often driven by very different motivations. The Northern League has been extremely versatile in its manipulation of the image of female migrants in prostitution to generate fears related to migration and to consolidate its power as the 'defender against the invaders'. In its crusade to protect the ethos of 'northern Italian-ness', the League has created a system of values and traditions that identifies in the family the core of the natural order of Padanian[13] society. This claims that the family's integrity and unity have to be protected from 'foreign prosti-tutes' who are a menace to societal moral order. The leader and president of the Northern League, Umberto Bossi, has stated that 'foreign prostitutes' 'lead to the diffusion of paedophilia and homosexuality, because between all this there is a continuity'[14] (quoted in Danna, 2004: 7). The solution pro-posed is to either expel 'foreign prostitutes' from the country or relegate them into a confined space (an unsophisticated solution which nonetheless has found substantial support among the population) to ensure that the 'problem' is no longer visible.

On the other hand, the Catholic Church identifies prostitution as an immoral activity and a social scourge. The Catholic catechism states that

> [prostitution] does injury to the dignity of the person who engages in it, reducing the person to an instrument of sexual pleasure. . . . While it is always gravely sinful to engage in prostitution, the imputability of the offence can be attenuated by destitution, blackmail or social pressure.
>
> (Catholic catechism, 2355)

Interestingly, after the changes in the prostitution scenario brought about in Italy since the 1980s, the Church has significantly moved its discourse from what used to be the prevailing focus on the sinful nature of prostitution to aspects related to exploitation of victims of trafficking for sexual purposes. This shift was primarily the result of the awareness raised by religious people inside the Church, who had established contacts with migrant women sex labourers and had activated informal structures of support. For instance, don Benzi (a Catholic priest) claims to have been contacted directly by a woman who asked for his assistance in securing refuge from her abusive pimp. After this first experience, he started a more systematised outreach operation with other volunteers who brought hot tea to the women and invited them to pray, and over time they developed what is now one of the biggest organisations operating in this field in Italy.

The expansion in the number of Catholic NGOs active in providing sup-port to migrant women sex labourers soon gave rise to internal diatribes in the Church. This was the result of the plurality of views on issues such as the role of the woman in prostitution and the methods to apply in the provision of assistance. These issues were clearly expressed in an interview conducted with the co-ordinator of a Catholic NGO, who complained about the fact that the Church has not yet expressed an official position on 'foreign prostitution' and trafficking for sexual purposes. As a consequence, a few priests who have media appeal often appear on television programmes expressing their view, which is not, she stressed, the official stance of the Catholic world, although this is what it appears to be.

> It is not fair to ask only people like don Benzi to talk about the trafficking issue. In his own little world, however, he has some few clear ideas and has a large group of people following him. The first is that the client has to be condemned, and then all the women have to be saved because they don't want to do this job, but it's not true! There are some people who do want to do this job. They want to do it because it is the most remunerative, and then they want to go back home and buy a house . . . Even if you take away the coercion, they still want to keep doing the job! . . .
>
> Don Benzi again, once said that it's the wife of the client who is not good in bed with the husband, and that's why they go to prostitutes, that's what he came up with once, then fortunately he retracted the statement. The last thing we need is that he attacks women again, and then we're done! It's always their fault!
>
> The thing that annoys me the most is that don Benzi is seen as representing the Catholic Church, and the Church is not going to deny this, it's not going to touch a man who is doing a . . . salvific job!
>
> (Personal interview, summer 2002, author's translation)

By the second half of the 1990s an increasing number of local groups and associations – both confessional and lay – that were active in the field of social exclusion started to show interest in understanding who these women were, and instituted various infrastructures of support. As the co-ordinator of a major organisation in Turin told me, during the initial years the phenomenon was so new and unknown in its various manifestations that any method of intervention was experimented with, and in some cases these resulted in negative consequences for the women themselves.[15] Often methods drawn directly from their experience with drug addicts were applied. Thus, harm reduction practices, which are generally strategies that reduce negative consequences of drug use, were introduced among migrant women sex labourers – in this particular case, it consisted of distributing free condoms to reduce the infection with sexually transmitted diseases.

These organisations carried out their activities in circumscribed local communities, often ignoring each other's presence, receiving very little support from the state and with limited representation in the political realm for a few years until 1998, when the new migration law brought some order and regulation in the administration of these particular services.

Between discourse and policy: the case of Article 18 for the protection and support of victims of trafficking

In 1998 a number of Italian parliamentarians declared their intention to formulate a law to address the issue of trafficking specifically, as the current regulations in place had proven to be insufficient to respond to this new development in migration. An Interministerial Table (for the fight against trafficking) – a specific steering group including a large number of NGOs that had been working specifically with migrant women sex labourers – was set up to gather information on the issue, pursuant to the elaboration of a new law that became operative in 1999 as Article 18 of the Consolidated Act on Immigration.

Article 18 contains specific regulations on the provision of protection and settlement services for women trafficked for sexual purposes in Italy.[16] It authorises the issuance of a residence permit for social protection reasons when it is deemed that a foreign national is in a situation involving violence or severe exploitation 'and there emerges a real threat to the personal safety of this individual'. The actual granting of the permit is subjected to the applicant's participation in a programme of 'assistance and social protection' organised and managed by a recognised 'social service'.[17] The permit is valid for six months, giving the holder access to social and assistance services, public education and, in addition, it provides registration with the national employment agency. It can also be renewed if, upon expiration, the woman has found employment. The innovative and 'progressive' nature of Article 18 lies in the fact that the victim should be able to enjoy both protection and the residence permit by virtue of her being a victim alone, and is not dependent upon her collaboration with law enforcement and immigration officials in investigations and prosecutions,[18] as it is often the case in other countries' legislations.[19]

Whilst it is relevant to outline the constituting elements of this new law, the concern here is not to analyse its content or effectiveness per se; rather, the next sections present some reflections on how politico-discursive representations previously presented ultimately reflect the design and implementation of this particular legal provision. The significance of this new law in the broader context of immigration policies in Italy, will also be discussed.

Ideologies and interventions

One notable aspect on the interplay between regulation and representation derives from the analysis of the programme of assistance and social protection enacted under Article 18 vis à vis differing ideological approaches and scopes that various social services give to the programme itself. Some organisations envision the project as an opportunity for the women to be rescued, to learn how to shape their life according to a more 'proper' behaviour, and eventually to be re-socialised (Prina, 2002). For others, the programme is aimed at reconstructing women's self-determination and autonomy, with autonomy meaning not necessarily abandoning prostitution, but 'gaining means of control of one's own destiny, by acquiring the capacity to elaborate one's own life story and personal experience' (Signorelli and Treppete, 2001: 60).

The crucial distinction between the two approaches lies in the differing conceptualisations of the experience of the women they attempt to target. For the latter, the underlying assumption is that the experience of being a woman, or of being oppressed, is not shared, lived and negotiated in the same way, hence the object of the programme is to foster decisional auto-nomy and independence (Prina, 2002). This implies an awareness that being the agent of one's own life has different meanings for different people in different contexts. Prostitution is viewed as an expenditure of physical labour that is identical to any other service for wages. Hence within this frame, trafficking is considered in the perspective of the violence and exploitation that it involves, and is considered as one of the effects of the widespread poor social and legal position of women (Wijers and van Doornick, 2002). The other type of implementation model is based on the understanding that prostitution is an abjection of the body, hence the practitioner is invariably a victim of an organised trade, or specific agents of force and oppression, or socio-economic circumstances (Rajan, 2003). Within this approach, prostitu-tion and trafficking become practically identical, without regard for condi-tions of consent or coercion. For those who support this view, the scope of the programme is 'the woman's reconstruction, which regards not only her self-esteem and social and relational skills but also her morality' (Prina, 2002: 210).

Inclusionary policies and exclusionary practices

At first glance, Article 18 appears as a progressive measure, especially in the European context where national laws either lack specific provisions or have formulated some that are still at a very embryonic phase of implementa-tion.[20] However, a look at the broader context of immigration policies and practices in Italy reveals the critical co-existence of both inclusionary and exclusionary practices towards the same group of migrants. For instance, according to data produced by the Italian Equal Opportunity Unit, between March 2000 and February 2001, approximately 1,755 women participated in the programme of assistance and social protection prescribed by Article 18 (On the Road, 2002: 77). In the same year the Committee reports that 4,600 'foreign prostitutes' without a residence permit were expelled and deported back to their countries of origin.

The question here is why some women evidently have access to protection and others do not, and on what basis the exclusion of so many is rendered possible. As Demleitner points out, the explanation may be found in the dangerous construction of the victim of sexual trafficking as 'powerless, helpless and pure. The legal process may tend to declare any woman not fitting this childlike image – and most victims of unscrupulous traffickers will not conform to this model – as unworthy of support and protection' (Demleitner, 2001: 273). In the case of Article 18, the focus on the category 'victim' creates an obfuscating dichotomy between legally recognised victims entitled to protection, and non legally recognised victims who are treated as criminals, brutalised by the police and repatriated. The latter may be women who are voluntarily involved in the sex business, or women who, though abused, do not want or are not able to report to the authorities. Aghatise, for instance, mentions that 'if the women and girls do not collaborate with the police, refusing to reveal or give comprehensive information about their exploiters, they may be picked up by the police along the roadsides and deported to their countries of origin' (Aghatise, 2004: 16). Here is a point about the difference in the law's discursive promise, and the police praxis which treats women who refuse to co-operate very differently from those who do.

Surveillance of sexuality by the state

The observations above reveal the pervasive tension between, on the one hand, the public obligation to provide support to individuals who suffer abuse and, on the other, the political commitment of the government to close the borders to 'outsiders' and expel unwanted migrants. This dynamic is succinctly expressed by Berman, who states that the 'anxieties encapsulated in the crisis over boundaries encounter one another at the site of migrant sex workers, and via criminalisation, subject women to a violent regime of policing in the name of staving off or covering these crises' (Berman, 2003: 59).

The portrayal of sex trafficking as a vast, violent and horrific practice serves as an act of statecraft that authorises the state to reinstate its boundaries at a historically critical moment when the meaning of the nation is undergoing significant revision (Berman, 2003: 59). In pursuing this endeavour, the government reproduces and manipulates both the images of victimhood and deviancy ascribed to migrant women sex labourers, and ultimately transforms these images into governmental technologies 'through which authorities seek to embody and give effect to governmental ambitions' (Rose and Miller, 1992: 175). Moreover, immigration control serves as a site for the regulation of sexual norms, identities and behaviours, and to (re)construct the nation, the symbols of nationhood, and its people in particular ways (Luibhéid, 2002). Hence, officially designated identities, which are not just sexual but also gendered, racial, ethnic and class-based, are 'treated as evidence that undesirable sexual acts would likely occur' and have to be disciplined (Luibhéid 2002: xv). The treatment of racialised gender identities as presupposing particular sexual acts is still widely in place, and Aghatise's report is again quite revealing:

> In the spring and summer of 2003, hundreds of Nigerian-trafficked victims were deported. In the southern part of Italy, 100 Nigerians who had been held in one of the special detention centres without residence permits were identified as prostitutes, put on a chartered flight to Lagos, and deported as illegal immigrants (Comboniani Missionaries, 2003). Unfortunately, the victims were not given any chance to explain their situations, and in obvious violation of Article 18 of the Immigration Law, they were not given any information about possibilities of obtaining assistance under the trafficking protection program.
>
> (Aghatise, 2004: 17)

During the past three years in Italy, many Nigerian women have been stopped at the border and quickly repatriated, often on the assumption that once in the country they would engage in prostitution. In this case the surveillance of sexuality 'is employed as a basis for regulation' (Foucault, quoted in Stoler, 1995: 34) which stamps out individuality. Nigerian women are equated with prostitutes, and the preventative measures reveal society's 'strength': the state that 'victoriously' keeps 'vice' and 'moral degeneracy' out of the body politic.

Conclusion

As Lutz (2002) points out, the institutionalisation of racist, nationalist and ethnic forms of violence now have gender-specific forms of expression which can be observed specifically in the treatment of migrant women sex labourers. As this chapter has illustrated, dominant historical prejudices against prostitutes and migrants have coalesced in the construction of the image of the 'foreign prostitute' who is subjected to a variety of forms of discipline on the basis of pre-determined racialised and sexualised identities ascribed to her. Moreover, the essentialisation of female migrant sex labourers as either sex-slaves/victims or criminals contributes to further stigmatise the category of prostitute. It does this either by reinforcing the belief that women prostitutes who are not victims are 'truly' deviant and criminals, or by categorising them as victims of different forms of exploitation which denies their agency and their capacity to choose. Prostitutes and migrant prostitutes within this mainstream discourse are invariably constructed as outcasts and are thus kept in a position in which they are more easily governable. Even the opportunity offered by the putatively progressive Article 18 to provide support to women trafficked in the sex industry has reinforced divisions amongst the associations that provide various forms of support by polarising them further along ideological lines.

The key question of whether the final aims of Article 18 projects should be to rescue and re-socialise women into a new lifestyle, or simply to give them the means to conduct their lives as they desire, has proven to be contentious. All too often the dual hostility towards migrants and prostitutes masks the various aspects constituting the socio-economic, political and cultural systems and practices that shape the constellation of women sex labourers' migration patterns and the way they are continuously negotiated, the knowledge of which should be essential for the formulation of support initiatives.

Acknowledgement

I am grateful to Nidhi Trehan for her contributions to an earlier draft of this chapter.

Notes

1 Throughout this study the expression 'migrant women sex labourers' is used to refer to women whose migration experience is highly determined by their involvement in the sex industry. I chose the word labour, thus 'sex labour', in that it non-normatively indicates the exertion of bodily and mental activities, as opposed to 'sex work' which is used by 'sex workers' themselves to indicate an income-generating activity or form of employment that underlies voluntariness. 'Migrant women sex labourers' covers prostitution-related migrations in their complexity, beyond issues of choice or coercion, which however are addressed extensively when appropriate. In many instances, to avoid monotony, I refer to women sex labourers or sex labourers, as a shorthand for migrant women sex labourers.

2 Due to the hidden nature of the phenomenon and the high rate of mobility involved, there is no clear estimation of the number of female migrants operating in the sex industry in Italy; however the most quoted figure, calculated by the Italian research association on population and social interventions PARSEC, estimates that they comprise between 15,000 and 19,000 individuals (Carchedi, 2000). The largest groups are from Nigeria, Albania, Romania and Moldavia; there are also significant numbers of women from the former USSR, Bulgaria, Poland, Ghana, Colombia and Peru (Aghatise, 2004; CABIRIA, 2004; Carchedi, 2000).

3 The expression 'foreign prostitutes' is used here as a direct translation of *prostitutite strainere* which is commonly employed both in Italian colloquial language and scholarly literature, and not as a term of choice by the author. It is used with inverted commas in order to highlight the semantic negativity that the expression conveys through the coupling of the terms foreigner (indicating not just a condition of non belonging, but also, and more significantly, one of rejection) and prostitute, all too often signifiers of deviance.

4 The adjective 'new' is adopted here exclusively in the context of the 'modern' history of Italy, i.e. since 1861; in fact for millennia, the Italian peninsula had been a destination and transition country for migrant people.

5 According to the most recent estimates (based on the number of migrants who are in possession of or have made a request for a visa, thus not inclusive of the number of undocumented migrants), the largest migrant communities in Italy are originally from Romania, Morocco, Albania, Ukraine and China (Caritas/Migrantes, 2004). Compared to other European countries such as Germany, France and the United Kingdom, their number is on a smaller scale; however, the quantitative dimension of the phenomenon assumes particular relevance when one considers the velocity with which the turnaround took place. In this sense, Italy's situation is closer to other southern European countries, such as Greece, Spain and Portugal, which went through similar transitions in their migration patterns (King and Black, 1997).

6 Italy's first Republic was proclaimed in 1948 and lasted until 1991.

7 Founded as Lega Lombarda (1984), the party became Lega Nord (Northern League, i.e. covering the entire North of Italy) in 1991. It has been in the 2000–2006 governing coalition, and also in a previous legislature from 1994 to 1995.

8 I came across this picture for the first time in Dal Lago's excellent book on the exclusion of migrants in Italy (Dal Lago, 1999: 47).

9 Abolitionism in the prostitution debate generally indicates abolition of regulations over prostitutes.

10 Soliciting for instance, applies to anyone who 'in a public place . . . invites to libidinous acts in a scandalous or harassing manner or follows persons in the street' (Article 5 of the 1958 prostitution law). It was supposed to protect primarily prostitutes from the harassment of clients, but ended up being one of the most frequent charges against prostitutes themselves.

11 The concept of 'encountering' is drawn from Ahmed, who adopts the dynamic nature of encounters – 'a meeting which involves surprise and conflict' – to examine and reveal the social relationships that are concealed by stranger fetishism (Ahmed, 2000: 6).

12 TAMPEP stands for Transnational AIDS/STD Prevention Among Migrant Prostitutes in Europe Project. Also known as the Dutch Institute for Prostitution Issues, it was launched in 1993 by the Mr A de Graaf Stichting, with headquarters in Amsterdam.

13 Padania is a geographical region in Italy which covers a large part of the North of Italy. It is used metonymically to indicate the entire Northern region, i.e. north of the river Po (*Padus* in Latin).

14 In Italy, knowledge on paedophilia, pornography, prostitution and homosexuality is often extremely blurred and these issues are treated almost as interchangeable problems, and are often represented as the scourges of modern society.

15 For instance, many women were beaten up by their pimps for accepting free condoms, while others used two condoms on the same client in order to increase protection, apparently not knowing that this practice leads frequently to the breakage of the condom itself.

16 Article 18 applies to adult people (for minors other legal provisions are in place) who have been trafficked for labour or sexual exploitations. So far it has been enforced almost exclusively in the case of migrant women trafficked for sexual purposes. In the following sections of the chapter, I refer to Article 18 exclusively in its application to this target group.

17 The term 'social service' (*servizio sociale*) used in the text of Article 18 refers to one of the registered organisations entitled to offer protection to victims of trafficking by the Department of Social Affairs.

18 However, as the majority of NGOs operators I interviewed told me, the fastest (and often the only) way for a woman to obtain a temporary permit is to start a criminal procedure against her traffickers.

19 Suffice to mention here the European Commission proposal for a Council Directive 'on short-term residence permit issued to victims of action to facilitate illegal immigration or trafficking in human beings who co-operate with the competent authorities' of July 2002. This provision requires victims of trafficking to co-operate in criminal investigations in order to enjoy a protection that lasts only for the time of the co-operation, a necessary condition that has been widely criticised by major human rights organisations.
20 Belgium is the only other country in the EU with specific provisions of support for women trafficked in the sex industry.

References

Aghatise, Esohe (2004) 'Trafficking for prostitution in Italy. Possible effects of government proposals for legalization of brothels', *Violence Against Women* 10(10), pp 1126–55

Ahmed, Sara (2000) *Strange Encounters*, London: Routledge

Andall, Jacqueline (2000) *Gender, Migration and Domestic Service: the Politics of Black Women in Italy*, Aldershot: Ashgate

Balbo, Laura (1991) 'Il modello italiano per gli immigrati', *Politica ed Economia* 9, pp 3–4

Barry, Kathleen (1984) *Female Sexual Slavery* (1st edn 1979), New York: New York University Press

Barry, Kathleen (1995) *The Prostitution of Sexuality*, New York: New York University Press

Berman, Jacqueline (2003) '(Un)Popular strangers and crisis (un)bounded: Discourses of sex-trafficking, the European political community and the panicked state of the modern state', *European Journal of International Relations* 9(1), pp 37–86

Bhabha, Homi (1994) *The Location of Culture*, London: Routledge

Bonifazi, Corrado (1992) 'Italian attitudes and opinions towards foreign migrants and migration policies', *StudiEmigrazione/Etudes Migrations* 29(105), pp 21–41

CABIRIA (2004) *Women and Migration in Europe. Strategies and Empowerment*, Lyon: Le Dragon Lune Editions

Campani, Giovanna (1993) 'Immigration and racism in southern Europe: The Italian case', *Ethnic and Racial Studies* 16(3), pp 507–33

Carchedi, Francesco (2000) *Considerations on Foreign Prostitution in Italy*, Rome: PARSEC

Caritas/Migrantes (2004) *Dossier Statistico Immigrazione 2004*, Rome: Idos – Centro Studi e Ricerche

Corso, Carla (2003) *E Siamo Partite! Migrazione Tratta e Prostituzione Straniera in Italia*, Florence: Giunti

Corso, Carla and Landi, Sandra (1991) *Ritratto a Tinte Forti*, Florence: Giunti

Dal Lago, Alessandro (1999) *Non-Persone*, Milan: Feltrinelli

Danna, Daniela (2004) 'Italy: The never-ending debate', in Outshoorn, Joyce (ed), *The Politics of Prostitution*, Cambridge: Cambridge University Press, pp 165–84

Demleitner, Nora (2001) 'The law at a crossroad: The legal construction of migrant women trafficked in prostitution', in Kyle David and Koslowski Rey (eds), *Global Human Smuggling: Comparative Perspectives*, Baltimore: Johns Hopkins University Press, pp 257–93

Dworkin, Andrea (1981) *Pornography: Men Possessing Women*, London: Women's Press

Ferrarotti, Franco (1988) *Oltre il Razzismo Verso una Società Multirazziale e Multiculturale*, Rome: Armando

Gabaccia, Donna (2000) *Italy's Many Diasporas*, Seattle: University of Washington Press

Gibson, Mary (1999) *Prostitution and the State in Italy, 1860–1915*, Columbus OH: Ohio State University Press

Indra, Doreen (1999) *Engendering Forced Migration: Theory and Practice*, New York: Berghahn Books

IOM (2001) 'Italy, the image of migrants through the media, civil society and the labour market'; accessed at: http://www.iom.int/en/archive/PBN261102.shtml#item2

Jeffreys, Sheila (1997) *The Idea of Prostitution*, North Melbourne: Spinifex Press

King, Russell and Black, Richard (eds) (1997) *Southern Europe and the New Immigration*, Brighton: Sussex Academic Press

Luibhéid, Eithne (2002) *Entry Denied: Controlling Sexuality at the Border*, Minneapolis: University of Minnesota Press

Lutz, Helma (2002) 'The long shadows from the past. The new Europe at a crossroad', in Lenz, Ilse *et al.* (eds), *Crossing Borders and Shifting Boundaries. Vol. II: Gender, Identities and Networks*, Opladen: Leske & Budrich pp 57–73

On the Road (2002) *Tratta e Prostituzione*, Milan: FrancoAngeli

Prina, Franco (2002) 'The projects and the forms of implementation of the law: Organisational models, systems of meaning, articulation of practices', in *Article 18: Protection of Victims of Trafficking and Fight against Crime*, Martinsicuro: On the Road Edizioni

Rajan, Sunder (2003) *The Scandal of the State: Women, Law, Citizenship in Postcolonial India*, Durham, NC: Duke University Press

Rose, Nikolas and Miller, Peter (1992) 'Political power beyond the state: Problematics of government', *British Journal of Sociology* 43(2), pp 172–205

Saunders, Rebecca (2003) *The Concept of the Foreign: An Interdisciplinary Dialogue*, Lanham, MD: Lexington Books

Signorelli, Assunta and Treppete, Mariangela (2001) *Services in the Window*, Trieste: Arterios

Statham, Paul (1998) 'The political construction of immigration in Italy: Opportunities, mobilisation and outcomes', *Wissenschaftszentrum Series*, FS III 98–102, pp 1–60

Stoler, Ann (1995) *Race and the Education of Desire: Foucault's History of Sexuality and the Colonial Order of Things*, Durham, NC: Duke University Press

Wijers, Marjan and van Doornick, Marieke (2002) 'Only rights can stop wrongs: A critical assessment of anti-trafficking strategies', paper presented at EU/IOM conference on Preventing and Combating Trafficking in Human Beings, Brussels

Wrench, John and Solomos, John (1993) *Racism and Migration in Western Europe*, Oxford: Providence, RI, Berg

INDEX